SNITCH

SNITCH

Informants, Cooperators & the Corruption of Justice

ETHAN BROWN

PublicAffairs / New York

PublicAffairs books are available at special discounts for bulk
purchases in the U.S. by corporations, institutions, and other organizations.
For more information, please contact the Special Markets Department
at the Perseus Books Group, 2300 Chestnut Street, Suite 200,
Philadelphia, PA 19103, call (800) 255–1514, or e-mail
special.markets@perseusbooks.com.

Library of Congress Cataloging-in-Publication Data
Brown, Ethan, 1972–
    Snitch : informants, cooperators, and the corruption of justice / Ethan
Brown. — 1st ed.
        p.   cm.
    Includes bibliographical references and index.
    ISBN-13: 978-1-58648-492-7 (hardcover : alk. paper)
    ISBN-10: 1-58648-492-3 (hardcover : alk. paper) 1. Informers—United
States. 2. Informers—United States—Case studies. 3. Sentences
(Criminal procedure)—United States. 4. Drug control—United States.
5. Law enforcement—United States. I. Title.
HV8141.B74 2007
363.25'2—dc22   2007030592

10 9 8 7 6 5 4 3 2 1

This book is dedicated to my wife, Kristen,
for being so patient with me—and for believing in
the importance of what I'm writing about here.

"Twenty years ago defendants were expected by their criminal associates to take their medicine and keep their mouths shut. Now sentences are so strong they all know that when they get caught they're gonna talk, their buddies are gonna talk—*everyone* is gonna talk. There is no more honor among thieves. And that is progress for law enforcement."

—*Alabama Republican Senator Jeff Sessions*

CONTENTS

ACKNOWLEDGMENTS

THANKS TO: CLIVE PRIDDLE, SUSAN WEINBERG, AND THE ENTIRE PUBLICAFFAIRS crew for their guidance, editing, and early enthusiasm; Jud Laghi at LJK for his vision both here and in *Queens Reigns Supreme*; my wife and my entire family for their patience and support; everyone who took the time to speak with me for this project—inmates such as Walter "King Tut" Johnson, policy experts like Eric Sterling, and a vast cast of criminal defense attorneys including Gerald Shargel, Martin Stolar, Leonard Goodman, Renato Stabile, Joseph Tacopina, Robert Simels, Marc Fernich, and Andrew White; special thanks to Katie Charles at *New York* magazine for her research assistance and her willingness to take on this project so early; Greg "Grouchy Greg" Watkins at Allhiphop.com for his friendship and unwavering support; Felicia Palmer and the entire staff of sohh.com for their support; William Sewell for his insights and assistance with my investigative work; Seth Z. R. for being such a great reader; Thomas Bentil at the Osborne Association and all the guys at Riker's Island for being great listeners and readers; Eskay at nahright.com for the on-point blogging; the fans of *Queens Reigns Supreme* for their enthusiasm and encouragement, particularly when it came to taking on this new project; Mary Zajac and E. Edward Richardson at the Maryland U.S. Attorney's Office for the trial transcripts; Rodney Bethea of One Love Films for the interview and the great conversation; Rick Doblin at MAPS for his longtime guidance; C. S. for his insights and generosity with his sources; Soulman Seth and Diane of Gorilla Convict for their smart input and constant correspondence; Alexander T. Riley of Bucknell University for sharing *Queens Reigns Supreme* with his students and for being such a warm and gracious host; and my friends—Nick, Jon B., Joe, Josh, Seth, Ana, Derek, Disco D (RIP), Juan Carlos, Jason L., Kate, Matt—for their sense of humor and support.

PROLOGUE

Says Who? Cooperators and Informants Replace Investigative Work

"SAYS WHO?" IT WAS EARLY IN THE MORNING OF NOVEMBER 16, 2005, AND Gerald Shargel, the legendary New York criminal defense attorney best known for representing John Gotti, had just begun his opening arguments in the federal money laundering trial of hip-hop impresarios Irv "Gotti" Lorenzo and his brother Christopher. Shargel began by savaging the credibility of the government's witnesses in the case. "I'm going to make a chart," Shargel continued sarcastically, mocking the opening statements made by the assistant U.S. attorneys, which had featured a series of PowerPoint presentations meant to demonstrate that the Lorenzos laundered cash from Queens-based drug kingpin Kenneth "Supreme" McGriff. Shargel paced through the courtroom looking for a prop until he found a large piece of blank poster board propped up against the defense team's table. After holding it aloft for the jury to see, Shargel picked up a Magic Marker with a dramatic flourish and scrawled "SAYS WHO?" on the poster board in capital letters. "Says who?" Shargel thundered again. "Who says they're laundering money?"

Challenging the truthfulness of cooperators—defendants who agree to offer information to prosecutors in hopes of receiving a reduction in their prison time—is a defense so familiar in criminal cases that it's become a cliché. Indeed, prosecutors often prepare jurors for this tried and true defense attorney strategy. In his opening arguments in the Lorenzo case, one assistant U.S. attorney warned jurors, "You're not going to like these witnesses. You might find them despicable. . . . All that we ask is that you listen to their testimony and you see whether it matches up with the other evidence in the case." But toward the end of his opening statements, Shargel moved far beyond the typical "you-can't-trust-the-cooperators" argument. "I'm going to make a promise to you," Shargel said of one government witness, "I'm going to promise that I'm going to show you by the end of the day tomorrow, assuming that he takes the stand on time and I can cross[-examine] him, that I will show him to be a shameless liar who has lied about everything in every situation he's ever been in." Shargel then offered an even bolder claim: the government had no evidence to corroborate their money laundering charges against the Lorenzo brothers, and, worse, since the raid on their offices two years earlier, federal investigators trolled the streets and prison system looking for cooperators instead of doing investigative work. "Do you know that after you were selected as jurors in the case," Shargel continued, this time speaking directly to the jury, "the government is *still* out looking for witnesses?" Shargel explained that a longtime member of McGriff's drug-dealing crew, the Supreme Team, had signed a cooperation deal with federal prosecutors just three days before the trial began. "If I had more hair," Shargel said, pointing to his bald pate, "I'd pull it out."

As I sat in the courtroom watching Shargel on that mid-November day, I suspected that he wasn't engaging in typical criminal defense attorney bluster. While researching the Lorenzo case for my book *Queens Reigns Supreme*, I found that the feds had made a number of serious allegations in the case that were easily, provably false. One federal agent, citing testimony from a cooperating witness, claimed that Irv Lorenzo was the "public face" of Murder Inc. while McGriff was the "true owner" of the company; even cursory investigatory work would have revealed that Lorenzo received start-up funds for the label in 1999 from entertainment giant Universal Music Group. "Rather than inquire with Universal or Def Jam as to the true origins of Murder Inc," Shargel wrote in a 2005 memorandum of law in support of the pretrial motions of client Lorenzo, "[one federal agent] chose to rely on a confidential witness whose own 'knowledge' that Murder Inc was founded with drug money appears to have been based on street gossip and rumor."

Still, I was hoping that Shargel's claims were exaggerated. If they were true, they would paint a devastating portrait of federal investigations. The Lorenzo case, after all, was a multiyear, joint investigation spearheaded by a number of federal agencies, including the Drug Enforcement Administration (DEA), FBI, and IRS. Furthermore, the January 2005 press conference announcing the indictment of the Lorenzo brothers featured federal and local law enforcement heavies from New York Police Department (NYPD) Chief Ray Kelly to U.S. Attorney Roslynn Mauskopf, a tenacious Brooklyn-based prosecutor who indicted "Mafia Cops" Louis Eppolito and Stephen Caracappa. "In Irving and Chris Lorenzo," Mauskopf thundered at the press conference, "McGriff found two willing allies and a network of businesses at the ready. The Lorenzos and Kenneth McGriff became partners—crime partners—and together they laundered over $1 million in illicit drug proceeds though Murder Inc. and through companies that they owned and controlled."

If such high-level members of law enforcement were simply stringing together cooperator testimony in a major case involving a massive, multimillion-dollar expenditure of the federal government's resources without any evidence to corroborate it—or, worse, if this was how investigations are typically conducted—then something was terribly wrong with the criminal justice system.

Astonishingly, during the Lorenzos' three-week trial, Shargel's initial assertions about the investigatory practices of the feds turned out to be understated. Not only did the credibility of the cooperators in the case implode on the witness stand, but prosecutors also offered little evidence to support charges of money laundering and were not even able to present coherent theories to explain their case. Donell Nichols, a former Murder Inc. intern fired by the Lorenzos for recruiting applicants for highly paid jobs at the record label that did not exist, was perhaps the most untrustworthy and comically inept witness of all. It was revealed that Nichols lured a North Carolina man named Glen Williams to take one of his $1,500 per week "jobs" at Murder Inc. After Nichols's ruse was exposed, he and Williams brawled in the record label's conference room, leading to Nichols's firing. On the stand, Nichols admitted that after he was fired, he called the FBI and offered to assist them in their investigation of money laundering by the record label. He also acknowledged that he made the decision to offer information to prosecutors while watching an MTV News story about the 2003 raid on Murder Inc.'s offices.

Relying on testimony from a fabulist like Nichols was a risky move for the feds. When he took the stand, Nichols contradicted what he had told the grand jury under oath. During his grand jury testimony, Nichols provided novelistic tales of cash bundles being hauled into Murder Inc.'s offices—$70,000 worth of "fives and tens" stuffed into a shoebox—but in the courtroom his memory about the money laundering was suddenly much less clear. "I have general ideas," Nichols responded when asked on the stand if he could specify the amount of cash the Lorenzos received from

McGriff. (Shargel pointed out sarcastically, "I guess you had a better memory of it then.") A former Navy man, Nichols was also exposed for posing as a Navy SEAL: he once sent e-mails from a navyseals.com address (legitimate e-mails from the military come from a .mil domain). Most embarrassingly, Nichols admitted that his claim to have run a nonprofit group that advised synagogues and mosques on security issues was actually false (the organization was revealed to have been merely a post office box in Georgia). "I probably just did a common thing and just bluffed the resume up," Nichols explained. U.S. District Judge Edward Korman characterized Nichols's behavior as "fraudulent conduct," which was "clearly relevant to his credibility."

Former Supreme Team member Philip "Dalu" Banks fared no better on the witness stand. Like Nichols, Banks contradicted his grand jury testimony: he previously had said that Irv Lorenzo was an intern at Def Jam in 1995, but under cross-examination acknowledged that this was false. A startling exchange between Shargel and Banks followed in which Banks proclaimed that he would gladly commit perjury if it would help him receive leniency from prosecutors at sentencing. (Banks began cooperating with federal prosecutors in the Murder Inc. investigation after a 2005 arrest.)

> SHARGEL: If telling a lie about Irv Lorenzo could get you
>   out of jail and prevent you from facing the sentencing you're
>   facing, you would do it?
> BANKS: Yes, sir.
> SHARGEL: You would?
> BANKS: Yes.

Banks also acknowledged that just after he was arrested on February 17, 2005, on charges ranging from credit card fraud to attempted assault with a firearm, he told the officers, "I want to talk to you about Supreme." Yet Banks had previously been in prison from 1997 to 2004 and did not have firsthand knowledge of McGriff and Irv Lorenzo's relationship (which began in the mid-1990s and lasted until McGriff's arrest in late 2002). "So you were, in effect, trying to tell the police about ten-year-old information in some respects, correct?" Shargel asked. "Yes," Banks replied.

The feds—who presented little evidence at trial other than co-operators offering fantastic tales—seemed as confused as their co-operators. A handwritten note found by investigators in Chris Lorenzo's office during the Murder Inc. raid, which read, "Preme gets 100, Owes 35K," was introduced as evidence of money laundering. Yet Assistant U.S. Attorney Sean Haran couldn't explain what the document proved. In one of the trial's most bizarre moments, Shargel stepped in to help Haran explain what the note meant, suggesting that it represented "cash for checks." Judge Korman then turned to Haran and asked him, "Is that your argument?" to which Haran replied "I like it, but . . . it's actually a good idea." "Is it or not?" Korman shot back. "It's the truth," Harman responded. "The argument . . ." Haran continued, stammering this time, "The document is . . . ," and then trailed off.

As the Murder Inc. trial came to a close in early December, the prosecution's theories about the case had become so convoluted that the reporters I was seated with in the courtroom had conflicting ideas about where exactly McGriff's money was being laundered. Was drug money laundered through *Crime Partners*, a straight-to-DVD movie that McGriff and the Lorenzos produced together? Or was it a straight "cash for checks" scheme in which McGriff hauled hard cash into Murder Inc.'s offices and received checks in return? None of the reporters I spoke to seemed sure. Yet the confusion about the case did not necessarily mean that the Lorenzo brothers would be acquitted of the money laundering charges against them. Indeed, the vast number of money laundering theories floated by the feds could leave the jury with the notion that *something* illegal was going on between McGriff and the Lorenzos. Though juries are not supposed to convict based on the implication of wrongdoing, they often do anyway, a reality Shargel acknowledged during his closing arguments in which he thundered, *"REASONABLE DOUBT!"* after repeating each and every one of the prosecution's inconsistencies.

When the jury went into deliberations on December 1, 2005, and did not return quickly with a "not guilty" verdict as many in the courtroom had expected, it appeared that the feds' cooperator-centric strategy was about to pay off. As deliberations extended into the next day, the defense team's mood darkened further. After Judge Korman's case manager told defense attorney Gerald Lefcourt that she expected a guilty verdict, he started to panic. "I was a wreck," Lefcourt remembers. "I didn't even tell Irv. When six PM rolled around, I was squeezing Irv's hand so hard it probably still hurts."

The reporters and Lorenzo family members were packing up their belongings in expectation of another day in court when, just after six fifteen, Korman's clerk announced that the jury had reached a verdict. After a tense silence punctuated only by low weeping sounds, the jury delivered a "not guilty" verdict on *all* the money laundering counts. Rapturous applause followed from Murder Inc. stars Ja Rule and Ashanti. Outside the Brooklyn courthouse, the scene was even more striking. The jurors—middle-aged, middle-class men and women from the outer boroughs who could hardly be described as hip-hop fans—waited for the Lorenzos so they could celebrate the verdict. "It was a very weak case," a sixty-year-old juror from Staten Island named Gloria Menzies told the *New York Daily News.* "I'm very happy because from the beginning these two kids were innocent."

■ ■ ■

While the jurors in the Lorenzo trial returned to their families that night in early December and probably quickly forgot about the case, I was shaken by the experience for months afterward. Though I had covered several major federal investigations in the 1990s and beyond—from a racketeering case involving New York made man Chris Paciello to a first-of-its-kind application of the so-called crack house statute against New Orleans rave promoter Donnie Estopinal—I was stunned that the investigation into Murder Inc. was built almost entirely on falsehoods promulgated by informants and cooperators. My faith in the criminal justice system was shaken to the core. I felt, as neocon godfather Irving Kristol famously said, "mugged by reality." That the collapse of the Murder Inc. case coincided with a rise in anti-informant sentiment, made me wonder: What was the basis for the growing animus against cooperators and informants? Do cooperators and witnesses provide reliable information to prosecutors, or do they, as some inner-city residents complain, "lie on" suspects? Was the cooperator-centric Murder Inc. case an anomaly in the federal criminal justice system—or the norm?

INTRODUCTION

Section 5K1.1 and the Rise of the Cooperator Institution

ON APRIL 19, 2007, HARLEM RAPPER CAM'RON APPEARED ON *60 MINUTES* and glibly told Anderson Cooper that he would never cooperate with cops even if a serial killer lived next door. "No, I wouldn't call and tell anybody on him," Cam'ron coolly explained. "But I'd probably move. . . . But I'm not gonna call and be like, you know, 'The serial killer's in 4E.'" Soon after the segment aired, Cam'ron was denounced by everyone from CNN's right-wing talker Glenn Beck to Al Sharpton, who compared Cam'ron's anti-snitch ethos to a "slave mentality." It was a classic moral panic with a predictable denouement: Cam'ron issued a public apology in which he acknowledged the "dark reality" that "where I come from once word gets out that you've cooperated with the police that only makes you a bigger target of criminal violence," but nonetheless "my experience in no way justifies what I said."

The Cam'ron controversy also felt familiar because it had been preceded by a nearly identical uproar in December 2005, when

Boston mayor Thomas Menino vowed that he would confiscate T-shirts bearing the slogan "Stop Snitchin'," which were inspired by a DVD produced in Baltimore in 2004 called *Stop Fucking Snitching, Vol. 1.* "It's wrong," Menino said of the T-shirts. "We are going into every retail store that sells the shirts and [removing] them." After civil liberties groups protested, Menino backed off the plan, but many Boston retailers voluntarily removed the "Stop Snitchin'" T-shirts from their racks anyway. Nonetheless, anti-snitch sentiment persisted in pop culture. In June 2006, rapper Busta Rhymes graced the covers of two major hip-hop magazines (*Vibe* and *XXL*) primarily because he had garnered huge headlines—and aroused the ire of the NYPD—for refusing to cooperate with cops in an investigation into the murder of his bodyguard, who was shot near Rhymes on a Brooklyn video shoot in January 2006. Rhymes's *Vibe* cover alluded to his reluctance to talk to law enforcement: the rapper was photographed with duct tape covering his mouth. (The Rhymes incident was also covered in the *60 Minutes* Cam'ron segment.)

Law enforcement, unsurprisingly, became increasingly concerned about the prevalence of the "Stop Snitchin'" phenomenon, which they viewed as a middle finger to cops or, worse, witness intimidation in a T-shirt. "Everybody in law enforcement is beside themselves," David Kennedy, director of the Center for Crime Prevention and Control at John Jay College told *USA Today. New York Times* columnist Clyde Haberman, meanwhile, clucked that the "Stop Snitchin'" ethos was merely a cover for rappers to avoid cooperating with cops. "Since some members of the Hip-Hop Nation seem to regard themselves as belonging to a separate land, perhaps we need creative ways to deal with the criminals among them," Haberman wrote. "Ah, but we should be more culturally tolerant, some say. It is very difficult, they say, for a big-time rapper to cooperate with the police. He would be seen as a snitch. He would lose credibility on the street. Worse, album sales might suffer. Poor Mr. Smith. What an ordeal this must be for him." Like most controversies, "Stop Snitchin'" was marked by overheated rhetoric with no effort by pundits or politicians to explore and examine the complex tangle of legal and cultural issues that helped create the phenomenon. Perhaps this was because a critical examination of the "Stop Snitchin'" movement would reveal that, as I told Andrew Jacobs of the *New York Times* during the spring of 2006, it's often propelled not by a reflexive anti–law enforcement mentality but a "real sense that the federal system is out of whack and that people are being put away for the rest of their lives based on [testimony from] informants."

The rise in anti-informant sentiment—and the government's increasing reliance on cooperators to make cases—can be directly traced to a series of anticrime bills passed by Congress in the mid-1980s and early 1990s that established severe mandatory minimums for drug offenders while offering the promise of drastic reductions in prison sentences for cooperators. Because the anticrime bills established significant jail time for even low-level drug game players—simple possession of five grams of crack, which weighs about as much as a nickel, could bring five years behind bars—entering into cooperation agreements with federal prosecutors became a near necessity for many defendants. Cooperation is so crucial because it can yield the much coveted "5K" motion from a prosecutor, which acknowledges "substantial assistance" on the part of defendants. The prosecutor's 5K motion—which takes its name from a section of the United States Sentencing Guidelines—recommends that the judge make a "downward departure" from the guidelines. "The anticrime bills created a scenario where there is only one way to escape a mandatory minimum sentence," says Robert Simels, a New York–based criminal defense attorney who has represented clients ranging from "GoodFellas" snitch

Henry Hill to drug kingpin Kenneth "Supreme" McGriff, "and that is to cooperate. 5K motions say 'Ignore the sentencing guidelines because he or she has substantially assisted us in this case.'"

Because drug organizations are highly compartmentalized, low-level drug defendants bear the brunt of harsher sentences: they often do not have information deemed significant enough by prosecutors to receive the 5K motion. "Defendants who are most in the know, and thus have the most 'substantial assistance' to offer, are often those who are most centrally involved in conspiratorial crimes," wrote New York University law professor Stephen J. Schulhofer in the *Wake Forest Law Review*. "Minor players, peripherally involved and with little knowledge or responsibility have little to offer and thus can wind up with far more severe sentences than the boss." Simels says that the targeting of low-level drug offenders by the sentencing guidelines has turned the criminal justice system on its head: "The more culpable you are and the more information you provide, the less time in prison you get." Indeed, the percentage of low-level powder cocaine offenders sentenced in federal courts rose from 38.1 percent in 1995 to 59.9 percent in 2000, while the percentage of low-level crack offenders sentenced increased from 48.4 percent to 66.5 percent during that same period.

The highly punitive punishments meted out as a result of the anticrime bills—particularly to those charged with crack cocaine–related offenses—has substantially increased the percentage of defendants serving decades-long (or lifelong) sentences. Nearly 127,000 people—about one in eleven inmates—is currently serving life behind bars, according to *The Meaning of "Life,"* a 2004 report by the Sentencing Project. "If I can keep my clients out of federal court," says Andrew C. White, a former prosecutor with the Maryland U.S. attorney's office who is now a criminal defense attorney in Baltimore, "that's a huge win in itself." Prior to the passage of the anticrime bills, a different sentencing structure existed in which judges weighed factors such as economic hardship and sexual abuse. By contrast, the anticrime bills stipulated that judges could depart from the guidelines when the "court finds that there exists aggravating or mitigating circumstances of a kind . . . not adequately taken into consideration" by the Sentencing Commission in formulating the guidelines. Still, judges had to provide a "specific reason" for making a departure. "In the pre-guidelines era judges considered an individual's background *and* the crime they were charged with and tried to fashion an appropriate sentence," New York criminal defense attorney Martin Stolar says. "The guidelines, conversely, created a cookie cutter system of justice."

Unsurprisingly, with the broad declines in crime nationwide in the mid- to late 1990s, support for such a highly punitive approach to incarceration—which spurns the notion of rehabilitation in favor of "just deserts" for criminals—was broad among both Democrats and Republicans. But while there are legitimate reasons to support the anticrime bills, their allure is primarily political: garnering a reputation for being "tough on crime" is almost as appealing as being viewed as a "hawk" in the war on terror. Viewed outside the prism of politics, mandatory minimums are disastrous as public policy, both burdensomely expensive and ineffective in combating the drug trade. "Mandatory minimum sentences are not justifiable on the basis of cost-effectiveness at reducing cocaine consumption, cocaine expenditures or drug related crime," wrote Rand Corporation drug policy analyst Jonathan P. Caulkins in a 1997 report called *Mandatory Minimum Drug Sentences: Throwing Away the Key or the Taxpayers' Money?* Mandatory minimums, Caulkins continues, cost taxpayers more than "enforcement under the previous sentencing regime."

The sentencing guidelines—which are by design highly mechanistic—have so eroded judicial discretion that not only has the balance of power in the courtroom tilted too far in favor of prosecutors, but justice itself is badly harmed. "Over the past thirty years, Congress has been granting the Department of Justice a virtual wish list in terms of passing new statutes," explains criminal defense attorney Gerald Lefcourt. "Combine that with a very conservative Supreme Court appointed by Republican presidents over the past few decades, and you have all the power in the hands of the prosecution." Similarly, Andrew White characterizes provisions in the sentencing guidelines such as 5K1.1 as "nuclear weapons in the government's arsenal." With the system so gamed in favor of federal prosecutors, investigative work is often spurned in favor of simply lining up informants and cooperators. "The attitude is 'We have ten informants; that's good enough; let's indict,'" Simels says. "Then, just before trial, they prep the witnesses. Very little investigative work is done."

One would think that such poor prosecutorial practices would lead to a substantial number of acquittals. But in fact the exact opposite is true: faced with mandatory minimums imposed by the anticrime bills, the overwhelming majority of defendants choose to plead out and/or cooperate rather than go to trial. When cases do go to trial, the "nuclear arsenal" prosecutors have at their disposal gives them overwhelming advantages over defendants. One of the most powerful tools is Rule 404(b) of the Federal Rules of Evidence, which stipulates that prosecutors can introduce *uncharged* evidence relating "other crimes, wrongs or acts" to prove "motive, opportunity, intent, preparation, plan, knowledge, identity, or absence of mistake or accident" behind a crime. Under Rule 404(b), prosecutors can introduce uncorroborated evidence relating to even serious crimes like murder, though some U.S. district court judges are reluctant to allow prosecutors such latitude.

Under Rule 404(b), prosecutors can also introduce evidence connected to crimes in which a defendant was previously acquitted. "When I was a prosecutor, I had a defendant who was previously charged with a drug dealing crime in which he was found not guilty," explains Andrew White. "Not only was I allowed to introduce evidence relating to that crime, I was also able to prevent the jury from hearing about the acquittal." Unsurprisingly, evidence introduced under Rule 404(b) heavily prejudices juries, a fact that has been acknowledged by even highly conservative judges. U.S. Supreme Court Justice Samuel Alito once wrote of Rule 404(b) that judges should take care to "exercise particular care in admitting such evidence," because it "sometimes carries a substantial danger of unfair prejudice."

Though Rule 404(b) requires that prosecutors provide criminal defense attorneys with "reasonable notice in advance of trial" that they will be introducing uncharged acts, often such evidence is not shared with the defense until just days before court proceedings begin. "Generally 404 notice only comes to you one week to ten days before trial," Simels explains. "You simply don't have time to investigate the evidence." A defendant able to hire a pricey attorney such as Simels might have a shot at investigating 404(b) evidence. But for defendants with a court-appointed CJA attorney—so-named because the Criminal Justice Act of 1964 stipulated that legal representation must be provided "for any person financially unable to obtain adequate representation"—the chance of examining "uncharged acts" is virtually nil, thus further unbalancing a criminal justice system that already favors the rich and well-connected.

One result of punitive criminal justice policy such as mandatory minimums and prosecutors who've grown accustomed to relying on cooperator testimony is a high rate of wrongful convictions: a 1997 study by the Northwestern University Law School's Center on Wrongful Convictions found that 46 percent of wrongful death penalty convictions can be attributed to false information provided by "incentivized witnesses." The anticrime bills have also created a skyrocketing federal inmate population. As of year-end 2005, the United States had a rate of incarceration of 737 inmates per 100,000 population—the highest rate in the world, far surpassing the Russian rate of 611 inmates per 100,000. Moreover, black and Hispanic men make up the overwhelming share of inmates in the federal and state systems. According to studies cited in a 2006 front-page article in the *New York Times*, "incarceration rates [for black men] climbed in the 1990s and reached historic highs in the past few years. In 1995, 16 percent of black men in their 20s who did not attend college were in jail or prison; by 2004, 21 percent were incarcerated. By their mid-30s, 6 in 10 black men who had dropped out of school had spent time in prison." Incarceration rates are so high in the black community that even middle-class and upper-middle-class black men have some level of contact with the prison system. A June 2006 *Washington Post* poll found that even among black men with college degrees and household incomes of $75,000 a year or more, six in ten said someone close to them had been murdered, and six in ten said a family member or close friend had been in jail or prison, putting them in the same camp as working-class, less-educated black men.

It is the most profound crisis in black American life since segregation. Indeed, U.S. District Judge Robert W. Sweet calls U.S. sentencing policy "the new Jim Crow law." Sweet's characterization of the federal criminal justice system isn't much of an exaggeration: as of mid-2005, 12 percent of black men in their twenties were in prison or jail, according to Bureau of Justice Statistics. It's a crisis that goes mostly unrecognized in left-leaning political magazines like the *New Republic* and the *Washington Monthly* as well as by civil rights leaders and black organizations.

The "Stop Snitchin'" phenomenon, then, deserves much greater scrutiny than simply brushing it off as witness intimidation promulgated by street thugs: it is instead the poisoned fruit of two decades of highly punitive sentencing policy and the secretive, sprawling, and mostly unregulated cooperator and informant insti-

tution. In the following chapters, beginning with the anticrime
bills passed by Congress in the 1980s, I trace the draconian policy
changes in the federal criminal justice system (such as the elimi-
nation of parole) that have fueled our high incarceration rates
while fostering a mistrust of law enforcement among the communities that need crime solving most. My focus here is on the federal system because of both the drastic changes in federal law and
the sheer numbers of prisoners in U.S. penitentiaries. (As of June
2005, there were 1,438,701 people incarcerated in the federal and
state systems versus 747,529 in the local jails, according to Bureau
of Justice Statistics. Findings from the Bureau of Justice Statistics
released in June of 2007 prove that incarceration rates continue to
climb. In the year ending June 30, 2006, the number of people incarcerated in U.S. prisons and jails jumped by more than 60,000
from 2005, the largest increase since 2000.) I do not argue for a total ban on the use of informants and cooperators—who are crucial
in building drug, organized crime, and corruption cases—nor do I
ignore the fact that the victims of the anti-snitch mentality are often crime victims themselves (though it's worth noting that the
high rate of unsolved crimes in cities like Washington, DC, and
New Orleans can also be attributed in large part to ineffective district attorneys and homicide departments in disarray). Instead,
this book is a call to reform the cooperation process and the sentencing guidelines themselves, which are at once enormously
costly to taxpayers, ineffective in solving the problems caused by
drug traffickers and drug users, and inequitable in terms of whom
they imprison.

Because the cooperation process—and even the statistics regarding the number of cooperators themselves—is shrouded in
secrecy, I demonstrate the corrupting influence of the informant
and cooperator-coddling approach to law enforcement through
a series of case studies: the first New York state resident to be

sentenced under federal three strikes legislation, who I believe not only is innocent of the armed robbery charges against him but also was wrongly suspected in the murder of Tupac Shakur in 1996; a Chicago man who is serving life in prison thanks to a drug conspiracy case built on a casting call of cooperators and informants assembled by a federal prosecutor in the late 1990s; a retail-level Ecstasy dealer who faced a stiff prison sentence under revised sentencing guidelines for Ecstasy-related offenses (which were instituted in 2001 as a result of poorly conducted scientific studies about the drug's effects) and, as a result, became a cooperator; a Pakistani immigrant living in Queens sentenced to thirty years' imprisonment in 2007 for his role in an alleged plot to bomb Penn Station in New York City, a plot that was concocted by a well-compensated NYPD informant who created a fictional terrorist organization called The Brotherhood; an assistant U.S. attorney in Baltimore who was slain during a 2003 trial of a drug trafficker that fell apart thanks to a renegade cooperator; a pair of extraordinarily dangerous cooperators—one in Richmond, Virginia, the other in New York City—who perpetrated perhaps the ghastliest crimes of 2006, all committed soon after they received 5K motions from federal prosecutors; and finally, two crooked Baltimore cops exposed by the infamous *Stop Fucking Snitching, Vol. 1* DVD in 2004. In every case, what's abundantly clear is that justice is poorly served by the culture of snitching, cooperator testimony is notoriously unreliable yet can often result in undeserved guilty verdicts for defendants, and the dangers posed by violent criminals released early because of cooperation agreements are potentially lethal.

Chapter One

FEEDING THE FEDERAL BEAST

Giuliani Day, Congress's Anticrime Bills, and Candy Bar Justice

ON JANUARY 8, 1984, A BITTERLY COLD DAY, EIGHTEEN-YEAR-OLD HUSTLER Ricardo Ortiz stood solemnly in front of U.S. District Judge Kevin Duffy and implored his family not to shed any tears for him. "Don't start crying," Ortiz said stoically as he stood in shackles in front of Judge Duffy. Ortiz was putting on a brave face because Duffy had just sentenced him to six years' imprisonment for selling $100 worth of heroin on the Lower East Side. Naturally Ortiz's parents—who were seated in the courtroom that day—were overcome with grief. But as U.S. marshals moved in and escorted Ortiz, who had been arrested more than half a dozen times since he was thirteen, from the courtroom, his calm facade slipped. "Six years," he cried. "I don't believe it."

Ortiz had ample reason to be surprised not just by his sentence but that he had ever attracted the attention of the feds in the first place. In August 1983, he was arrested during a new law enforcement campaign against low-level drug dealers on the Lower East Side launched by Rudy Giuliani, who had just been sworn in as the U.S. attorney for the Southern District of New York. The plan for stepped-up drug enforcement on the Lower East Side—dubbed "Federal Day" because the feds would choose a day, without advance notice, to prosecute low-level dealers in federal court—came during a tour of the drug-plagued neighborhood that Giuliani took at the invitation of Manhattan Borough President Andrew Stein and Congressman William Green. "I was shocked by what I saw," Giuliani told the *New York Times* on February 19, 1984. "Hundreds of people bought drugs in the open."

Federal Day brought harsh sentences for retail-level dealers like Ortiz as well as a moralistic glee from a few federal judges who handed them out. After Ortiz's attorney made a plea for mercy just before sentencing, Judge Duffy railed at him, "You're going to get two things: you're going to get dried out, and you're going to get out of the Lower East Side. Then you'll realize that lying won't get you any place.'" Ortiz was not alone in his fate. Drug dealers who would have received a sentence of just a few months in the state system were suddenly being sent away for years by the feds. Unsurprisingly, in a city wracked by high crime rates—in 1984, there were more than five thousand crimes per hundred thousand population in New York state—Federal Day was well-received by both local politicians like Mayor Ed Koch and newspaper editorial boards. A February 1984 piece in the *New York Times* praising Federal Day described the streets of the Lower East Side as cleansed—at least temporarily—of drug dealers: "No longer were teen-agers steering out-of-state drivers to dealers' dens in abandoned buildings owned by the city. Gone were the queues of addicts buying drugs on the street."

Because it gave crime-weary New Yorkers the impression that the feds were making great strides in their battle against the downtown drug trade, Federal Day quickly became a signature accomplishment for Giuliani, and he would later boast of its success when he ran for mayor. But Federal Day actually yielded very few indictments of drug dealers. "It was a disaster," former New York Special Narcotics Prosecutor Robert Silbering told me. "The feds are accustomed to handling big, long investigations. I used to handle more indictments in a month than the Southern District would handle in a year. In those days if they were doing 750 indictments a year, that would be a lot. We were doing 7,000 a year. They simply couldn't handle the numbers." An examination of Federal Day by the *New York Times*—conducted just as Giuliani was running for mayor in 1989 on his crime-busting credentials—supported Silbering's contention. According to the *Times*, Federal Day yielded only a few hundred drug arrests—"a small fraction of the 67,000 people arrested on narcotics charges in the city that year." Many of the 351 people indicted by Giuliani in the Southern District, according to the *Times*, "would have been arrested on Federal charges even without the special program." Giuliani brought indictments of just 64 more people than the U.S. attorney for the Eastern District of New York, which did not have any sort of Federal Day–like program.

What infuriated judges and state law enforcement officials was not necessarily the insignificant number of indictments brought by Giuliani but the cases themselves, most of which involved petty hustlers. "The judges would say, 'What do you mean, you're bringing me a guy who sold a packet of coke or a vial of crack?'" Silbering remembers. But if Federal Day did little to combat New York's flourishing drug trade, it nonetheless was crucial in shaping the image of Giuliani as a dynamic, almost revolutionary crime fighter. "It got so much press," Silbering remembers. "The feeling was 'The feds are coming in!' But other than publicity it wasn't getting them anywhere." In fact, Silbering says, among state law enforcement officials Federal Day was so widely viewed as a grab by Giuliani for headlines that it was nicknamed "Giuliani Day."

...

Federal Day may have been a failed anticrime program crafted by a PR-savvy U.S. attorney. But it is also a potent symbol of a trend during the 1980s toward extending federal jurisdiction over crimes once prosecuted by state and local law enforcement. Soon after Federal Day was implemented in New York City in 1984, Congress enacted the first in a series of tough anticrime bills that abolished parole for federal offenders, established mandatory minimum sentences for drug-related crimes, expanded the number of crimes eligible for the death penalty, and established a three strikes provision for violent offenders. Because they faced such steep prison sentences under the new federal anticrime legislation, many defendants would plead out to their crimes and cooperate with prosecutors. The small percentage of defendants who did go to trial would face almost certain conviction in federal court, with conviction rates at around 84 percent.

University of Illinois law professor Andrew D. Leipold attributes this phenomenon to the sentencing guidelines. "The guidelines took away a huge amount of sentencing discretion," Leipold wrote in a study for the *Washington University Law Quarterly*, "which meant that judges were more often faced with cases where they knew that a conviction would result in a harsh—maybe too harsh—sentence." Leipold also argues that juries are less able to discern flaws in prosecution arguments. "Judges are more likely to acquit because defense counsel direct weak cases toward the bench, and they do so because they trust judges more than juries to find the genuine flaws in the government's case. In contrast, juries convict more because they see stronger prosecutions, and they see these cases because defense counsel believe that their chances are better before a jury, even if the odds are slim in absolute terms." Unsurprisingly, the outcome of such harsh sentencing policy has been explosive growth of the prison system for at least the past decade. Since the mid-1990s the federal prison system has grown at a much faster rate than the states, according to the Bureau of Justice Statistics; in the first half of 2005, for example, the number of federal inmates increased 2.3 percent, more than twice the rate of the states.

Such historic changes naturally did not occur overnight. Efforts to overhaul federal criminal law—which prosecutors and lawmakers believed to be outdated with the rise of burgeoning areas of crime, such as drug trafficking and money laundering—had begun in the late 1970s. In 1978 Senator Edward Kennedy, then head of the House Judiciary Committee, co-sponsored legislation that would recodify federal criminal laws, restrict parole, and establish a sentencing commission to set sentencing guidelines. An amended version of the bill passed the Senate, but then stalled in the House. When Kennedy introduced similar legislation—the Criminal Code Reform Act of 1979—it also stalled. Efforts to revise criminal law continued during the waning years of the Carter administration, when the judiciary committee sought to revise Title 18 of the U.S. Code ("crimes and criminal procedure"). Title 18 provided an alphabetized, laundry list of crimes from arson to robbery, which was considered a relic from the time of its passage (1948). But when President Ronald Reagan took office and the Republicans gained control of the Senate in 1981, the policy goals of the Judiciary Committee—whose new chair was Southern archconservative Strom Thurmond—shifted from revising Title 18 to addressing the explosion in drug use and trafficking. This change in tack was understandable: according to Monitoring the Future, the study funded by the National Institute on Drug

Abuse, in 1981 approximately 66 percent of twelfth graders had used "an illicit drug by the time they left high school." This was an all-time high in the history of the study, a record that stands more than twenty-five years later.

Spectacular violence accompanied this spike in drug use: Cuban and Colombian drug traffickers battled over the rapidly expanding markets for cocaine, then the drug of choice among both teenagers and adults. "There were shoot-outs with military-style weapons," Eric Sterling, who was legal counsel to the U.S. House of Representatives Committee on the Judiciary from 1979 to 1989, told me. "Things got so bad that there were even efforts to get the military involved." President Reagan's secretary of defense, Caspar Weinberger, opposed the militarization of the drug war (he didn't think it was an appropriate use of the armed forces), frustrating lawmakers in the House and Senate, particularly those from Florida, where much of the cocaine-related carnage occurred. Cocaine-related crime spiked with such ferociousness in South Florida that kidnappings and targeted killings became an almost daily fact of life. One of the most notorious incidents in Florida's cocaine wars came on July 11, 1979, when assassins working for Medellín Cartel underboss Griselda Blanco murdered a pair of drug kingpins as they shopped at a liquor store in the Dadeland Mall in Dade County. The killers drove to the mall in an armored van outfitted with one-way glass and gunports and then carried out the hit by spraying their targets and the mall's parking lot with gunfire, injuring two employees and sending shoppers running for their lives. Such brazen acts of violence earned the Medellín hit men the nickname "Cocaine Cowboys."

With warlike conditions in South Florida and cocaine use increasing dramatically, Delaware Senator Joseph Biden, who was then a member of both the Judiciary and the Intelligence Committees, proposed the creation of a cabinet-level "drug czar" to coordinate antidrug efforts among federal agencies like the FBI, DEA, and IRS. "We need one person to call the shots," Biden proclaimed to the *New York Times* on October 9, 1982. The Reagan administration rejected Biden's proposal, dubbing it "bureaucratic" and offering instead to initiate a program that would hire eight hundred to a thousand agents for the DEA and FBI at a cost of nearly $200 million. Biden pushed ahead with his drug czar bill regardless, but while it had crucial support from Strom Thurmond, Reagan vetoed it in January 1983. There was enormous consternation in Congress over Reagan's veto, and anger toward Reagan's rejection as well as expectations about the upcoming election in 1984 inspired lawmakers to craft even tougher anti-crime measures.

During the spring of 1983, Thurmond and Nevada Senator Paul Laxalt began working on the Comprehensive Crime Control Act (CCCA), a revolutionary piece of legislation that would replace the United States Parole Commission with the United States Sentencing Commission (USSC), thus abolishing parole for federal prisoners. The role of the USSC—an independent agency within the judicial branch whose seven members were to be appointed by the president and confirmed by the Senate—would be to draft "sentencing guidelines" for federal courts, which U.S. district judges would then consult in a mechanistic manner. Indeed, the sentencing guidelines were to be defined by a kind of rigid calculus: crimes would be assigned a specific "offense level" between one and forty-three (one being the lowest), with a defendant's criminal history ranked between one and six (one being the least severe). The judge would then consult a "sentencing table" featuring a matrix of offense levels and criminal history with a 258-box grid of punishment ranges for defendants. By locating the point at which the matrices of crime and criminal record met on the sentencing table, the judge would arrive at the applicable guideline range for a defendant. Most importantly, in drug cases the weight of narcotics would become the central basis for determining a defendant's sentence. "The sentencing guidelines took into consideration the weight involved but made little distinction between someone running a massive drug operation and an addict dealing to support his problem," Eric P. Berlin, a Chicago-based attorney who has written law review articles about the sentencing guidelines, told me. "It's a *quantitative* versus qualitative approach to penology."

While the Comprehensive Crime Control Act standardized sentencing, it also put dozens of crimes ranging from arson and murder-for-hire to trademark violations and credit card fraud under federal jurisdiction. In an attempt to rein in the cocaine-related crime plaguing the streets, CCCA also contained a series of provisions targeting drug traffickers. Judges were permitted to refuse bail if it could be determined that the source of the bail was illegal profits; the value of property that could be seized administratively without a court order was raised from $10,000 to $100,000; and ringleaders of drug organizations could be charged under a continuing criminal enterprise statute defined as a "continuing series of violations" of drug laws. "'You can go back many years before you'd find such an effort to enact serious crime legislation," Deputy Attorney General Edward C. Schmults boasted to the *New York Times* on October 3, 1983. Schmults may have been understating the case: under the CCCA, the very nature of the federal criminal justice system shifted from rehabilitation of prisoners to punishment. "Sentencing is no longer for rehabilitating offenders into good citizens," wrote Eric P. Berlin in a *Wisconsin Law Review* article, "The Federal Sentencing Guidelines' Failure to Eliminate Sentencing Disparity: Governmental Manipulations Before Arrest." "It is based solely on the ideology of punishment and deterrence." The sentencing guidelines replaced the concept of "indeterminate sentencing"—whereby prisoners were released before serving the full term if the parole commission determined that they were rehabilitated—while greatly curtailing judicial discretion. Even the composition of the United States Sentencing Commission represented a shift in power away from the bench (no more than three of its seven voting members could be judges), a departure from Senator Kennedy's concept of the commission, which he intended to be judge-dominated.

Given the sweeping changes promised by the Comprehensive Crime Control Act, a serious debate should have taken place in Congress over its provisions. But thanks to external pressures—a looming presidential election, fury with Reagan's veto of Biden's drug czar bill, and a fear among Democrats of being perceived by voters as being "soft on crime"—the legislation was hurriedly enacted in October 1984, just one month before election day. "The whole process had the speed of an auction," Sterling remembers, "because the Democrats were anxious about both the upcoming election and getting politically beaten up as soft on crime and drugs. It was like 'Time's up. Do we have a deal?'" Berlin says that while the goal of sentencing uniformity was reasonable, CCCA was driven by "blind ideology of getting tough on crime and the notion that rehabilitation is simply a fool's errand."

■ ■ ■

The fevered lawmaking behind the Comprehensive Crime Control Act in the mid-1980s was circumspect compared to the manner in which Congress crafted its next major piece of antidrug legislation. On June 19, 1986, twenty-two-year-old University of Maryland basketball star Len Bias collapsed in his dorm room and then died hours later from a heart attack triggered by "cocaine intoxication." Lawmakers quickly worked themselves into a frenzy over the drug crisis, surpassing the apocalyptic mood surrounding South Florida's cocaine killing fields. "During the summer of 1986, every committee—agriculture, ways and means, education, veterans affairs, you name it—was directed to do something about the drug problem," remembers Sterling. Because Bias had been drafted by the Boston Celtics just before his death, antidrug legislation became a priority for Massachusetts lawmakers, particularly Speaker of the House Thomas Phillip "Tip" O'Neill. "When Tip went back to his district, the feeling was 'Our Larry Bird successor has died,'" Sterling says. "It was the 9/11 of athletics."

A new drug on the streets—crack—was also fueling the legislative momentum, particularly from black lawmakers, like New York Congressman Charlie Rangel, who witnessed the effect it was having on their constituents. Because crack was inexpensive to prepare—dealers simply mixed cocaine and baking soda and "cooked" it over a stove—the drug democratized the drug trade, which was once dominated by established cocaine and heroin crews run by street CEOs. A former hustler who once plied his trade in Queens' "40 Projects" told me that with the rise of crack "the privates became generals." The old generals, needless to say, were not happy with the new drug business arrivistes and fought fiercely to protect their territory. "He's like a wounded lion now," New York Special Narcotics Prosecutor Sterling Johnson said of southeast Queens kingpin Lorenzo "Fat Cat" Nichols after the arrival of crack on the scene, "and the jackals are nipping at his heels." Fueling the tension was the behavior of crack users themselves, whose short, intense highs caused them to come back for drugs like clockwork and, worse, commit crimes big and small to support their addiction.

Crack was an authentic crisis, but there were ample amounts of hysteria surrounding the drug. A 1985 study in the *New En-*

gland Journal of Medicine concluded that the newborns of twenty-three cocaine-using women were less interactive with others and moodier than babies who were not exposed to cocaine; the report was picked up by the media and transformed into a furor about a generation of "crack babies." Medical studies would later dispel the "crack baby" myth. "Exposing fetuses to cocaine may or may not have lasting consequences," wrote pediatric health expert Dr. Gary A. Emmett in a study called "What Happened to Crack Babies?" "but current research demonstrates that by the time the child reaches age five, the effect of the disastrous social situation that many crack cocaine users share with other economically deprived children washes out any measurable effect of the cocaine itself on these children's school performance."

Instead of tamping down the panic, Democratic legislators—still smarting from their electoral losses in 1984—seized on it in hopes of reclaiming the White House in 1988. Hysteria about the drug war was so prevalent on Capitol Hill that when Eric Sterling presented a proposal to redirect law enforcement efforts toward high-level drug traffickers, he was told, "We're never going to have these kinds of prosecutions in towns like Louisville." This claim was technically correct—major drug traffickers use metropolises such as Miami, New York, and Los Angeles as points of entry, therefore reducing the chances of big prosecutions in smaller towns—but it was also an excuse to direct drug enforcement toward low-level dealers.

When Congress returned to work in the fall of 1986, they did just that, drafting and passing the Anti-Drug Abuse Act of 1986, which imposed a mandatory minimum sentence of ten years in prison for anyone convicted of selling or possessing fifty grams of crack. Defendants in powder cocaine cases, by comparison, faced ten years' imprisonment for the sale of five thousand grams, a 100:1 disparity. Even though crack dealers can "rock up" with small amounts of cocaine, fifty grams is still such an insignificant amount of the drug that drug policy experts use the term "Candy Bar Justice"—so-named because a Hershey bar weighs about forty-three grams—to describe the act. "Congress was totally illiterate about the metric system," says Sterling. Legislators also seemed uninterested in having experts weigh in on the bill: neither federal judges, nor members of the Bureau of Prisons, nor state law enforcement officials (most notably, those in New York who had experience with the Rockefeller drug laws, which made the penalty for selling certain amounts of cocaine and heroin the same as that for second-degree murder) were invited to testify before Congress.

Those caught selling fifty grams of crack faced not just ten years behind bars but denial of bail under the Comprehensive Crime Control Act. "The bail denial becomes very effective because suddenly just about everyone charged in a drug case is facing ten years," explains Robert Simels. "They contain you throughout the proceedings, and obviously by putting someone in jail it creates an incentive to get out of jail. By the time you get to your client after their lockup, they have been schooled by everybody in the institution about the sentencing guidelines and how you get out of the guidelines, which is cooperating." Indeed, immediately following the passage of the Anti-Drug Abuse Act of 1986, Congress directed the USSC to craft major incentives for cooperators. Under 5K1.1, a new section of the sentencing guidelines, judges could make a "downward departure" from a guideline sentence if the defendant provided "substantial assistance" to prosecutors. Though section 5K1.1 was enthusiastically backed by the Justice Department, some lawmakers worried that with even retail-level drug dealers facing significant prison time under the sentencing guidelines, the temptation to fabricate evidence in order to receive a "downward departure" would be too great. There was also concern that section 5K1.1 provided too generous rewards to cooperators, who could then feel emboldened to return to the streets to commit even more crime. "We fought the Department of Justice on this because we thought that they [cooperators] were fiendishly bad people," Sterling remembers, "but the DOJ insisted that 'substantial assistance' be part of the legislation. They told us, 'We need this to build cases.'"

While section 5K1.1 was an invaluable tool to federal prosecutors—"flipping" was suddenly a foregone conclusion for most defendants—it also created huge incentives for defendants to fabricate evidence, particularly when faced with harsh prison terms. And as nearly every flashpoint of the drug war—from the Dadeland Mall murders in South Florida to the overdose of Len Bias in Maryland—brought increases in the sentencing guidelines, the prosecutor's 5K motion became a brass ring for defendants.

Unsurprisingly, the February 1988 murder of rookie NYPD cop Edward Byrne at the hands of henchmen working for Lorenzo "Fat Cat" Nichols was greeted by yet more increases in the sentencing guidelines for drug-related offenses. In the wake of Byrne's murder, members of Congress and local New York politicians seemed to be engaged in a competition over who could devise the most florid metaphor about the drug trade or the most strained comparison to historic assassinations. In a speech about Byrne, New York Mayor Ed Koch managed to compare the cop's slaying to the death of FDR and assassinations of John F. Kennedy, Robert F. Kennedy, *and* Martin Luther King. "If drug traffickers have become so emboldened that they can engage in the assassination of a young police officer, then our whole society is at risk and we will have anarchy," Koch said then. "That is why his death rivals the others. Not because he is Edward Byrne, but because of what it means to have this police officer assassinated."

With the publicity surrounding Byrne's murder and major anticrime legislation becoming a priority in Congress, crime was the dominant issue in the 1988 presidential campaign. George H. W.

Bush hit the campaign trail with Byrne's badge in his pocket, and his strategists created an ad called "Revolving Door," in which Democratic opponent Michael Dukakis was criticized for vetoing mandatory sentences for drug dealers. "Now Michael Dukakis says he wants to do for America what he's done for Massachusetts," the ad's narrator intoned ominously. Another Bush ad—which featured a mug shot of a convicted Massachusetts murderer named Willie Horton who had raped a white woman while on furlough—was even more effective, putting a frightening (and black) face on criminal justice issues. "If you look at the way [Dukakis's] negatives grew in July," Gallup's Andrew Kohut told the *National Journal*, "you see that it occurred at the time when people were becoming aware of the Massachusetts furlough story."

As Bush and Dukakis debated Massachusetts's incarceration policies, the Democrat-controlled Congress put the finishing touches on yet more sweeping anticrime legislation, the Anti-Drug Abuse Act of 1988. Along with creating a cabinet-level drug czar, the bill offered punishments far harsher than even its predecessor in 1986: mandatory minimums of five years in prison for simple *possession* of five grams of crack; a twenty-year sentence for continuing criminal enterprise (and possibility of life in prison if the quantity of drugs were large enough); and the death penalty extended to drug traffickers and, in a nod to Byrne, to "anyone who intentionally kills . . . any law enforcement officer during or in relation to a Federal drug felony." But the get-tough posturing of the act didn't resuscitate the Democrats' political fortunes, at least in the short term: Bush handily defeated Dukakis on November 8, 1988, and, just days later, President Reagan signed the Anti-Drug Abuse Act of 1988 at a White House ceremony, flanked by Byrne's parents. "With us today are Matthew and Ann Byrne," Reagan said, "who join us as we give their son's comrades the valuable tools they need to carry forth the fight for which young Eddie so valiantly gave his life. . . . We salute his family for their determination that his death will not have been in vain."

Byrne's death did not usher in a new era of killings of law enforcement officials as Congress and the White House feared. Instead, it was a signpost that the most intense violence of the crack era was finally coming to an end. Even high-ranking members of Fat Cat's organization had grown weary of violence and were furious with his lieutenant Howard "Pappy" Mason for ordering the Byrne hit, which they rightly viewed as bad for business. So, after spiking in the early 1990s—in 1990, there were over 6,300 crimes per 100,000 population in New York State, an all-time high—crime rates began to fall precipitously in New York and around the country. From 1991 to 1998 the overall crime rate declined by 22 percent, violent crime fell 25 percent, and property crime dropped 21 percent, according to the FBI Uniform Crime Reports. On its face, the dramatically falling crime rates of the 1990s appeared to validate the anticrime bills of the 1980s. But while increasing incarceration rates *did* contribute to the drop in crime in the 1990s—economist Steven D. Levitt estimates that increases in the prison population accounted for a 12 percent decline in homicide and violent crime—Canada experienced similar crime declines in the 1990s as its incarceration rates declined, according to University of California at Berkeley criminologist Franklin Zimring. In addition, there were other factors behind the reductions in crime beyond increased incarceration rates: namely, a beefing up of state and local law enforcement resources. During the 1990s, the ranks of the NYPD swelled by 35 percent, with violent crime dropping 56 percent in New York City during that period. There were also less measurable but equally important factors behind the substantial drop in crime, foremost among them a generational rejection of crack and its accompanying violence. Inner-city youth watched as crack wiped out not only friends and relatives but even drug kingpins, making for a powerful form of deterrence. "Younger brothers of the gang bangers looked at the [street] life and said, 'Maybe not,'" Mark Kleiman, director of the Drug Policy Analysis Program at UCLA's School of Public Policy, told me.

Yet during the 1990s, politicians, law enforcement, and the media tended to ignore these other factors contributing to the steep crime declines, instead attributing them solely to increased incarceration rates and policing strategies like COMPSTAT, a program developed by the NYPD in the early 1990s in which the department brass reviewed a weekly summary of statistics on crime complaints and arrest and summons activity. So at the beginning of 1994 lawmakers began crafting yet another sprawling anticrime bill, in the mold of the Anti-Drug Abuse Acts of 1986 and 1988, with punitive punishments such as a three strikes provision for violent offenders that would once again ratchet up incarceration rates. The political climate in Washington in early 1994 was uncannily similar to that which preceded the anticrime legislation of the 1980s. Though Democrats controlled the White House and Congress, polls suggested that they could lose their majority in the fall elections; worse, Democrats battled the "soft on crime" image foisted upon them by Republicans, an ironic (and unfair) label, given that the party's most prominent lawmakers, such as Senator Joseph Biden, were key players in the passage of anticrime bills of the 1980s.

Caught in the political crosswinds, the Democrat-dominated Congress crafted legislation—dubbed the Violent Crime Control and Law Enforcement Act of 1994—that was an awkward mix of classic big government liberalism (nearly $2 billion to help prevent and investigate acts of violence against women) and Republican-styled "just deserts" for defendants. Under the legislation, inmates were to be denied Pell grants for higher education, and a defendant who had been previously convicted in federal courts of a serious violent felony and had two or more prior convictions in federal or state courts (at least one of which was a "serious violent felony") would receive life imprisonment under a three strikes provision. The proposed law seemed to be, as the *New Republic*'s Peter Beinart later characterized it, "tough on crime, tough on the causes of crime." But while the bill was politically appealing to the Washington pundit class represented by Beinart, most of its provisions were ineffective at reducing crime and economically burdensome to states. The legislation offered incentives for states to pass so-called truth-in-sentencing laws, which require violent offenders to serve at least 85 percent of their sentences. These laws would quickly become extravagantly expensive to taxpayers: a 2004 report by the *Milwaukee Journal Sentinel* on Wisconsin's truth-in-sentencing laws—which are among the toughest in the nation—found that the program will cost the state's taxpayers an estimated $1.8 billion for inmates admitted through the year 2025. Wisconsin wardens also complained to the *Journal Sentinel* that truth-in-sentencing laws led to an increase in bad conduct and caused inmates to forgo drug and alcohol treatment programs. "They know they are not going to get out any earlier," one warden explained, "so they simply don't want to take the time to do the programming and don't want to invest in it. It is a shame, because we have excellent programs here."

The Violent Crime Control and Law Enforcement Act of 1994 should have at least worked as great politics for Democrats. "How did such a misbegotten piece of legislation become law?" *New York Times* op-ed columnist Anthony Lewis wrote then. "The answer is simple: politics. Democrats wanted to take the crime issue away from Republicans. Republicans responded by sounding 'tougher.' The Justice Department did not work effectively against the worst features because President Clinton wanted something—anything—labeled 'crime bill.'" But while the bill was a boon to

President Clinton's legacy—its COPS program, which provided funding for 100,000 new police officers, was remembered by the *Chicago Tribune*'s Steve Chapman as "Bill Clinton's most bally-hooed domestic program"—it failed to deliver on its political promise. Soon after the bill became law on September 13, 1994, Republicans took control of the House for the first time since 1954.

As crime fell steadily around the country throughout the 1990s, the "lock 'em up" policies of the anticrime bills seemed vindicated. But did the almost threefold increase in the number of federal drug offenders from the mid-1980s to the late 1990s—and the profound shift in the balance of power in the courtroom from the bench to prosecutors that took place during that period—actually reduce the availability of drugs or curb drug use? It should be noted that traditionally the aims of drug enforcement are to raise the price of drugs and lower their purity and that there is very little research on drug prices to support those aims. Federal agencies like the FBI or DEA do not conduct such research, and most drug-related studies focus on treatment and prevention. Conversely, in the UK, the FBI-like Serious Organised Crime Agency tracks heroin prices so closely that the *Economist* criticized it for reading too much into market fluctuations to measure its success in combating the drug business. The few studies that do exist mostly gauge drug usage, not availability or pricing.

One exception is DAWN (Drug Abuse Warning Network), funded by the U.S. Department of Health and Human Services. DAWN monitors drug-related visits to hospital emergency rooms and drug-related deaths investigated by medical examiners and coroners. Its statistics provide a sense of how problematic certain drugs are at a given moment, and, as its name implies, it serves as a warning system for future crises. By the end of the 1990s, DAWN's statistics were prescient in predicting the explosion in Ecstasy use.

Similarly, a pair of national studies—the aforementioned Monitoring the Future and the National Survey on Drug Use and Health (funded by the U.S. Department of Health and Human Services)—offer a broad sense of trends in drug use and availability since the passage of the anticrime bills. But they do not provide a complete picture of the drug problem because, as drug policy expert Peter Reuter notes, "heavy users of cocaine, crack, and heroin are often socially isolated and thus beyond the reach of general population surveys." Nonetheless, it's clear from both studies that prior to the passage of the federal anticrime bills, drug use among young adults was worryingly high; in 1981, 66 percent of Monitoring the Future's respondents (which included a sample of 18,267 twelfth graders) used "an illicit drug by the time they left high school." In the years following the enactment of the anticrime bills, the percentage of Monitoring the Future's respondents using "any illicit drug" declined to an all-time low of 41 percent in 1992. However, since 1992 the percentage of respondents saying they used "any illicit drug" climbed to 55 percent (in 1999) followed by only a slight decline, to 50 percent (in 2005). This led Monitoring the Future's authors to conclude that "while use of individual drugs . . . may fluctuate widely, the proportion using any of them is much less labile."

Seemingly major successes in combating specific drugs—such as cocaine—are also elusive and follow the plateauing trend of other drugs, according to Monitoring the Future. From 1985 to 1992, annual cocaine usage declined steeply among young adults (from 12.7 percent to 3.1 percent). But that trend quickly reversed course, and by 1999 6.2 percent of its respondents said they used cocaine, a 100 percent increase from 1992. Statistics from the National Survey on Drug Use and Health mirror this up-down-and-up-again arc. "The percentage of young adults aged 18 to 25 who had ever used cocaine . . . rose steadily throughout the 1970s and early 1980s," the survey's authors wrote, "reaching 17.9 percent in 1984. By 1996, the rate had dropped to 10.1 percent, but climbed to 15.4 percent in 2002." On the twentieth anniversary of Len Bias's death, in June 2006, a spokeswoman for the Substance Abuse and Mental Health Services Administration admitted to the *Washington Post* that cocaine use has been steadily rebounding since the mid-1980s.

If cocaine usage has fluctuated, one metric has remained constant: the percentage of Monitoring the Future's respondents who say that the drug is "fairly easy" or "very easy" to obtain. In 1975, just under 40 percent of respondents said that drug was easy to obtain, and by 1989 (near the peak of the crack/cocaine era) nearly 50 percent said the drug was easy to obtain. Since then, the percentage of respondents saying the drug is easy to obtain has remained at nearly 40 percent. An examination of the percentage of the study's respondents who say that marijuana is "fairly easy" or "very easy" to obtain tells a similar story about the availability of drugs: the percentage has remained over 80 percent since 1975.

At the very least, locking up thousands of drug dealers should make drugs much more expensive. Drug dealers, after all, calculate levels of risk when determining their prices. But the opposite is true: prices for most drugs have *declined* since the early 1980s. From 1981 to 1995, the inflation-adjusted prices of cocaine and heroin fell by two-thirds. In a May 1997 *Drug Policy Analysis Bulletin* for the Federation of American Scientists, Peter Reuter concluded that "the number of people dependent on cocaine and heroin has been fairly stable over a long period of time," while at the same time, "an increasing share are being locked up." Indeed, Reuter found that from 1981 to 2000, heroin and cocaine arrests *increased* tenfold as the retail price of cocaine *declined* by two-thirds. The anticrime bills, then, have been somewhat effective in curbing violent crime associated with the drug trade (though not nearly so much as one might think, given the extremely harsh sentencing guidelines), very effective in stigmatizing drugs (Reuter says that "the most proximate cause of the decline" in drug use over time can be attributed to "a shift in attitudes concerning the risks of use"), but remarkably ineffective in reducing availability and pricing—perhaps the most important metrics of all when sizing up the costs and benefits of drug enforcement efforts. "The situation with illegal drugs should not look like this," says Eric Sterling. "We're spending $50 billion per year, and we end up with better and better drugs—for less and less money."

■ ■ ■

Perversely, the great achievement of the anticrime bills is the sprawling federal prison system itself. Direct expenditures on crime at the federal level *doubled* from 1990 to 1999 (from $10 billion to more than $20 billion) according to the Bureau of Justice Statistics. Thanks to section 5K1.1 and the persistent ratcheting up of the sentencing guidelines, it's a criminal justice system under which cooperators thrive. "The use of criminal informants in the U.S. justice system," says Loyola University law professor Alexandra Natapoff, "has become a flourishing socio-legal institution unto itself." This should be no surprise: the Comprehensive Crime Control Act and the twin Anti-Drug Abuse acts of 1986 and 1988 established such steep prison sentences for even minor crimes (like possession of five grams of crack) that cooperating is a necessity for many defendants. "They'll even volunteer to cooperate as they are being arrested," says Washington, DC–based criminal defense attorney Cheryl Stein. "In fact, deals are often worked out even before a defendant has reached a lawyer." As the cooperation process is shrouded in secrecy by the feds, it's difficult to discern the number of defendants who have struck cooperation deals, though Natapoff estimates that "approximately 20 percent of federal offenders received on-the-record cooperation credit under 5K1.1 as did 30 percent of drug defendants." But, according to Natapoff, "those recorded percentages . . . represent less than half of defendants who actually cooperate: some cooperators receive no credit, while others escape the process altogether by having charges dismissed or never being charged at all."

While there is no doubt that cooperators are critical in building drug conspiracy, public corruption, and organized crime cases, the centrality of the 5K motion in receiving a "downward departure" from the sentencing guidelines creates a nearly overpowering motive for defendants to lie. Worse, the cooperator-driven criminal justice system has turned the role of prosecutors and drug enforcement on its head. "Targets are selected by informants and cooperators," says Eric Sterling, "not by DEA intelligence." Indeed, cooperators eager for a 5K motion will often induce targets into cooking powder cocaine into crack in order to trigger the maximum possible sentence for them under the sentencing guidelines (and thereby increasing the chance of the cooperator receiving a glowing 5K motion from a federal prosecutor). "Cooperating witnesses claim that the defendant sold them crack in certain amounts, knowing full well that they will be rewarded commensurate with the defendant's sentence," A. J. Kramer, the federal public defender for the District of Columbia, told the United States Sentencing Commission in November 2006. "These tactics produce more bang for the buck in crack cases than in any other kind of drug case because a very small increase in quantity results in a very large increase in the sentence, and because the simple process of cooking powder into crack results in a drastic sentence increase."

With low-level dealers the focus of the sentencing guidelines those targeted are often street corner hustlers, not drug kingpins: in 2000, for example, the DEA made 3,866 seizures of crack with the average seizure yielding eighty-eight grams of the drug. Similarly, in 2001 the DEA made 3,916 seizures of crack, with an average seizure of seventy-two grams. Candy Bar Justice, indeed. The targeting of low-level players in the drug game has brought a dramatic increase in the percentage of federal drug defendants (from 11,854 in 1984 to 29,306 in 1999), all of which comes at an enormous cost to taxpayers and, more importantly, the minority communities most affected by such policies. As of year-end 2005, 40 percent of all inmates in federal prisons serving more than one year were black, and 31 percent self-identified as Hispanic, according to Bureau of Prisons statistics. Such profoundly inequitable policies inspire animus toward law enforcement and suspicions that minority groups were purposefully targeted by the lawmakers who crafted the anticrime bills of the 1980s and 1990s (even though black legislators like Charlie Rangel pushed for the bills out of a genuine concern about crack's effects on inner-city communities). Anger burns the brightest, though, at the cooperators who help fuel the skyrocketing incarceration rates by assisting prosecutors not in bringing justice to kingpins but in triggering the longest possible prison terms to retail drug dealers under the sentencing guidelines.

Chapter Two

BAD TO WORSE

Snitching Scandals, Coddled Cooperators

ON NOVEMBER 1, 1987, THE SENTENCING REFORM ACT WENT INTO EFFECT. This was the portion of the Comprehensive Crime Control Act of 1984 that created the United States Sentencing Commission and instructed it to create sentencing guidelines for federal courts. It was an epochal moment in criminal justice history: parole was abolished (reflecting a lack of faith in what legal scholars call "the rehabilitative ideal"), and the role of judges was essentially reduced to choosing a sentencing from within the guidelines' range—unless the judge could identify a factor that would result in a downward departure, namely the provision of "substantial assistance" to prosecutors. Cooperation thus became a necessity for many defendants looking to reduce their sentences. Besides a few scattered protests from criminal defense attorneys, few voices rose in opposition to this cooperator-centric approach to law enforcement—a surprisingly quiet response, since there was already a history of informants fraught with corruption and scandal.

Though the use and misuse of cooperators in prosecuting drug cases is a relatively recent phenomenon, informants have long played a critical role in mafia, public corruption, and counterterrorism cases brought by federal prosecutors. Still, the history of the FBI's use of informants has been plagued by corruption and a lack of oversight, which has resulted in the establishment of extensive guidelines about their use. Guidelines governing the use of informants actually arose from the abuses stemming from covert domestic surveillance programs conducted during the 1950s and 1960s. These programs monitored "revolutionary-type subversives": suspected communists, civil rights workers, anti-war activists, and even Ku Klux Klan members. To help keep an eye on potential threats, FBI Director J. Edgar Hoover cultivated a stable of informants among these groups. Later investigations of Hoover's informants would reveal that under the FBI director's watch, the domestic surveillance informants were given free reign to commit serious crimes—including murder.

Perhaps the most notorious of Hoover's informants was Gary Thomas Rowe, a member of the Eastview Klavern No. 13, a chapter of the Ku Klux Klan based in Birmingham, Alabama. Rowe, a part-time bartender and machinist, was recruited to be an informant in 1960 by FBI agent Barrett G. Kemp, who believed that he would make an ideal Klan informant because he loathed civil rights workers (he referred to them as the "white nigger allies" of Southern blacks) yet also harbored fantasies of one day joining the ranks of law enforcement. Agent Kemp "rescued him from a dreary existence," wrote University of Delaware history professor Gary May in a 2005 biography of Rowe. "He was transformed into an undercover agent of the FBI, entering a world of midnight meetings, code names, mail drops, dangerous scrapes, bizarre adventures and the chance to raise hell without worrying about the consequences." Indeed, just one year after becoming an informant

Rowe attacked a group of Freedom Riders. And from 1962 to 1963, Rowe associated with white supremacists who conducted a series of bombings in Birmingham, a campaign of terror that culminated in the September 1963 bombing of the city's Sixteenth Street Baptist Church, which left four young girls dead. Though there is no evidence that Rowe was involved in the Sixteenth Street Church bombing, he may have had prior knowledge that the church was going to be attacked, according to May.

It was not long before Rowe would be directly involved in violent acts. On March 25, 1965, the night after the Selma-Montgomery voting rights march led by Martin Luther King Jr., Rowe and three other Klan members piled into a car and tailed an Oldsmobile driven by civil rights activists Leroy Moton and Viola Gregg Liuzzo. Soon after they passed Edmund Pettus Bridge in Selma, the Klansmen drew their pistols and fired on the Oldsmobile, killing Liuzzo. The next morning, Hoover telephoned President Lyndon Johnson to boast that he could solve Liuzzo's murder because the FBI had one of its men in the car. Hoover also offered a wildly implausible story to President Johnson of informant Rowe thwarting a plan by his fellow Klansmen to throw the murder weapon into a "blast furnace where they work." At the end of the call, Hoover assured Johnson—falsely, as it turned out—that Rowe "had no gun and did no shooting."

Nearly a decade after the Liuzzo murder, the Church Committee, a Senate subcommittee named after its chair, Idaho Senator Frank Church, conducted a wide-ranging investigation into the FBI's domestic surveillance programs under Hoover, including an investigation of Gary Thomas Rowe. The committee stated that Rowe committed a number of illegal acts while working as an FBI informant, including beating civil rights workers severely, kicking them off buses, and attacking them in restaurants with "blackjacks, chains, and pistols." Rowe was also present during a series of major acts of violence against civil rights workers throughout the 1960s, such as the 1961 beating of Freedom Rider Walter Bergman and the 1965 killing of Liuzzo. His FBI handler admitted that Rowe did not intervene in these situations because Rowe "couldn't be an angel and be a good informant." Bergman and the Liuzzo family later sued the U.S. government under the Federal Tort Claims Act, claiming that the FBI violated its common law and statutory duties by ignoring threats against civil rights workers and failing to report them to the Justice Department. Bergman's suit was successful; the Liuzzo family's was not. In the Liuzzo case, the judge actually hailed Rowe as "a model public servant—perhaps the best informer in the South," even though Rowe himself would later admit that he was essentially useless as an informant because the identities of the members of the Eastview Klavern No. 13 were well-known.

The Church Committee wisely recognized that Rowe was more than merely a rogue informant; he was a symptom of a Justice Department with no rules governing its use of informants and no independent oversight of federal law enforcement's relationship with such individuals. The committee's report noted that "informants can be used without any restrictions . . . and there is nothing that requires a determination be made of whether less intrusive means will adequately serve the government's interest." The use of informants was unique in this manner: other "intrusive techniques," such as wiretapping, were subject to a range of checks and balances.

In response to the Church Committee's findings, Attorney General Edward Levi issued the first Domestic Security Investigation Guidelines on April 6, 1976. In addition to curtailing the FBI's monitoring of individuals or groups that held "unpopular or controversial political views," Levi sought to rein in the FBI's use of informants because, as Rowe had proved, "government itself" could "become a violator of the law." Under the Levi Guidelines, FBI agents still had latitude in the handling of informants, but they also were obligated to notify the Department of Justice or the U.S. attorney they worked with when an informant committed an "unauthorized criminal act" in connection with an assignment from the FBI. The Levi Guidelines had an almost instantaneous effect on the FBI's investigatory practices: in the two years that followed, the number of domestic security investigations fell dramatically from 4,868 to 102. On May 3, 1978, FBI Director William Webster declared that the bureau was "practically out of the domestic security field."

Soon after the Levi Guidelines went into effect, laws regarding the FBI's use of informants were revised yet again, this time to specify precisely what criminal acts informants could participate in. Attorney General Benjamin Civiletti divided these criminal acts into two distinct categories: "ordinary" and "extraordinary." The former (defined as misdemeanor crimes) required authorization from an FBI field office supervisor, while the latter ("any activity involving a significant risk of violence, corrupt actions by high public officials, or severe financial loss to a victim") required approval from either a special agent in charge of the investigation or the U.S. attorney handling the case. The Civiletti Guidelines, which went into effect on December 4, 1980, also required agents to advise informants that their relationship with the FBI would not necessarily protect them from prosecution for violations of federal, state, or local law.

Both the Levi and Civiletti guidelines were drafted under Democratic administrations, but when Ronald Reagan took office in 1981, guidelines regulating use of informants—and even domestic security investigations—were dramatically revisited, perhaps because conservatives tend to favor fewer restrictions on (and oversight of) federal law enforcement. From 1982 to the spring of 1983, the Senate Subcommittee on Security and Terrorism held a series of hearings that recommended sweeping changes to the Levi Guidelines, foremost among them relaxing restrictions on the recruitment and use of new informants. After considering the Senate subcommittee's recommendations, Reagan's attorney general, William French Smith, issued the Smith Guidelines on March 7, 1983; these rejected fears of FBI law-breaking that had guided the Levi and Civiletti guidelines. Smith lowered the evidentiary thresholds for domestic security investigations and stipulated that informant guidelines should be loosened because FBI agents had "demonstrated their professional competence, integrity, and ability to adhere to requirements."

This would prove to be wishful thinking on Smith's part. About two years after the Smith Guidelines were passed, a Justice Department investigation into the establishment of nonworking, "ghost" jobs at Teamsters Union 507 in Cleveland revealed that Jackie Presser, the union's secretary-treasurer who also held the top position at the International Brotherhood of Teamsters, was a high-level FBI informant. Starting in the late 1970s, Presser provided the FBI with information about his union rivals and even his uncle Allan Friedman, who was sentenced to three years' imprisonment for embezzling $165,000 from Teamsters Union 507 as a so-called ghost worker. But during the summer of 1985, the Justice Department mysteriously dropped its investigation into Presser, spurring a Senate investigation into whether the DOJ's decision was motivated by improper reasons.

The Senate probe found that the Justice Department had made its decision to end the Presser investigation at least in part because his FBI handlers claimed that they authorized Presser to create the ghost jobs. But when it was later discovered that one of Presser's FBI handlers—Robert S. Friedrick—concocted the defense to protect his valued informant, federal prosecutors renewed their investigation into Presser and, in 1988, jailed Friedrick after he refused to testify in a racketeering case against Teamsters Local 507 recording secretary Anthony Hughes, which involved the payment of $700,000 to ghost workers. As the federal investigation into Presser continued that spring, Presser was diagnosed with cancer, and in July 1988 he succumbed to the disease. Presser's death was of little comfort to the Mafioso he ratted out, as he had never faced the consequences of his behavior. Indeed, soon after Presser's passing, his imprisoned uncle vowed that he would urinate on his nephew's grave.

The sticky legal and ethical issues raised by the murky relationship between Presser and his FBI handlers paled in comparison to an agent's close relationship to a pair of Boston's most infamous made men: James "Whitey" Bulger and Stephen J. "The Rifleman" Flemmi. When Bulger and Flemmi were indicted by the feds on multiple charges of racketeering including acts of extortion, murder, and bribery in January 1995, a special agent in charge of the FBI's Boston field office revealed that both men had worked as FBI informants from 1975 until the early 1990s, when their handler retired. Just as Presser and his FBI handlers had done a few years earlier, attorneys for Flemmi argued that the indictment should be dismissed on the grounds that the FBI had authorized their client's illegal activity. The FBI, they said, promised Flemmi immunity from prosecution as long as he provided information about the mob. During Flemmi's trial, his attorneys introduced evidence that FBI agent John Connolly Jr. and Special Supervisory Agent John Morris maintained an illicit relationship with Bulger and Flemmi that involved ignoring major criminal acts committed by the men and filing false FBI reports. More dramatically, Flemmi testified that on November 30, 1984, he murdered Boston fisherman John McIntyre after Connolly warned Flemmi that McIntyre was a cooperator. A federal judge in the case ruled that the FBI "had ignored the essential point of the Attorney General's Guidelines," which required agents to consult the assistant attorney general for the Criminal Division when the FBI wants to hold on to an informant who has committed a crime, rather than reporting the informant to law enforcement.

In December 1999, Connolly was charged with obstruction of justice and racketeering. Federal prosecutors alleged that he provided Bulger and Flemmi with the names of cooperators who were murdered and that in 1994 he tipped off Bulger to his impending indictment, allowing him to flee. While Bulger remains at large, Connolly was convicted of obstruction of justice and some of the racketeering charges, though he was acquitted on the racketeering charges related to the murdered cooperators. Still, when Bulger and Flemmi were indicted yet again in September 2000 for committing twenty-one murders while working for the feds, the scandal surrounding Connolly's relationship with the men was revived.

Mindful of the decades of abuses committed by Bulger and Flemmi's FBI handlers, in early 2001 Attorney General Janet Reno issued sweeping new guidelines governing the use of informants. Reno's guidelines addressed the FBI's multiple failures in the Bulger case: agents were prohibited from making promises of immunity to informants, a Confidential Informant Review Committee was established to approve and monitor high-level informants, and it became a requirement that federal prosecutors be notified when an informant was under investigation.

The Reno Guidelines, along with the embarrassment to the FBI caused by the Bulger and Flemmi case, should have spurred a sea change in the agency's handling of informants. But a few years later, a sprawling 314-page report on the FBI's compliance with informant guidelines by Department of Justice Inspector General Glenn Fine suggested that the agency continued to routinely violate the attorney general's guidelines governing the use of confidential informants. After examining more than 120 informant files from around the country, Fine found that FBI agents violated the attorney general's guidelines on informants in 87 percent of their cases. In an interview with the *Washington Post* just after the report's release in the fall of 2005, Kevin R. Brock, the FBI's assistant director of the Office of Intelligence, defended the agency's mistakes in handling informants as mere "administrative failures," adding "it's not like we had sources running around, willy-nilly breaking the law." But Fine found that not only did agents largely fail to inform prosecutors when informants were permitted to engage in illegal activity (dubbed "otherwise illegal activity" under the attorney general's informant guidelines and defined as a set list of misdemeanors or felonies, etc.), they also didn't tell prosecutors when informants committed unauthorized crimes—which gave informants a wide berth to engage in criminal activity.

But in a criminal justice system dominated by drug offenders— the number of adult drug arrests has risen from just under 500,000 in 1970 to more than 1.5 million in 2005—confidential informants (or CIs) play a more limited role than cooperating witnesses (CWs), who provide testimony in hopes of receiving a "downward departure" from the sentencing guidelines. "Informants are an investigative tool," explains Gerald Shargel. "They provide information for search warrant affidavits that lead to indictments. Cooperating witnesses, on the other hand, are a prosecutorial tool; they have a written agreement with the prosecutor in which they agree to offer information to prosecutors in hopes of receiving leniency at sentencing." Though both CIs and CWs are commonly referred to as "informants," they play separate, distinct roles in the federal criminal justice system—and are subject to different rules and regulations as to their use. The attorney general's guidelines governing the use of informants, for example, do not apply to cooperators.

The lack of oversight of cooperating witnesses is particularly dangerous, as a "cottage industry of cooperators" has emerged in the wake of the establishment of the sentencing guidelines in the mid-1980s. While confidential informants have some incentive to lie—they are often compensated monetarily—cooperators have even more motivation to be untruthful, since their very freedom is at stake. Because cooperation is critical in bringing about a downward departure from the sentencing guidelines, there is strong incentive for defendants to "perform" for prosecutors in hopes of receiving a 5K motion. And as prosecutors have wide discretion in the kind of 5K motions they make, defendants not only lie in proffer sessions and in grand jury testimony but also commit perjury on the witness stand. "Defendants know that 5K motions come in all shapes and sizes," Gerald Shargel says, "from getting a few years shaved off a sentence to decades. The goal for a defendant is to get [as] glowing [a] 5K letter as possible." Incredibly, defendants who do not cooperate at first can receive a reduction if they decide to offer information to prosecutors even *after* they are sent to prison. Under Rule 35 of the Federal Rules of Criminal Procedure, the court may reduce a sentence if the defendant, after sentencing, is deemed to have provided substantial assistance in investigating or prosecuting another person.

Informants and cooperators have long been loathed as "snitches," "rats," and "stool pigeons" (so named because a "stool pigeon" was a decoy bird usually attached to a stool to lure other pigeons into a trap). Indeed, former FBI Director William Webster once admitted that "there is a tradition against snitching in this country." But in the era of harsh mandatory minimums for drug-related crimes—in which cooperators induce dealers into making sales that will trigger the longest possible sentence, therefore giving them the best possible shot at a sparkling 5K motion from a prosecutor—snitching is now seen as little more than entrapment, particularly in inner-city neighborhoods. In these neighborhoods, slang phrases like "snitching" or "telling on" have now been replaced with the much more apt "lying on." Admittedly, some of the anti-snitch sentiment is promulgated by criminals who seek to intimidate witnesses from testifying against them. But there is genuine outrage that cooperators often lie about defendants and commit far worse crimes than those they are cooperating against, all to maintain a system of highly punitive drug laws, much of which has been recognized as unjust by drug policy experts and even the United States Sentencing Commission. (In a May 2007 report, the USSC found that punishments for crack cocaine–related offenses "overstate the seriousness" of those offenses, "mostly impact minorities," and "apply most often to lower level offenders.")

In our cooperator-coddling system, the little fish face the most severe punishment while the big fish get off the hook. One need look no further than Whitey Bulger's street muscle Kevin Weeks, who received just seventy-two months in prison after he struck a cooperation deal with the feds. "A lot of people, particularly the families of the victims, have been outraged," said Ed Bradley during an interview of Weeks on 60 Minutes. "I mean they look at it, 'We lost a loved one, and this guy's walking out on the street.'" Weeks replied, "I mean, if someone killed a loved one of mine, I'd want to kill them. I wouldn't want them in jail. I'd want to kill them. So . . . you know . . . they're probably correct."

Chapter Three

KING TUT'S THIRD STRIKE

The Murder of Tupac, Three Strikes Legislation, and the Fall of Brooklyn's Most Storied Hustler

Former street hustler Walter "King Tut" Johnson, probably best known for his alleged connection to the nonfatal shooting of rapper Tupac Shakur in New York in 1994 and the rapper's murder two years later in Las Vegas, is now serving life without parole for a series of armed robberies in Brooklyn he did not commit. Since his arrest and subsequent indictment in 1996, Johnson has been given the opportunity to cooperate against some of hip-hop's major players, but he declined to do so and remains in prison. Johnson was brought down not by careful police work and thorough investigation but by informants who eagerly provided false testimony about a man the feds desperately wanted to take down.

Just after nine AM on October 4, 1996, Johnson strode into the courthouse at 360 Adams Street in downtown Brooklyn feeling confident about facing the robbery charges against him. Though Johnson had a criminal record that one prosecutor characterized as "extraordinary," he'd been acquitted in several major cases, most notably the shooting of an off-duty cop in a Brooklyn barbershop in 1993. Johnson's attorney Stephen Flamhaft had told him that there was a strong possibility of a "not guilty" verdict, or even a dismissal of the case entirely, so Johnson's spirits were high.

But when Johnson—a small, wiry African-American man barely over five feet tall who speaks in a thick Brooklyn brogue—passed through the courthouse metal, he encountered a group of men waiting for him. "What's up, Wally?" one said to Johnson menacingly. "You got the wrong person," Johnson replied. "What's the problem?" A brief altercation ensued, in which the men demanded he go with them.

Johnson broke free and straggled to the courtroom with the group of men following close behind. "I got a problem," Johnson told his attorney inside the courtroom. Flamhaft turned to the man tailing Johnson and demanded that he identify himself. He refused and then pointed to Johnson angrily and said, "He's going with me." When the judge entered the courtroom and announced that he was dismissing the case against Johnson, one of the men who had accosted Johnson stepped forward and identified himself as NYPD detective William Oldham and slapped handcuffs on him. Realizing that he was about to be hauled off to jail, Johnson asked Oldham if he could give the claim ticket for his truck (which was parked in the courthouse garage) to Flamhaft. When Oldham refused, he and Flamhaft got into a shoving match, which Flamhaft says ended with Oldham shoving him violently to the ground. Flamhaft later filed a complaint against Oldham with New York City's Civilian Criminal Complaint Review Board (CCCRB), but the board cleared Oldham in the incident, a decision Flamhaft calls a "whitewash."

After Johnson was trundled by Oldham and a group of U.S. marshals into a car headed to U.S. District Court on Cadman Plaza East in downtown Brooklyn, he began to panic. This was his first run-in with the feds, and his long criminal record nearly guaranteed a decades-long prison sentence. His fear turned to paralysis when the marshals in the car accused him of shooting Tupac Shakur at the Quad Studios in New York in 1994 *and* murdering the rapper in September 1996 in Las Vegas. The agents said that Johnson had carried out the shootings at the behest of New York hip-hop impresario Sean "Puffy" Combs, who had been embroiled in a years-long, often violent rivalry with Death Row, the Los Angeles–based record label Shakur recorded for. "You crazy—I didn't do either one of them," Johnson shot back. "I didn't kill nobody. I didn't kill Tupac." The agents didn't believe Johnson's claims of innocence; they were so sure that he'd killed Shakur that they asked to search his truck in hopes of finding the murder weapon. "Puffy is a piece of shit just like you," the agents told him, "but people don't know it. We want to expose who Puffy really is. All you have to do is cooperate."

As the car closed in on Cadman Plaza East, Johnson says the agents delivered a blunt warning: "If you don't play ball and you don't give us Puff," they said, "you goin' down." Told of Johnson's recollection of his arrest, Samuel Buell, a former assistant U.S. attorney in Brooklyn who was closely involved in Johnson's case, says, "That sounds ridiculous to me. I can't speak for everyone involved in the case, but I have no knowledge of anyone having said that. That's inconsistent with the way we generally discuss plea negotiations. Saying 'If you give us piece of information X, you will get benefit Y' is not helpful to the process or to anyone's credibility."

■ ■ ■

Though Johnson has the most regal of street names, and would turn out to be a key player in hip-hop's greatest unsolved crime, he has unremarkable roots. Born on September 8, 1963, Johnson was raised in the Cypress Hills housing project in the East New York section of Brooklyn by a homemaker mother and an ex-Marine father who fought in both World War II and the Korean War. During the early 1970s, Johnson and his friends attended the hip-hop block parties sprouting up across the borough, but by the end of the decade he was drawn to a much more sinister side of the streets. The late 1970s was the era of the "stick-up kid," a time when hustlers could earn respect by committing robberies with a ski mask and a pistol. As a self-proclaimed loner uninterested in joining the gangs and drug crews that dominated New York, Johnson had the ideal personality for the moment, and he was soon executing robberies with relish. "I was angry," Johnson admits, "you could say disturbed." Having grown up in a household competing for the attention of his parents among five brothers and sisters, Johnson reveled in the adulation his high-wire hustlers brought him. "When you're young and you're ignorant and rebellious," he explains, "you allow yourself to be manipulated into situations that will affect you for the rest of your life."

It didn't take long for Johnson to experience the consequences of his thuggish behavior. Though he attended Franklin K. Lane high school on the Queens/Brooklyn border, he was forced to earn a GED at Riker's Island because of an arrest. But Johnson's role as a significant player in the stick-up kid scene ended during the spring of 1978, when he was picked up in Brooklyn on a robbery charge. When his mother came to pick him up, the police asked her if her son had any nicknames. "Tut," she told them. The cop turned around and told his superior about the nickname, calling Johnson "King Tut" instead.

Johnson's mother tried to correct him, but the superior responded that "King Tut" was more appropriate, as Johnson hailed from "the County of Kings." (Brooklyn is also known as "Kings County.")

Though the nickname was given to him by a cop, it stuck because it was grandiose—it made Johnson feel as though he reigned over the entire borough. In the wake of his crowning as "King Tut," Johnson's stick-up schemes grew much bolder. On October 7, 1982, he robbed six passengers on a Queens-to-Brooklyn bus; that same year he pulled off a hold-up of nearly three hundred congregants at a Jehovah's Witness kingdom hall in East New York—a brash and almost sacrilegious act for Johnson, who had been raised a Jehovah's Witness himself. Johnson racked up one of the most extensive criminal records in New York City while managing to serve short prison terms of two to six years. He was often paroled before finishing out the sentences.

But Johnson's luck with the law ran out in spectacular fashion on January 15, 1993, when he took his young son to get a haircut at a Brooklyn barbershop. Soon after sitting down for a haircut, a patron who Johnson says was "dressed like a thug" pulled a weapon on him without provocation. Johnson pulled out a gun and fired at his assailant, leaving him partially paralyzed. When the cops arrived on the scene, they handcuffed Johnson and informed him that the man he had just shot was actually an off-duty NYPD officer named Richard Aviles. Though Johnson was charged with shooting the cop, his longtime attorney Flamhaft convinced a Brooklyn jury that Johnson had acted in self-defense. In a ruling that infuriated the NYPD, Johnson was acquitted on all of the charges against him.

Unfortunately for Johnson, even the allegation of wrongdoing in the Aviles shooting represented a violation of his parole on a previous robbery charge, and he was sentenced to eighteen months in prison. It was a hugely depressing outcome to a case in which Johnson had been found innocent, and when he came home in 1994, he swore to finally put the streets behind him. He knew just how fortunate he was to emerge unscathed from a fire-fight with an undercover cop; the next time he had a brush with the law, he couldn't expect to be so lucky. The unforgiving nature of the streets also spurred Johnson to make dramatic changes to his life. The Giuliani era of aggressive policing had just begun, and, more importantly, the federal anticrime bills of the late 1980s were putting career criminals like Johnson in prison for decades.

Like his more savvy peers on the streets, Johnson looked to hip-hop as a way out of a life of crime. In the mid-1990s hip-hop was beginning its commercial ascent thanks to emerging superstars such as Tupac Shakur, Jay-Z, and the Notorious B.I.G. (aka Biggie Smalls), all of whom were enjoying far more lucrative careers than the music's icons of the 1980s. To make their rhymes seem more street credible, these rappers borrowed heavily from the stories of hustlers like Johnson and his longtime friend from Brooklyn Jimmy "Henchmen" Rosemond, whom Biggie affectionately referred to as "Big Brother." Because Biggie was close with pal Rosemond and because he was a fellow Brooklynite, Johnson surmised that he'd have the best luck breaking into his camp. So, during the winter of 1995, Johnson staked out Daddy's House, the midtown Manhattan recording studio owned by Biggie's mentor, Sean "Puffy" Combs. One January day, Johnson followed Puffy into the studio in hopes of holding a meeting with him. When the front desk employee refused to grant him entry, Johnson persisted and was allowed in. He offered his assistance to Puffy, saying that he wanted no money, only to learn about the music business. Puffy was doubtful at first—he had heard that Johnson was a dangerous stick-up kid—but when Johnson swore that he had changed his ways, Puffy was finally swayed. He sent a messenger to retrieve a copy of Donald S. Passman's book *All You Need to Know About the Music Business*, and when it arrived, he autographed it for Johnson. "I need you to take this book, and I want you to study this book," Puffy told him. "Learn the book by heart. I want to know that you really read it in order to be part of this industry."

Johnson wanted to obey Puffy's wishes, but he had other plans in mind. Though Johnson had a long history on the streets, he watched worriedly as hustling became a huge influence on the hip-hop scene, symbolized by such songs as Biggie's stick-up kid anthem, "Gimme the Loot." Johnson was worried that rap fans could fall victim to street culture. He wanted to start a group to attend to hip-hop artists, preventing them from using drugs or, in the case of female artists, "make sure that she is not dating somebody who is a dope dealer or a gunslinger."

However, Johnson's plans to save hip-hop from the streets never came to pass. Though he did not realize it at the time, the timing of his meeting with Puffy only fanned rumors that he had been involved in the 1994 nonfatal shooting of Tupac Shakur. In 1995, when Shakur was incarcerated at the Clinton correctional facility on rape charges, his fellow inmates told him that it was Johnson who shot him under orders from Biggie and Puffy. During the spring of 1995, speculation that Biggie and Puffy ordered the hit moved from the prison system to the hip-hop scene, when Shakur gave a jailhouse interview with *Vibe* magazine in which he implicated both Biggie and Puffy in the shooting.

Though Shakur didn't name Johnson in the interview, it wasn't hard to believe that he was the triggerman at the Quad. Like Biggie, he was from Brooklyn; he had a reputation as the borough's wildest stick-up kid; and he had grown up with Biggie's mentor Rosemond, who had invited Shakur to the Quad that night to record a song with his protégé Lil' Shawn.

Most importantly, the shooting had the appearance of an armed robbery, Johnson's stock-in-trade. Shakur told *Vibe* that soon after entering the Quad's lobby at Times Square, he was ambushed by a pair of men toting 9mm weapons who demanded that he hand over the nearly $45,000 in jewelry dangling from his neck. When Shakur refused, he claimed that the gunmen shot him five times and his manager, Freddie "Nickels" Moore, once.

But a source who was with Shakur that night told me that while it's true that two men ambushed Shakur in the Quad's lobby, they fired no shots intentionally, preferring to pistol-whip the rapper instead. A panicked Shakur, believing he was being robbed, tossed his jewelry at his attackers, and when this failed to placate them, he grabbed at one of their weapons, which went off and hit him in the hand. After Shakur fired his own gun in response, he ended up shooting himself in the testicles (which passed through to his thigh) and Moore in the stomach. These accounts contradict Shakur's claim that he was shot five times and law enforcement's belief that Shakur was an armed robbery victim.

The physician who treated Shakur after the shooting also contradicted claims made by Shakur and the NYPD. Dr. Leon Pachter said that Shakur was not, as police reports stated, shot in the head; he also said that the rapper's wounds were concentrated "mainly" in his scrotum, confirming my source's account. Finally, Pachter admitted that when he treated Shakur, he was "limited by family and everybody else on disclosure of the entire picture" and suggested that the rapper did not allow himself to be fully examined. Indeed, after undergoing surgery on his injuries to his groin, Shakur checked himself out of Bellevue Hospital in Manhattan against the wishes of his physicians. Perhaps because he had been injured in a manner that would have caused him huge embarrassment in the hip-hop world, Shakur was intent on exaggerating his wounds, even showing up in court on the rape charges wrapped in bandages and in a wheelchair.

To make matters worse for Johnson, in countless songs and interviews, Shakur characterized the Quad shooting as an East Coast conspiracy against him comprised of Puffy, Biggie, Rosemond, and

Johnson. Sadly, Shakur's fears that he was in the crosshairs of his enemies were realized on September 7, 1996, when the rapper was shot several times as he sat in a BMW stopped at a traffic light at a Las Vegas intersection. Shakur had just come from a boxing match featuring Mike Tyson and Bruce Seldon at the MGM Grand Hotel, and he was strafed with a barrage of bullets as he sat in the vehicle with Death Row founder Suge Knight. Shakur survived the initial attack, but he succumbed to his wounds nearly one week later (Knight escaped mostly unscathed; he was hit in the head by shattered glass). Though Shakur was captured on surveillance videotape beating Orlando Anderson, a member of feared Los Angeles gang the Southside Crips inside the MGM Grand Hotel just hours before his own murder, law enforcement and some journalists suspected that the rapper was slain as a result of his rivalry with Puffy and Biggie. Indeed, Pulitzer Prize–winning *Los Angeles Times* investigative reporter Chuck Philips would later claim that Biggie had actually flown to Las Vegas to personally order Shakur's murder (Biggie's family angrily denied the allegations, claiming he was home in New Jersey at the time when Philips said he was in Las Vegas).

The theory that Johnson attacked Shakur at the Quad—and perhaps even murdered the rapper in Las Vegas—all at the behest of Puffy was buttressed when, just weeks after Johnson was picked up by the feds in the Brooklyn courtroom in October 1996, a posthumous Shakur album was released called *The Don Killuminati: The 7 Day Theory*, in which Shakur implicated Biggie, Puffy, Johnson, Rosemond, and an associate of Rosemond's named Jacques "Haitian Jack" Agnant (Shakur's codefendant in the 1993 rape case) in the Quad shooting.

The song—"Against All Odds"—became an instant hip-hop classic because Shakur addressed the Quad shooting in his bluntest language yet (that the song was released after Shakur's death added to its strange power). One of its most powerful verses ended with a vow to exact revenge against Johnson: "gunshots to Tut, now you stuck." With so much misinformation clouding the Quad shooting, Johnson quickly became a prime suspect in the shooting.

■ ■ ■

When Johnson arrived at U.S. District Court in Brooklyn the afternoon of October 26, 1996, he expected to be indicted for the Quad shooting by the U.S. attorney for the Eastern District of New York. Johnson had refused the government's entreaties to cooperate by implicating Combs in the Quad shooting, even though it would have guaranteed Johnson a sharply reduced sentence. By refusing to cooperate, Johnson was not adhering to street code against snitching; rather, he believed he was being asked by federal investigators to falsely implicate innocent people.

Not long afterwards, a small army of informants came forward to provide evidence that Johnson was involved in both the shooting at the Quad and Shakur's slaying in Las Vegas. One informant claimed that soon after the Quad shooting, Johnson said that Shakur wasn't a "real gangster" and that he had shot him. Yet another informant was quoted as saying that Johnson shot Shakur at the Quad because he "needed to be disciplined." Even more damaging, NYPD detective Derrick Parker, who would later become known as the "Hip-Hop Cop" because of his role in investigating rap-related crimes, said that his most trusted informants all implicated Johnson in the Quad incident. Federal investigators, unsurprisingly, appeared to be swayed by the overwhelming amount of informant chatter about Johnson and leaked to the press that they expected him to be charged in both the Quad shooting and Shakur's murder. "We hope this [Johnson's arrest] will lead to a solution of the murder of Tupac," an anonymous law enforcement source told the *Daily News*, while (presumably) another anonymous cop source told the paper just a few days later, "We expect he'll be charged" in the attack on Shakur at the Quad.

Shakur and a gaggle of informants may have fingered Johnson, but when federal investigators searched his truck on that late October day in 1996, they found not the weapon in the rapper's killing but Halloween costumes worn by Johnson's young son. Johnson's refusal to cooperate in the investigation into Shakur's slaying—which centered around Puffy's alleged involvement in the incident—threw up yet another roadblock in the effort to pin the murder on Johnson. As he prepared for trial in the early fall of 1996, the foundations for the allegations against him in the Shakur slaying were crumbling fast. Nonetheless, under the federal three strikes provision Johnson faced a lifetime behind bars if he was convicted on any of the robbery, drug distribution, and witness intimidation charges. Worse, after incurring huge legal expenses from his multiple run-ins with the law, Johnson could no longer afford trusted attorney Stephen Flamhaft. Johnson's hopes lay in the contradictory accounts of the witnesses in the robberies, but even that was of little comfort to him. The act of the feds picking him up in state court and charging him under an "instant indictment" was a dramatic demonstration that he was unlikely to escape his three strikes fate.

■ ■ ■

The air of suspicion surrounding Johnson after the Quad shooting may have put him back on law enforcement's radar, but, unknown to him at the time, a series of armed robberies committed in Brooklyn in the spring of 1995 would bring about his downfall.

Early in the morning of March 15, 1995, after a long night out, Brooklyn hustler Jay-Tee "Tee Tee" Spurgeon came home to the apartment he shared with his girlfriend, Crystal Lacey Winslow, on Hoyt Street in downtown Brooklyn. A cocaine dealer who trafficked in wholesale amounts of the drug and often hauled in more than $10,000 per week, Spurgeon made a tempting target for a robber, particularly since he and Winslow lived in an easily accessible ground-floor brownstone apartment. It didn't help matters that on the morning of the fifteenth, Spurgeon left both the door to his building *and* his apartment door open soon after arriving home. As Spurgeon readied himself for bed, he and Winslow began arguing about the time he'd been spending away from her. Spurgeon spent most nights hanging out at a Brooklyn nightspot called the Q Club, and he'd recently flown to Los Angeles without Winslow to party at the Soul Train awards. As the fight with Winslow dragged on, Spurgeon saw two men armed with 9mm weapons standing menacingly in his doorway. Spurgeon vaguely recognized the pair from his Brooklyn neighborhood. He also remembered seeing them just a few weeks earlier, standing on the street in front of his building.

As Spurgeon struggled to focus on the pair in the early morning darkness, he noticed a third man in the apartment, whom he did not recognize. This man stood by the front windows of Spurgeon's apartment and quietly closed the blinds, presumably to make Spurgeon's job of identifying him difficult. When the blinds blocked out the remaining light, the trio forced Spurgeon and Winslow down to the floor and demanded thirty kilos of cocaine. "Where the money at?" they barked. "Where the dough at?" Spurgeon protested that he had neither money nor drugs, which only infuriated them. The robbers smacked him in the face with a pistol, and, as he lay on the floor nursing his wound, the shadowy third man (who was still standing by the window) tossed a thick roll of duct tape in the air toward his partners. In a fake Jamaican accent—Spurgeon instantly knew it wasn't real because he partied with the heavily Jamaican crowd that frequented the Q Club—the man ordered his partners to bind both Spurgeon and

Winslow with duct tape. After they completed the job a few minutes later, one of the men growled, "You are going to die for this fucking money!" Winslow hysterically burst into tears. "Tell her everything is going to be all right," one of the men shouted. Spurgeon managed to calm Winslow down, but their ordeal was far from over. The robbers popped Spurgeon's gold earrings from his earlobes, snatched the thick gold chain that hung from around his neck, and took $650 in cash from his pocket.

Meanwhile, the third man remained in the background to keep an eye on Spurgeon and Winslow. As his partners took the last of Spurgeon's belongings, he moved into the bedroom, where he found Spurgeon's gun hidden under his bed. "You think you're bad, *bwoy*," he taunted Spurgeon from the bedroom, once again speaking in a faux Jamaican patois. The third man then emerged from the bedroom with a pillowcase in hand and snarled, "You're going to die for this money." With that, he cocked his gun back, aiming it squarely at Spurgeon. Suddenly, Spurgeon's phone rang, making everyone in the apartment freeze. When Spurgeon's answering machine picked up, a voice on the line bellowed, "It's the police! Pick up the phone! Pick up the phone!" Spurgeon recognized the voice as his friend Leroy, not the cops—Leroy had been paging Spurgeon all night, and when Spurgeon didn't return his pages, he phoned posing as the cops—but the robbers fell for the ruse and made a hasty retreat.

When they were gone, Spurgeon wriggled out of the duct tape binding his hands and feet and freed Winslow. The couple then ran upstairs to their landlord's apartment and called the cops. But before the cops arrived, Spurgeon wanted to ensure that the house was clean. He went back downstairs and hid his gun back under his bed. His efforts were for naught, however: when the cops arrived, they found an AK47, a triple beam scale used to weigh drugs that had cocaine residue on it, a bulletproof vest, and a police scanner.

A night that began with Spurgeon and Winslow as robbery victims ended with Spurgeon indicted on numerous weapons and drugs charges by the U.S. attorney for the Eastern District of New York.

There was, unsurprisingly, one way out of his predicament: cooperate with federal prosecutors in Brooklyn in an investigation they had just begun into Walter "King Tut" Johnson. "They wanted me to snitch on people," Spurgeon said later. The cops promised Spurgeon that he could go home that night if he cooperated, but he refused, insisting, "I'm not a snitch; I'm not cooperating against anyone." While negotiations with investigators were at a stalemate, Spurgeon decided to face trial and posted $250,000 bail, returning home about one week later. But Spurgeon didn't go back to Hoyt Street. The robbery frightened him, so he and Winslow moved to the apartment where her mother, Henrietta, lived at 92 Woodruff Ave. in Brooklyn.

The change of address did little to shield Spurgeon from the dangers of his profession. On April 21, 1995, the robbers struck again, this time late in the afternoon as Henrietta prepared dinner for Tahara, the young daughter of Spurgeon's cousin who had been placed in his custody after she had been abused by her mother. To keep Tahara occupied as she made the meal, Henrietta slid a copy of *The Lion King* into the VCR. But just moments after the movie's credits rolled, Henrietta's doorbell rang. "It's Cris," Crystal Winslow shouted through the intercom. Henrietta buzzed her in, and when she met her daughter at the front door, a dark-skinned man with a light moustache suddenly appeared behind Winslow. After pushing his way through the front door he ordered Winslow and Henrietta to the living room, where Tahara was sitting watching TV. Henrietta nervously flipped the light switch on in order to get a better look at her assailant, but he moved in to stop her, growling, "Don't be turning no lights on." When Henrietta turned the lights off, she and her daughter were instructed to lie face down on the floor. As she lay motionless on the floor, Henrietta heard her front door slowly creak open, followed by the sound of a new voice. "Hold your head up, Momma," the man said in a fake Jamaican accent. Henrietta dared not look at the assailant as he placed duct tape over her eyes. Blinded by the duct tape, Henrietta could only make out a cacophony of angry demands by the robbers. "Where is it at? Where is the drugs?" shouted one, while another said menacingly that he would not leave the apartment without "thirty keys and the money," a request nearly identical to the one made during the first armed robbery at Hoyt Street. Then Henrietta heard someone walking toward the bedroom. Moments later, a same voice shouted that they had found the "two mink coats!" Spurgeon had given Winslow as a gift.

Henrietta was hoping that the expensive coats would satisfy the robbers, but then she heard something strange, once again coming from the bedroom: "Did you all see a stick around here?" After an excruciating period of silence that seemed to last hours but was actually just minutes, Henrietta heard loud footsteps coming out of the bedroom followed by the sound of the front door slamming shut. "Tahara," Winslow cried from the bedroom, "take the tape off grandma's eyes." When Tahara peeled the duct tape from her face, Henrietta ran into the bedroom to check on her daughter. There, Henrietta remembered later, she found Winslow lying naked on the bed with "brown stains . . . like bowel movements" covering the bedspread and, even more disturbingly, a broomstick lying on the floor. Her daughter, Henrietta realized then, had been raped. As Henrietta struggled to take in the grisly scene in front of her, the phone rang. It was Spurgeon. When Henrietta told Spurgeon about the rape and robbery, he was surprisingly unsympathetic. "I told you all they was out there," Spurgeon said angrily. He explained that he had seen the robbery crew that very morning at a neighborhood hair salon called Maribel's. Furious at Spurgeon's callousness, Henrietta slammed the phone down.

When cops arrived at the scene, Winslow refused to go to the hospital to be examined for her injuries—though she would later check into Kings County Hospital for treatment on her own, under an assumed name—and Henrietta threw the broomstick used in the rape into the garbage. In the weeks after the incident, cops showed Henrietta pictures of potential suspects, but none of them matched the faces of the men who had been in the house that day.

Frustrated by the lack of progress into the investigation, Henrietta began to lose hope that any arrests would be made. But during the late spring of 1995, she received an offer to help apprehend the robbers from a man named Walter Johnson, who lived nearby and had been friendly with Winslow's first cousin, Benjamin Shim. "If you have any problems, if anybody bothers you, let me know," Johnson told her. But Johnson—"King Tut"—had a menacing street rep and, worse, was so persistent in his offers of assistance (he once left a greeting card under Henrietta's door quoting a biblical verse) that Henrietta became suspicious of his motives. When Johnson showed up one day outside her house, she told him, "Listen, I want this to stop. I want me and my family left alone. I want us to go on with our lives." Johnson admits now that he was too aggressive in his communications with the Winslows, but says that his offers to protect them were sincere. The robbery and run-ins with Johnson made Henrietta weary of life on Woodruff Street.

By the spring of 1996, when Henrietta found herself nervously looking out of the peephole of her apartment at even the slightest sound outside, she decided that it was time to move. That the always-tense relationship between her daughter and Spurgeon had degenerated into all-out warfare did not help matters. So, in April, after living in the Woodruff apartment for more than a decade, Henrietta finally moved her family. Despite the move, the robbery still cast a pall over the Winslow family. An NYPD detective named William Oldham, who worked closely with the

U.S. attorney for the Eastern District of New York, was investigating the incident. Oldham was constantly phoning Henrietta at work, causing her to get into trouble with her boss.

Worse, her daughter and Spurgeon bickered about the robbery constantly; she believed it had been committed by Johnson, while he insisted that a Brooklyn drug-based kingpin named Spencer "Scooter" Bowens was responsible, with good reason: Bowens often spoke in a fake Jamaican accent; he committed robberies of drug houses with a militaristic precision; and, most importantly, had confronted Spurgeon at the Q Club before the first robbery about the "thirty keys" of cocaine. Yet Spurgeon didn't dare let his suspicious about Bowens be known outside of the Winslow family because Bowens ran a fearsome crack-dealing crew called the Poison Clan, whose Brooklyn-based distribution network extended all the way to Baltimore, Boston, Washington, DC, Richmond, Virginia, and Raleigh, North Carolina. Most frightening to Spurgeon, Bowens was skilled at evading law enforcement: in June 1996, when the U.S. attorney for the Eastern District of Virginia charged twenty-three Poison Clan members with conspiracy to distribute crack cocaine, Bowens escaped indictment. Bowens would not be brought down until 1998, when he was indicted by the feds on drug conspiracy, money laundering, and obstruction of justice charges.

Spurgeon and Winslow's starkly different accounts of the robberies didn't stop prosecutors in New York from charging Johnson with them in the early spring of 1996. At first, Johnson was unworried by his prospects in the case; he maintained his innocence and had longtime attorney Flamhaft representing him. Indeed, when Johnson arrived in state supreme court in Brooklyn on that fateful day, he was expecting that the charges would be dismissed. The case against him *was* dismissed, but he was charged with the same robberies, as well as hit with obstruction of justice and drug distribution charges, under an "instant indictment" by the U.S. attorney for the Eastern District of New York in October 1996.

"For fifteen years or more, Johnson has waged a campaign of violent crime in this community," Assistant U.S. Attorney Samuel Buell wrote in a letter to the court, in which he argued that Johnson should be sentenced to life in prison without parole under the three strikes provision.

Under the three strikes provision of the Violent Crime Control and Law Enforcement Act of 1994, he could be sentenced to life in prison without parole. Johnson might have avoided this grim fate if he had cooperated against Combs, whom federal investigators believed ordered both the nonfatal shooting of Shakur and his murder. "That was the worst day of my life," Johnson remembers. "I knew I was innocent, and I knew that I'd face serious consequences for not cooperating."

Still, even though federal investigators were never able to charge him with hip-hop's most high-profile crime, they could claim victory by putting Johnson—whom they considered a profound menace enjoying a lucky streak of beating cases—behind bars under the three strikes provision. A *Daily News* headline said it all: "Feds Hope to Bury 'King Tut.'"

■ ■ ■

"I am not a snitch." In mid-November 1997, Jay-Tee Spurgeon testified as a witness for the prosecution in Johnson's much-anticipated trial in U.S. District Court in Brooklyn. As federal prosecutors conducted their direct examination of him, Spurgeon repeated "I am not a snitch" mantra-like throughout the trial. There was some truth to his claim: throughout the court proceedings, Spurgeon did not once implicate Johnson in any of the robberies. Instead, he voiced his suspicions that Poison Clan CEO Spencer "Scooter" Bowens was responsible. Spurgeon explained that about one month before the first robbery at his Hoyt Street apartment, Bowens confronted him at the Q Club and asked when he was going to receive a delivery of thirty kilos of cocaine. So when the Hoyt Street robbery occurred and the assailants repeatedly demanded "thirty keys," Spurgeon assumed that Bowens had to have been involved. "I had my mind set on one person," Spurgeon said. But because Spurgeon only referred to Bowens by his street name throughout the course of the trial, neither the prosecution nor Johnson's defense attorney offered any questions about the mysterious "Scooter," an understandable omission, as Bowens had yet to be indicted by the feds and was probably unknown to both the assistant U.S. attorneys—and even Johnson's own attorney—at the time.

Spurgeon's identification of Bowens as the perpetrator of the robberies was far from the only unusual aspect of Johnson's trial, which was marked by wildly inconsistent testimony from the Winslow family. Henrietta couldn't say who committed the robberies and admitted on the stand that she had filed false police reports in the past. And the charges against Johnson—in one robbery, Johnson was alleged to have stolen a mink coat and earrings from Crystal Winslow—were not the kind of allegations usually prosecuted in federal court. "The U.S. Attorney's Office bundled together old allegations made in state court," explains Johnson's attorney Kevin Keating, "in hopes that Johnson would cooperate. But Johnson did not bite." Former Assistant U.S. Attorney Samuel Buell defends the Johnson case as representing "a long tradition in Brooklyn federal court of prosecuting individuals who have thwarted the system on the state side. Individuals who have a long record of arrests and convictions that don't seem to have resulted in any significant prison time or are successful in obstruction of justice are often targeted."

On December 8, 1997, a Brooklyn jury delivered a verdict as inconsistent as the testimony during the trial: Johnson was acquitted on nearly half of the counts in the twelve-count indictment. In a court filing soon after the verdict was handed down,

Keating characterized the outcome as a "confusing verdict which undoubtedly reflects concern" about Henrietta and Crystal Winslow's credibility. Crystal Winslow was the sole witness in the case to implicate Johnson in the robberies. But Johnson's conviction meant that he would be sentenced to life imprisonment without parole under the three strikes provision anyway. Johnson was the first New York resident to face such a punishment, and more than ten years after the verdict, he is incarcerated at a federal penitentiary in Lewisburg, Pennsylvania.

It's disturbing that a case like Johnson's—marked by wildly inconsistent testimony, false leads from informants who purposefully sought to distract law enforcement from the true culprits in the Shakur shooting at the Quad and his murder in Las Vegas, and, most strangely of all, petty state crimes that were amplified into gravely serious federal charges—resulted in New York state's very first three strikes conviction. The credibility of primary witness Jay-Tee Spurgeon is particularly questionable: on April 25, 1996, about one year after his 1995 indictment on federal drugs and weapons charges, he suddenly pled guilty in the case and had most of the charges against him dismissed on the government's motion, resulting in a sentence of fifty-seven months in prison with three years of supervised release. Tellingly, it was at that moment that the case against Johnson began to gain serious momentum. Though Johnson attorney Keating told me that Spurgeon "claimed to have received no benefit" for his testimony, his cooperation could have been acknowledged after Johnson's sentencing (or he could have received off-the-record acknowledgment of his cooperation). This would help explain why Spurgeon insisted "I am not a snitch" at Johnson's trial—even *while* testifying against Johnson. Furthermore, Crystal Winslow's first cousin Benjamin Shim told me that immediately following Spurgeon's arrest in 1995, both Spurgeon and Winslow were questioned relentlessly by federal investigators about Johnson. "Ya'll know a Walter John-son?" Shim says they were asked. "Ya'll know a Tut?" Shim also told me that he is certain that Johnson did not commit the Brook-lyn robberies. "If Tut was responsible," Shim says angrily, "I would have killed him myself." Shim says that he is coming forward now because Johnson's predicament is the source of overwhelming guilt for him and his relatives. Crystal Winslow, who is now an au-thor of popular "street lit" novels such as *The Criss Cross* and *Life, Love and Loneliness*, refuses to comment on Shim's claims, claim-ing that the case was "too traumatic" to discuss.

Shim isn't the only person to come forward to support Johnson's claims of innocence in the Brooklyn robberies. In the spring of 2002, an inmate at the Leavenworth penitentiary named Burgess Chad Flowers wrote in a sworn affidavit that soon after he be-friended a much-feared Brooklyn hustler named Dexter Isaac there, Isaac confessed to committing the robberies of the Spurgeon and Winslow apartments. "Dexter said that Tut is in prison for crimes that he committed with his boys," Flowers wrote. Another Leavenworth inmate—James A. Mitchell—also said that Isaac confessed to his role in the robberies to him. In a sworn affidavit signed in May 2000, Mitchell wrote, "Dexter admitted that he per-sonally committed the robberies that Johnson is now serving time for." Interestingly, Isaac has long been suspected—but never charged—in the shooting of Tupac Shakur at the Quad, in which he emphatically denies any involvement. Even more tellingly, a source close to Spencer "Scooter" Bowens recently told me that Bowens, along with Dexter Isaac, were the principle players in the shooting of Shakur at the Quad. (Bowens, who is currently incar-cerated at the U.S. penitentiary in Allenwood, Pennsylvania, re-fused to comment on the allegations through a private investigator working with him.) Perhaps most importantly, the shooting of Shakur at the Quad and the Brooklyn robberies in 1995 and 1996 share remarkably similar traits: in both incidents attackers wielded 99mm weapons, and the attacks were committed in a militaristic fashion. It's also worth noting that in 1998, Isaac was indicted by the U.S. attorney for the Eastern District of New York on robbery, murder, fraud, and witness intimidation charges and was sentenced to life in prison, while Bowens is serving life imprisonment on drug conspiracy and obstruction of justice charges.

■ ■ ■

More than a decade after Johnson's conviction, it is Shakur's murder that continues to haunt him. During the spring of 2005, federal investigators moved Johnson from a prison cell in Jonesville, Virginia, to the Metropolitan Correctional Center (MCC) in downtown Manhattan, an administrative facility used to house pretrial and holdover inmates being prosecuted by the feds. At first, Johnson was unsure of why he was being flown to MCC, as the U.S. marshal accompanying him on the trip refused to answer any questions about the move. "The marshal said that I wasn't in any trouble but that they needed my testimony," Johnson remembers.

But once he arrived at MCC and found himself incarcerated with Shakur's former associate Jacques "Haitian Jack" Agnant, he surmised that the feds were yet again seeking his cooperation in the ongoing investigation into the rapper's murder. Johnson also worried that, just as they had done after his arrest in 1996, federal investigators wanted him to implicate Sean "Puffy" Combs in Shakur's slaying. This theory had gained credence in law enforcement circles after *Los Angeles Times* reporter Philips's September 2002 article, which claimed Biggie ordered the hit on Shakur while secretly visiting Las Vegas. When Johnson was moved into an intake room in MCC for questioning, he announced that he would not cooperate with investigators. "I'm not testifying *for* anybody, I'm not testifying *against* anybody," Johnson proclaimed, "and as a matter of fact I need my lawyer." The questioning ended before it even began. As Johnson prepared to return to Jonesville the next day, his suspicions about the direction of the investigation were confirmed during a conversation with Agnant, in which he "constantly spoke about a guy named Bill Courtney." Agnant told Johnson that Courtney was pursuing hip-hop industry executives.

Though Johnson was not aware of it at the time, William Courtney is a detective with the New York City Police Department, assigned to the High Intensity Drug Trafficking Task Force, who is cross-designated as a special agent of the Intelligence Squad of the FBI. Courtney was a major player in the federal investigation into hip-hop impresario Irv "Gotti" Lorenzo's ties to Queens drug kingpin Kenneth "Supreme" McGriff. Furthermore, just as Johnson finished his trip to MCC, *Newsweek* reported that investigators working with the U.S. attorney for the Southern District of New York were looking into a long list of crimes, including the unsolved murder of Shakur. And a *New York* magazine piece about Johnson's transfer to MCC suggested that federal prosecutors "could be on the verge of a breakthrough in the '94 shooting [of Shakur], which might in turn help solve the murder." It was obvious to Johnson that they wanted him to snitch on Puffy.

Though federal investigators involved in Johnson's case deny it, it's clear that his case has been driven—and continues to be driven—by his alleged connections to the nonfatal and fatal shootings of Shakur. It is not unusual for the feds to indict someone whom they suspect in a high-profile murder on lesser charges. For example, when law enforcement suspected that Kenneth "Supreme" McGriff ordered the murder of Run-DMC DJ Jam

Master Jay, he was hit with gun charges related to visits he made to a Baltimore area shooting range between January 1999 and June 2001. A source close to the case admitted then that prosecutors were using the weapons charges to keep McGriff "on ice" as they investigated the more serious allegations against him, including money laundering, drug conspiracy, and murder charges—though he, nor anyone else, has ever been charged in Jam Master Jay's slaying. Johnson's attorney Keating will not say if federal prosecutors prodded his client to cooperate against Puffy in the investigation into Shakur's murder. But he does admit that, just like in any other case with the government, they would have been interested in Johnson's cooperation on a wide variety of subjects.

Sam Buell, the former assistant U.S. attorney who was closely involved in Johnson's case, insists that while some investigators believed that Johnson might have information about a number of crimes, including the attacks on Shakur, Johnson's alleged role in the rapper's slaying "was certainly not the driving force behind the case."

To Shakur's millions of fans, however, Johnson will always be known as the "Tut" of the rapper's revenge anthem "Against All Odds." 50 Cent has also name-checked Johnson in the song "Many Men" from his multiplatinum debut album *Get Rich or Die Tryin'*. "I can understand why the Tupac fans would not like me, and I respect their loyalty to him," Johnson explained to me from the Lewisburg Penitentiary. "But I want the Tupac fans to know that I'm not responsible for his attempted assassination, nor did I have anything to do with his assassination. It's important that they look at the Biggie Smalls case and a lot of cases that involve law enforcement officers who break the law. With this story, there's only one way to find the truth: remove the lies and inconsistencies. I guarantee that if you come into the case, you will find cover-ups and smoke screening." Johnson cleared his throat.

"This is America; you have the right to ask questions. 'Why is this guy being targeted? Is he involved, or isn't he?' I'm coming to the public, and I'm sacrificing myself. Find me guilty if I'm wrong. Prosecute me to the fullest degree of the law possible if I'm guilty. But if you got an innocent man lying in jail . . ." he trails off. "Even though I was a bad guy in my younger years, I didn't do this. And I don't deserve to be here for this."

Chapter Four

LINE 'EM UP AND INDICT 'EM

The Cooperator Casting Call that Brought Down Euka Wadlington

WHEN THE FEDS CAME FOR MARK THOMAS, HE WAS READY. THE FORTY-SIX-year-old native of Clinton, Iowa, had hustled cocaine in his hometown ever since he was discharged from the army in the mid-1970s after a tour in Vietnam as an artillery man. Thomas's involvement in the drug business was so extensive that he boasted connections to just about every distributor who supplied dealers in Clinton, a small town of about thirty thousand near the Iowa-Illinois border. Thomas first became involved in Clinton's drug trade—which was unusually active for a rural town because of its close proximity to Chicago (just 175 miles away)—via local cocaine boss Jack Jetter. When Jetter's operation was taken down in the early 1980s, Thomas moved up the ladder to a California-based wholesaler named José Mendez. By the mid-1980s, Thomas was moving up to two or three kilos of cocaine at a time—so much that he offered to share his California connection with a Clinton hustler named Terry Hildebrandt. But by the end of the decade, Thomas had become a cocaine addict himself, and, worse, he was allowing debts from his sprawling customer base in Clinton's housing projects to go unpaid. "I wasn't really taking care of business," Thomas admitted later. "I was using a lot of it [cocaine]. I would give it to a lot of different people. Some would pay me; some wouldn't. A lot of times I didn't even get enough money back to actually pay for it." So in the early 1990s Thomas quit using drugs, but he soon found out that he couldn't leave the easy profits of the drug business behind. He got a job at a local factory and allowed Hildebrandt to take a more central role in their organization. Under the new arrangement, Thomas would buy cocaine from Hildebrandt and then sell it to retail dealers in Clinton. "I was a drug addict who wasn't using drugs," Thomas explained. "I was like the middleman . . . a lot of times I wouldn't even see the dope."

By the mid-1990s, the feds began clamping down on Clinton's drug scene. In September 1996, a pair of the city's biggest cocaine distributors—George Harper and Deleon Gadison—were indicted by the U.S. attorney for the Southern District of Iowa on drug conspiracy charges. A few months later, in April 1997, Thomas's business partner, Hildebrandt, was also hit with drug conspiracy charges, this time from the U.S. attorney for the Northern District of Iowa. Thomas feared that he would be the next to go down.

Sure enough, one night in early September 1998 he arrived home, pushed play on his answering machine, and heard a bone-chilling message: "I'm Steve Cundiff from the Clinton County Sheriff's Department. I need to talk to you. Please return my call." The next morning, Thomas called Cundiff back, and he was instructed by Cundiff to come down to the U.S. attorney's office in nearby Rock Island, Illinois, the next day. When Thomas arrived the next morning, he was met by Cundiff and Mike Dasso, an agent from Iowa's Division of Narcotics Enforcement. During the meeting, Cundiff and Dasso delivered a blunt warning: Thomas was going to be indicted on drug conspiracy charges, and he was facing decades behind bars under the sentencing guidelines because of the drug arrests on his record. Right then, Thomas knew that his three-decade-long run in the drug game was over. "I guess I can best describe it by a line in the movie *Laramie* with Jimmy Stewart," Thomas explained later, "where the rancher says to him 'I don't know who you are, but I knew you were coming.' . . . I knew this was going to happen. I knew for two years that I was going to be sitting there talking to somebody."

Though Thomas's future looked dark, Dasso and Cundiff explained that there was one way for him to escape lifelong imprisonment. "If I could be of assistance, and if it proved to be of 'substantial assistance,'" Thomas explained later, using a surprisingly accurate definition of section 5K1.1 of the sentencing guidelines, "the prosecutor could ask for a departure from the sentencing guidelines." Without hesitation, Thomas signed a cooperation agreement with the feds. Just as quickly, however, he realized that there was a serious obstacle in his quest for that much-coveted "downward departure": Clinton's drug scene had been hit so hard by the series of indictments in the mid-1990s that there were few players left on the streets to cooperate against. But Thomas was undaunted. He set his sights on one of Clinton's most well-known black residents, an amiable, forty-one-year-old Chicago native named Euka Wadlington.

■ ■ ■

In Chicago, everyone from street hustlers to nightclubbers called Euka Wadlington "Smookie Smokin' Eukie." The nickname was

obviously ridiculous—it made Wadlington laugh whenever anyone used it—but as a teenager growing up in Chicago's infamous
Cabrini Green housing projects during the 1980s, having a sense
of humor helped Wadlington survive. Besides, the flamboyant
nickname fit him well. From his teens to early twenties Wadlington worked as a DJ and club promoter in Chicago, earning admir-
ers with his distinctly Southern, genial style—his stepfather was
raised in Mississippi, and he has ten stepbrothers and stepsisters
there—and a love of absurdist wordplay reminiscent of Andre
3000 from Atlanta hip-hop duo OutKast. Indeed, when I spoke
with Wadlington for the first time during the fall of 2006, the soft,
Southern lilt in his voice and his decidedly slangy speaking
style—he announced himself on the telephone by shouting, "Hey,
it's Euki *Euuuuk* here!"—were dead ringers for Andre's. Wadlington's wild eccentricity stood in stark contrast to his low-key,
working-class parents, both of whom were employed in the health
care industry (Wadlington's mother worked at a local veteran's
hospital; his stepfather worked for a taxi company that trans-
ported Medicare patients to clinics and hospitals). But while
Wadlington loved DJing and partying, he also possessed a strong
entrepreneurial streak. During the mid-1980s, Wadlington and a
team of promoters threw house parties in Chicago that were a fast
success because they created invites (nicknamed "pluggers")
promising door discounts for revelers. Pluggers were much sought-
after items in the city's club scene, and soon Wadlington and his
crew—who called themselves "Reflex"—moved from throwing
parties at homes and high schools to renting out entire halls.

By the late 1980s, however, Wadlington and his promoter pals
had become bored with their parties. They threw one last "Reflex" event and retired the name permanently. Not long afterward, when a friend from Wadlington's Chicago neighborhood
named Terrance McLoyd moved to nearby Clinton, Iowa, he

begged Wadlington to check out the party scene there and perhaps start promoting again. McLoyd lured Wadlington to Clinton by boasting about the small-town girls who would fight over
"fresh meat"—men—from Chicago, and the raucous, all-day barbeques the city's residents threw during the summer. His curiosity
piqued, Wadlington made a series of visits to Clinton in the late
1980s and early 1990s and, to his surprise, found that Clinton
was just as fun as McLoyd had promised. The girls loved city
guys, and the afternoon barbeques held in the backyards of Clinton's run-down single-family homes—which looked like little
more than shacks to the Chicago-bred Wadlington—were a
blast. After spending a series of weekends in Clinton, though,
Wadlington began to sense the city's shortcomings. "Clinton was
so small that you could hire a cab to comb the town twice and
clock no more than three dollars in cab fare," Wadlington told
me. "I just didn't feel the spirit of the town, so I never stayed
more than a weekend."

Back in Chicago, Wadlington abandoned the club scene altogether, working construction jobs and dreaming of one day running a small business of his own. But Wadlington was jolted out of
his nine-to-fiver's life during the spring of 1993, when he received
a frightening phone call from McLoyd. "I have a problem,"
McLoyd told him. "I had a few words with some dudes here from
the city." McLoyd said that street hustlers taunted him so relentlessly that life in Clinton had become unbearable. "I'm tired of
hearing their mouth, man," McLoyd lamented. So, Wadlington
gathered a huge group of friends—about sixteen in all—and drove
out to Clinton. Wadlington and his crew made the 144-mile trip
in a little more than three hours, arriving just after eleven thirty
that night at McLoyd's house, where they were greeted by his wife,
Phyllis. McLoyd was out drinking at a local club called Drummer's
Lounge, Phyllis explained, and she'd be happy to escort them

there. To Wadlington's surprise, when his crew arrived at Drummer's, McLoyd seemed completely at ease. Wadlington realized right then that McLoyd was using him to bolster his street credibility, and that his response to McLoyd's call made McLoyd more respected in the eyes of Clinton's street guys.

McLoyd had another motive in bringing Wadlington out to Clinton: he wanted him to see the thriving party scene at Drummer's. McLoyd introduced Wadlington to the club's owner, and after he ordered a round of Remy VSOP, they all reminisced about the Reflex parties and Wadlington's days as "Smookie Smokin' Eukie." As the night wound down, the proprietor of Drummer's turned to Wadlington and asked, "Have you ever owned a club, son?" Wadlington admitted that he hadn't but, sensing a great opportunity within his grasp, laid out his plans for Drummer's anyway. Drummer's was relatively successful, Wadlington explained, but it could do better by reaching out to Clinton's minorities. Because blacks made up a mere 3 percent of Clinton's population, they had few nightlife options and could be persuaded to become loyal patrons if the club was more welcoming. Wadlington's presentation was an impassioned one—and it got him in as the manager at Drummer's.

Though managing Drummer's was just the kind of entrepreneurial gig Wadlington had long hoped for, his timing in taking over the club was terrible. The drug business in Clinton was peaking, and federal, state, and local law enforcement were putting Drummer's—and the run-down motels nearby where its revelers rented cheap rooms to drink and do drugs—under constant surveillance. Fortunately, Wadlington was street-savvy enough to sense that Drummer's was becoming a dangerous place, so he moved back to Chicago the following year. With a $3,000 loan secured from a new friend he'd made in Clinton named Mark Thomas, he took over the lease at a car wash.

Drummer's, meanwhile, was rudderless without Wadlington, and in the late fall of 1996 the club's owner lured him back to Clinton. When Wadlington returned to Clinton's hustling scene, Drummer's was once again in law enforcement's crosshairs, thanks to the indictment of George Harper on drug conspiracy charges that September. In early 1997, Clinton cops finally raided Drummer's itself. The bust yielded neither guns nor drugs, but that didn't end law enforcement's suspicions about the nightclub—and Wadlington. Though Wadlington moved back to Chicago soon after the raid, and Clinton cops had never arrested him for selling or even possessing drugs, federal prosecutors in Iowa suspected that he was a drug kingpin who employed major players like George Harper. One Clinton cop even dubbed Wadlington the "Big Fish" of the city's drug game. But because the feds and local law enforcement had no evidence of Wadlington's involvement in the drug business—not even a single controlled buy from him or any of his alleged underlings—they sought out cooperators to corroborate their suspicions.

■ ■ ■

When Mark Thomas entered into a cooperation deal after agents Dasso and Cundiff threatened him with indictment, it was suddenly up to him to help the feds make their case against Wadlington. Though Thomas had significant connections in the drug business, he was a far from ideal candidate to help bring down Wadlington, as he had not even seen him for years. Nevertheless, as Thomas admitted later, "the idea of getting 'substantial assistance'" was on his mind, and he was determined to assist the feds in their investigation.

The investigation into Wadlington began clumsily, with Thomas begging just about everyone he knew in Clinton for a phone number in Chicago where Wadlington could be reached. When no one could be of assistance, Thomas turned to Wadlington's closest friend in Clinton, Terrance McLoyd. But the number McLoyd had for Wadlington turned out to be out of service, a huge embarrassment to Thomas because just before he made the call, he had Agent Cundiff attach a tape recorder to his phone. Thomas went back to McLoyd, who shrugged and offered to drive him to Wadlington's Chicago home. Out of options, Thomas agreed to make the trip, even though he knew that the surprise visit would make Wadlington suspicious.

Just after six thirty AM on October 4, 1998, Thomas and McLoyd set out for the Southside Chicago home where Wadlington lived with his fiancé, LaTonya, and their three children. The pair arrived just before nine that morning, and when they knocked on Wadlington's door, they managed to wake the entire family. A groggy Wadlington let Thomas and McLoyd in anyway, and the group sat down at the dining room table, sipped coffee, and reminisced about old times at Drummer's Lounge. As Wadlington refilled their cups, Thomas explained that he'd come to collect on the $3,000 he'd loaned him for the lease on the car wash. He was broke and hard up for cash. Wadlington replied that he, too, was broke—LaTonya was on public assistance—but Thomas insisted that he start paying back the loan immediately, asking if he could at least get 10 percent of the loan back. Wadlington reluctantly agreed to the arrangement and as he walked Thomas and McLoyd to the door, Thomas suddenly blurted out, "Do you have access to any keys?" It was an embarrassingly awkward attempt at making a drug buy, and it made Wadlington immediately suspicious that he was being set up, especially since he wasn't even involved in the drug business. "My instincts told me that I was being betrayed," Wadlington remembers. In a last-ditch effort to save the trip, Thomas got Wadlington's pager and telephone numbers—but still left without any sense that he'd ever buy drugs from him. "Nothing was definite that day," Thomas admitted later, "and it was pretty much left that way."

Soon after arriving back in Clinton that afternoon, Thomas called Agent Cundiff to let him know that he had reestablished contact with Wadlington. Cundiff then raced over to Thomas's house, and the pair got Wadlington on the phone. Thomas told him that he had a buyer—actually DEA agent Jon Johnson—who wanted to buy a kilo of cocaine. Wadlington said that he wanted no part of any drug deals, so Thomas gave him a stern reminder of his outstanding debt. "He hit me with the guilt trip about him helping me out and me not trying to help him out," Wadlington remembers. Against his better judgment, Wadlington suggested that they scam Thomas's buyer out of his drug money without ever giving him drugs. Wadlington knew the scheme was lame and potentially dangerous, but Thomas talked up the buyer as being flush with cash, so he seemed like an easy enough mark. "There should be some way to get this guy's money," Thomas told Wadlington. "He's got the money." Wadlington also hoped that Thomas might forget about the kilos of coke altogether if they pulled off the scam. A few weeks later, when Thomas and DEA Agent Johnson drove out to Chicago to meet Wadlington, he wisely decided not to show up. Furious, Thomas called Wadlington and demanded that they reschedule their rendezvous for November 17 at a divey Hampton Inn near Chicago's Midway Airport.

When Wadlington and a friend named Roberta Thomas arrived at the Hampton Inn that day, they knocked on the door of room 505 and waited for a reply. As they stood at the door, an older white man brushed close by them in the hall. Growing impatient and nervous, Wadlington knocked on the door again, and Thomas let the pair in. Suddenly, the white man who passed them in the hall grabbed Roberta from behind. Federal agents, joined by members of the Illinois Tactical Response Team, burst out of the bathroom and a connected hotel room and tackled Wadlington, forcing him to the ground so they could search him. To their chagrin, Wadlington, the purported "big fish" of Clinton's drug scene, didn't have drugs or weapons in his possession. In fact, Wadlington was barely carrying any cash; he had just $1 in his wallet that day. A search of his vehicle—a beat-up 1986 Nissan Maxima—also turned up nothing illicit. Yet the takedown of Wadlington—which involved nearly thirty agents from the Illinois Tactical Response team backed by air support—would bring him an indictment on federal drug conspiracy charges and the potential of life imprisonment. Unless, of course, he agreed to cooperate. As he was held at the Hampton Inn on that November day, Wadlington says agents implored him to "help yourself. Give us somebody, Eukie. You can walk out the door right now but you got to give us somebody." One of the arresting agents later confirmed Wadlington's account, testifying at his trial that Wadlington was asked "if he was interested in helping himself or talking with Inspector Cundiff or myself."

As Wadlington feared, just one month after the November 1998 bust at the Hampton Inn, the U.S. attorney for the Southern District of Iowa charged him with conspiring to distribute crack. Two superseding indictments followed in which Wadlington was hit with numerous counts of drug conspiracy; federal prosecutors also alleged that he had been a member of the sprawling drug organization run by George Harper and Deleon Gadison that had controlled much of the crack and powder cocaine business in Clinton's housing projects and nightclubs during the mid- to late 1990s. Despite the fact that Wadlington and his Chicago-based attorney Leonard Goodman knew that the investigation sting was kick-started by the call from cooperator Thomas, they were about to discover that the superseding indictments were even more informant and cooperator-driven.

•••

Though he'd spent just two years behind bars, George Harper was getting restless. It was the fall of 1998, and Harper, who was then housed at FCI Oxford, a medium security federal prison in Oxford, Wisconsin, confided to fellow inmate Romaine Dukes that he couldn't imagine completing his twenty-seven-year sentence on drug conspiracy charges. "It was too stressful," Harper told Dukes. People had lied about Harper at his trial, and Harper admitted that if he got an opportunity, he would lie about someone else, too, if it would get his time cut. "He asked me if I would be willing to lie about someone to cut my time," Dukes remembered. "I told him that I could not do it." Shortly after his conversation with Dukes, Harper disappeared from FCI Oxford. As cooperators are often moved from their place of incarceration to an administrative prison facility near a U.S. attorney's office, Dukes assumed that Harper had found someone to cooperate against.

Dukes was right. In early 1999, Harper testified in front of a grand jury that Euka Wadlington had been his distributor since 1992 and that Wadlington supplied the cocaine he sold at crack houses around Clinton. Harper also claimed that Wadlington made $450,000 from crack sales in Clinton from 1995 to 1996 alone. In exchange for his testimony in the Wadlington case, Harper received a significant reduction in his twenty-seven-year sentence; he is scheduled to be released on November 4, 2010.

As federal prosecutors in Iowa assembled their case against Wadlington, they began to encounter witnesses far less malleable than Harper. During the late fall of 1998, when Clinton narcotics cops arrested Terrance McLoyd's teenage son, Terrance Hood, with one hundred crack rocks, he rebuffed their attempts to get him to cooperate against Wadlington. When cops warned Hood, "You better start talking," and "You better start telling us because you're the one in trouble," Hood broke down sobbing. "I don't want to go to jail," Hood cried. The officers responded by couching their cooperation offer in more appealing language. "Well, talk to us," they continued. "Tell us what you know. And maybe we can help you." After a long pause, they suggested, "How about Eukie?" to which Hood replied "No, I never sold for him." The cops thought Hood was lying. "*Never?*" they asked. Hood repeated his claim that he'd never hustled for Wadlington. "Has he ever approached you to sell?" the officers continued. "No," Hood replied. Rather, Hood explained that Wadlington nagged him about staying in high school and even told drug dealers to stay away from him. Hood then went on to describe players in the hustling scene in great detail—without once implicating Wadlington.

Hood would soon have a change in heart. In early January 1999, just as George Harper was moved from FCI Oxford to testify against Wadlington, Hood was visited at the Clinton County jail by Agent Dasso. Dasso told Hood that if he entered into a cooperation deal he could avoid much of the prison time he'd face because of his arrest. Hood finally flipped; he had Dasso call his attorney and then signed the cooperation agreement. Once the deal was struck, Hood—who had never implicated Wadlington in any drug activity—started claiming that he'd stolen crack from Wadlington and that he'd seen Wadlington with cocaine at a barbeque in Clinton. Hood still maintained that Wadlington was not his drug supplier, until he was moved to Scott County jail that month, when he was visited by Dasso. During the interviews, Hood changed his story yet again, this time claiming that Wadlington supplied him with drugs since he was fourteen. Hood also told a chilling story about Wadlington doling out a punishment to his subordinates called a "one-minute violation" in which he'd shock them with a Taser gun.

Hood's cooperation was critical in building the case against Wadlington, but in the weeks before he was to go to trial, federal investigators still scrambled to line up more cooperators. On April 7, 1999, prosecutors flew Juanita Ellis, an ex-girlfriend of Wadlington's, from her home in Baudette, Minnesota, to the U.S. attorney's office in downtown Davenport, Iowa, in hopes that she would testify against Wadlington in front of a grand jury. Ellis, however, insisted to Assistant U.S. Attorney Clifford R. Cronk and his team of investigators that Wadlington had never been involved in the drug game and that she had never seen him with any drugs. She added that she hadn't seen Wadlington since they stopped dating in the early 1990s. The feds were not convinced. Their questioning of Ellis stretched well into the night, and Ellis, a mother of seven, later said that she was deprived of food during the interview. Despite the pressure from prosecutors, Ellis did not break, so just before the interrogation concluded, the feds threatened her with indictment. Federal agents told her they suspected that she'd lied to them throughout their interrogation even though they offered no proof of their claim. Such hardball tactics would provide the grounds for Wadlington's attorney, Leonard Goodman, to make a motion to dismiss the indictment based on "prosecutorial misconduct and abuse of the grand jury." Cronk and his team of investigators, Goodman alleged, "bullied and threatened defense witnesses until they recanted exculpatory statements."

Even after being threatened with indictment, Ellis could not be persuaded to testify against Wadlington. But when she arrived back at the U.S. attorney's office the next morning she was feeling weary and vulnerable, and feared missing her flight back to Minnesota later that afternoon. Ellis had to make a decision about whether or not she would cooperate—fast. At around 1:35 on

April 8, 1999, just one hour before her plane to Minnesota was to depart, Ellis huddled with her attorney, Patrick Kelly, in a conference room.

There Ellis told Kelly that she would, at last, testify against Wadlington. Seizing the moment, Assistant U.S. Attorney Cronk rushed Ellis before a grand jury. Though Ellis had long resisted the entreaties of federal prosecutors to cooperate, there was an air of inevitability about her decision. Federal investigators, after all, had been leaning hard on her for months. In a series of phone conversations before their April meeting in Iowa, Cronk had warned her that he would indict her on perjury and drug charges and would even have her children removed from her custody. "If I were you," Cronk told her, "I'd be afraid."

The case against Wadlington was built on a casting call of co-operators and informants, and only when he went to trial in April 1999 did it become clear just how thoroughly un-credible their testimony was. An ex-girlfriend of Wadlington's named Luwanda Kelly, who had agreed to cooperate an hour after arriving at the U.S. attorney's office in Iowa from her home in Georgia, testified that Wadlington packaged bags of powdered cocaine into ziplock bags, which he'd store in Tide detergent boxes. But under cross-examination from Goodman, Kelly admitted that when federal agents interviewed her at her home in Savannah, she told them that Wadlington was never involved in the drug business. When Goodman questioned Kelly on her conflicting accounts, she acknowledged that she had not been entirely truthful when interviewed by investigators in Georgia. "You're saying that you lied" in Georgia? Goodman asked Kelly. "Yes," Kelly replied. Kelly explained further that, like Juanita Ellis, she had told federal investigators that she'd never seen Wadlington with drugs only to have them threaten her with indictment. It was at that moment, Kelly explained on the witness stand, that she agreed to testify about Wadlington in front of the grand jury.

If Kelly's and Ellis's testimony sprang from pressure from prosecutors, their fellow cooperators seemed to cynically enter into cooperation agreements solely to receive a 5K motion. Though Mark Thomas was perhaps the most critical witness to the U.S. attorney's case, he could only vaguely describe how Wadlington was connected to Clinton drug business players such as Samuel "Big Ed" Miller and George Harper. Thomas testified that while he did not purchase drugs "directly from" Wadlington, Clinton's hustlers "were like runners for him." However, he could not specify who these dealers were nor how he knew that they worked for Wadlington. Even under the friendly, direct examination from Assistant U.S. Attorney Cronk, Thomas's testimony was so opaque and inconsistent that at one point Goodman quipped, "Mr. Thomas, do you make this up as you go along?" Most damningly, Thomas seemed all too savvy about the sentencing guidelines and the 5K process. Thomas explained that "there was something called 'substantial assistance'" and that if he cooperated with the government by providing it, he would be given credit. The "credit" Thomas would receive for his cooperation, he continued, would be the prosecutor asking the judge for a departure from the sentencing guidelines. During his cross-examination of Thomas, Goodman pointedly raised the issue of the cooperator's extraordinary grasp of the sentencing guidelines and section 5K1.1.

> GOODMAN: You know a little bit about the federal system,
>   do you not?
> THOMAS: I'm not sure what you're referring to.
> GOODMAN: Do you know how people get sentenced in
>   federal court?
> THOMAS: The sentencing guidelines.
> GOODMAN: You know about the sentencing guidelines,
>   don't you?

THOMAS: Just recently I've become aware of those.

GOODMAN: Do you know about mandatory minimums?

THOMAS: No, not necessarily. I'm not sure what you mean by that.

GOODMAN: Never heard of a mandatory minimum sentence?

THOMAS: I believe what that is like if it's a certain crime, the minimum amount of time you can get . . .

GOODMAN: Now are you aware, Mr. Thomas, that if you sell over five kilograms of cocaine and you have a prior conviction that you can go to prison for twenty years? Did you know that?

THOMAS: I knew that with quantity time increased.

GOODMAN: You didn't know that you were facing a minimum of twenty years for your crimes?

THOMAS: I would have guessed it was twenty-five years.

GOODMAN: How much time have you done in jail for all of these drugs that you've dealt?

THOMAS: Fourteen days.

Similarly, convicted cocaine dealer-turned-cooperator Sherman Bell admitted that he signed a cooperation agreement with the feds after a 1995 arrest because he was "familiar with the [sentencing] guidelines." Bell's acknowledgment was followed by a testy exchange with Goodman in which he admitted that he had no hesitation whatsoever about "telling on" whomever prosecutors sought information about.

GOODMAN: You . . . agreed to become an informant for the government.

BELL: Yes, sir.

GOODMAN: To do whatever they wanted you to do.

BELL: Yes, sir.

GOODMAN: To tell on whoever they wanted you to tell on.

BELL: Yes, sir.

Bell added that he hoped his cooperation would result in his release from prison—and a reunion with his girlfriend. "If I sat here and told you that I didn't want to be free out on the street with my beautiful girl," he proclaimed, "I'd be lying. I've been praying since the day I went to jail, from day one, that God would send me some miracle and release me—yes, sir." Goodman then sarcastically shot back, "Well, he sent Cronk, maybe not a miracle—but you got some hope now."

During his closing statements, Cronk appeared to acknowledge the poor performance of his cooperators when he told jurors that they should convict Wadlington if they found the word of *any* of the witnesses credible. "If you believe the testimony of *one* witness," Cronk said, "just one, if you believe their testimony, then you know you must find Mr. Wadlington guilty of conspiracy." It didn't matter that the feds had never made any crack or powder cocaine buys from Wadlington; that they had never found drugs in his home or in his vehicle; or that, as Goodman put it, "the government's case was built entirely on the word of compensated informants." The jury, Cronk said, should deliver a guilty verdict on all the drug charges.

On May 10, 1999, an Iowa jury found Wadlington guilty of three counts of drug conspiracy and acquitted him on one count of cocaine distribution. Because Wadlington had two state drug convictions from the late 1980s, he was sentenced to two concurrent life terms in prison. "Like any innocent person," Wadlington told me, "I was devastated. How could I have run crack houses in Clinton while at the same time work twelve hours a day, five days a week nearly two hundred miles away in Chicago?"

Goodman was less surprised, though no less angered, by Wadlington's guilty verdict, as he is well-accustomed to the astonishingly high conviction rate (nearly 90 percent by some estimates) by juries in the federal criminal justice system. "When a federal prosecutor says 'I represent the United States of America, and this guy is a drug dealer,' that is a very powerful thing," Goodman explains. Appeals can often be just as treacherous for defendants. Even though several of the witnesses in Wadlington's case (including Terrance Hood) recanted their testimony in sworn affidavits in the wake of his guilty verdict, an Eighth Circuit judge affirmed his conviction. In the spring of 2006, Goodman filed a petition for writ of certiorari—a document filed by a losing party in which the high court is asked to review the decision of a lower court—with the U.S. Supreme Court on Wadlington's behalf—to no avail. In January 2007, the Supreme Court declined to hear his case. When I spoke with Wadlington just before the Supreme Court's decision, he seemed less interested in the outcome of his case than in assisting his fellow inmates with their appeals. "I was dealt a bad hand in the legal system," Wadlington told me. "Maybe I can bring better luck to someone else."

Chapter Five

MARK'S BAD TRIP

The Shaky Science that Led to Increased Penalties for Ecstasy Dealing and the Dealer Who Turned Cooperator Because of Them

DURING THE LONG, STRANGELY STALE, AND UNEVENTFUL SUMMER THAT preceded the September 11 attacks, Mark had a recurring nightmare. He'd fulfilled his lifelong dream of traveling to Florida to witness a space shuttle launch. To his horror, soon after liftoff the craft broke apart in the sky and crashed to the ground in a fiery explosion. "As the shuttle came apart, I heard radio reports describing the disaster," Mark remembers. "It was all the more frightening because the voices on the radio were staticky. Visually and aurally the entire dream was bad news."

The nightmare particularly affected Mark because he had been so space-obsessed as a teenager growing up in the Boston suburbs that he enrolled in physics and engineering classes in hopes of one day becoming an astronaut. When Mark's low marks in college physics finally convinced him that he'd never make it into the ranks of NASA, he abandoned that dream, though he still followed the space shuttle's developments religiously. He also became a space hobbyist, poring through books on aeronautics whenever he was not working at his day job—selling Ecstasy.

After Mark graduated from college in the mid-1990s with a degree in political science, he had a moment every bit as revelatory as watching his first space shuttle launch on TV. During the fall of 1996, at the urging of a pair of friends whom he'd met his freshman year in college, Mark took Ecstasy for the first time at a downtown Boston nightclub. "I had tried pot before but thought it was really dull," Mark remembers, "but Ecstasy was a very powerful experience. So whenever these guys invited me out, I went because I wanted to do Ecstasy again." Mark's exciting nightlife stood in stark contrast to his dull, low-paying day job as a dispatcher for a taxi company. By the spring of 1997, Mark realized that if he sold drugs he could pay for his lifestyle.

As a drug business amateur, Mark didn't have the connections or the cash to make bulk Ecstasy, so he'd buy a handful of pills from the dealer who sold to his friends and then resell them in Boston clubs for a small profit. "It was just supplemental cash at first," Mark remembers, "but I needed it. I was bringing home something like $705 every two weeks after taxes from my job, and I had student loans maturing." The solution to Mark's money woes came during the late summer of 1997, when, after earning the trust of his dealer, he began purchasing dozens of Ecstasy pills at a time. By that fall, Mark had earned enough money from his modest drug business to take a long trip to Mexico. While on vacation, Mark realized that it was time to abandon his day job altogether. He knew that he could make real money if he immersed himself in the Ecstasy business. Use of the drug was spiking dramatically, and legal penalties associated with its sale were far less significant than those connected to cocaine and heroin. Prison sentences were relatively light for Ecstasy-related offenses—federal guidelines called for fifteen months in prison for trafficking eight hundred pills. Most importantly, Ecstasy's user base was comprised not of hard-core addicts but of weekend partiers with disposable income who simply needed a few pills for a Saturday night out. While retail co-caine dealers kept long hours (and fielded constant pages and cell phone calls from demanding customers), the Ecstasy dealers Mark had befriended in Boston set strict business hours, which their clients were happy to abide by as long as they were able to make a purchase early in the night before they hit the clubs later.

Mark quit his job as a dispatcher and, to get started in the busi-ness, purchased a beeper and a few dozen Ecstasy pills. As the drug could be purchased for $7–8 at the wholesale level and then sold for $25 at retail, Mark began to see significant profits fast. He'd move about one hundred pills every two weeks, earning him a profit of $1,700. The days of bringing home $700 from a boring forty-hour-per-week day job were now gone forever. Mark hustled in a particularly unsafe way—he sold Ecstasy on the dance floor in nightclubs—so he was vulnerable to both bouncers and, as law enforcement began to become aware of the growing use of Ec-stasy, undercover cops. So Mark was forced to shift his small, emerging drug business from nightclubs to his Boston apartment, a risky move because he wasn't sure if his club-hopping customer base would follow him. But after explaining his new business model to his clients—"Listen, I'll come to your house, or you can come to my house; it's safer"—they were understanding and even appreciative of his decision to leave the club scene behind. By 1999, as Ecstasy use peaked around the country, Mark had a thriving business conducted with an ease and simplicity rare in the drug game: after getting a phone call or a page from a client, he'd head over to their apartment with a knapsack stuffed with Ecstasy and then sell dozens of hits at a profit of around $17 per pill. As he moved his product, Mark would share a few drinks with his amiable clientele—and then return home, often to bed by midnight.

Though Mark was unaware of it at the time, while he was focusing on his growing business, law enforcement's attitudes about Ecstasy were changing dramatically. Seizures of Ecstasy by U.S. Customs increased sevenfold from 1997 to 1999, and drug counselors were reporting that use of the drug was spreading from urban club kids to suburban high school students. Perhaps the most profound shift in law enforcement's perception of Ecstasy came in 1998, when the medical journal *Lancet* published a paper demonstrating what appeared to be long-lasting damage among Ecstasy users. The study, performed by husband-and-wife team George Ricaurte and Una McCann, researchers at Johns Hopkins University, examined fourteen people who had used Ecstasy more than one hundred times on average and concluded that the drug "injures the brain for life." Ricaurte and McCann arrived at this conclusion by subjecting the study's participants to PET (Positron Emission Tomography) scans, in which chemical probes were stuck to serotonin transporter proteins, the area of the brain affected by Ecstasy (the drug causes surges of serotonin, which make users feel euphoric). The Johns Hopkins researchers concluded that because the serotonin synapses of Ecstasy users "glowed" less under the PET scans than the synapses of control subjects, it was likely that permanent damage to the brains of drug users occurred. Armed with Ricaurte and McCann's results, Alan Leshner, then director of the National Institute on Drug Abuse (NIDA), created a multimillion-dollar print and TV advertising campaign featuring PET scans of the brains of Ecstasy users and nonusers side-by-side, bearing the ominous warning "PLAIN BRAIN, BRAIN AFTER ECSTASY." In Leshner's ad, the "plain brain" looked bright and robustly healthy under the PET glow, while the "brain after Ecstasy" was shrouded in such deep darkness that it seemed as though parts of it had actually been permanently eliminated. Leshner's "PLAIN BRAIN, ECSTASY BRAIN" took the iconic "This Is Your Brain on Drugs" campaign by the Partnership for a Drug Free America to terrifying new heights.

With seizures of Ecstasy rising sharply and evidence accruing that the drug caused long-lasting brain damage, Congress decided to raise criminal penalties associated with its sale and, they hoped, curb its use with expensive public education campaigns like Leshner's. During the spring of 2000, Senators Chuck Grassley, Bob Graham, Craig Thomas, Evan Bayh, and Joseph Biden introduced the Ecstasy Anti-Proliferation Act, which sought to provide funds for treatment of Ecstasy users and amend federal sentencing guidelines to massively increase penalties for those involved in trafficking the drug. In his public comments about the act, Grassley claimed that while the drug produces euphoria, it raises the heart rate to dangerous levels—sometimes causing the heart to stop beating—and that longtime users could expect to suffer from depression, paranoia, and confusion. In a nod to Ricaurte and McCann's work, Grassley added that "scientists now believe that it causes irreversible brain damage. No one should ever call this a harmless drug." The Anti-Ecstasy Proliferation Act became law on October 17, 2000, despite testimony from drug policy experts such as the Rand Corporation's Jonathan Caulkins, who argued that extending sentences was the reform least likely to be successful in combating Ecstasy use.

Still, after the bill's passage, Congress directed the United States Sentencing Commission (USSC) to devise new sentencing guidelines for Ecstasy-related offenses. During the USSC hearings about Ecstasy in March 2001, Ricaurte and McCann's *Lancet* study was cited repeatedly by government officials such as USSC Chair Diana E. Murphy and acting Deputy Attorney General Robert S. Mueller III. "It kills the serotonin nerve cells in the brain," Murphy said of Ecstasy. "The damage to these nerve cells is particularly dangerous because nerve cells very well may not grow back. If they do not grow back, permanent impairment of memory functions can result." Mueller was even more emphatic about the drug's effects. Ecstasy "is quickly becoming one of the most abused drugs in the United States," he said, referring to Ricaurte and McCann's study that seemed to demonstrate that brain damage produced by Ecstasy is "significant and long term."

The scientists and drug policy experts who testified before the USSC offered far more skeptical analyses of Ricaurte and McCann's work. Dr. David Nichols, a professor of medicinal chemistry and molecular pharmacology at Purdue University, argued that while Ecstasy could "cause the degeneration of brain serotonin axons . . . these axons can 'resprout' and grow back." Dr. Charles Grob, a professor of psychiatry and pediatrics at the UCLA School of Medicine, lambasted Ricaurte and McCann's work (and other NIDA-sponsored medical studies) as suffering from "serious flaws in methodologic design and questionable manipulation of data, and misleading and deceptive reporting in the professional literature and to the media." Yet the testimony of Nichols and Grob did little to influence the USSC's decision making. As Rick Doblin, founder of the Multidisciplinary Association for Psychedelic Studies (MAPS), told me, "We left feeling like we were totally ignored." Doblin's fears were borne out during the spring of 2001, when harsh new sentencing guidelines for Ecstasy-related offenses were established. Defendants convicted of selling eight hundred pills would receive sixty-three to seventy-eight months in prison; under the previous sentencing regime, it took around eleven thousand pills to receive that sentence. "This is a wholly political act," declared Edward Mallett, president of the National Association of Criminal Defense Lawyers, "not one based on scientific evidence."

■ ■ ■

During the summer of 2001, just months after the USSC established new sentencing guidelines for Ecstasy-related offenses,
Mark began experiencing his space shuttle nightmare. But he
shrugged off the bad dreams because his Ecstasy business was still
booming. He was selling about a hundred pills per week, and, flush
with cash, he took a series of vacations to Spanish party destina-
tion Ibiza. He even moved from a small ground-floor studio in
Roxbury to a spacious, upper-floor, one-bedroom apartment in
Boston's Back Bay. As the summer of 2001 came to a close, Mark
received a tantalizing offer that solidified his status as an up-and-
coming drug business player in Boston: a friend who worked as a
club promoter offered to introduce him to a man who wanted to
buy a thousand Ecstasy pills. "This guy *really* wants to buy in quantity," the club promoter told Mark. Though Mark had never sold
wholesale amounts of Ecstasy, he was tempted to make the deal.
If he could convince the customer to buy a thousand hits at retail,
he would make $18,000; even if he offered the buyer a price
just slightly above wholesale—say, $10 per pill—Mark would net
$3,000.

Anxious to make the transaction, Mark hastily scrawled the customer's number on a piece of notebook paper and called him that
night. During the call, Mark and the potential buyer arranged to
meet the next day at a Spanish restaurant. Mark's plan was to suss
the guy out, gauge if he had the cash to cut the deal, and then
scrounge up enough money to make a wholesale buy from his distributor. But when Mark arrived at the restaurant the next day, he
was immediately suspicious of the buyer. "He was Italian-looking
with a thick build," Mark remembers, "*very* straight and clean-cut
looking." But Mark set aside his doubts because he was an acquaintance of a close friend. It didn't hurt that the buyer obviously had
the cash to buy hundreds of Ecstasy pills: he pulled up to the
restaurant in a black Mercedes. As Mark and the buyer finished

lunch that afternoon, they agreed to meet in the coming weeks to make the transaction.

Mark was excited at the prospect of pulling off the deal, but he had to save for weeks in order to make the unprecedented buy from his distributor. He delayed "going shopping" (slang for re-upping his drug supply) and instead liquidated his inventory to customers who would pay top dollar per pill. This meant break-ing his long-held rule of not hustling in nightclubs, but in the end it was worth it: clubbers will pay a premium for Ecstasy once they're at a venue because they have few other options for ob-taining drugs. In October 2001, he purchased a thousand hits of Ecstasy from his distributor, the largest buy in his history as a dealer. Mark then called his buyer to let him know that he had the product—and the pair arranged to meet toward the end of the month. Ominously, in the weeks after their meeting the buyer called repeatedly to ask if Mark could sell him five thou-sand more pills. Mark said that he didn't have the connections for such a large purchase. Mark rationalized the unusual request as perhaps that of a more experienced buyer, one accustomed to dealing in quantity.

Finally, during the last week of October 2001, Mark received an early morning call from the buyer. "I'm ready," he said and then slammed the phone down. Mark stuffed the thousand Ec-stasy pills into a knapsack and headed downtown. After breakfast with his girlfriend, Mark took the T train to the arranged meet-ing place, a park in downtown Boston. But when he arrived, the buyer wasn't there. Mark called him, and there was no answer; the line rang repeatedly and then went dead. Undeterred, Mark stood in the park and waited until the buyer showed up about twenty minutes later. He apologized for his lateness and told Mark that he had the cash in his car. "Follow me," the buyer said, motioning Mark to the spot where his car was parked. When they reached the car, Mark handed over the knapsack stuffed with Ecstasy. As the buyer opened the trunk to retrieve the cash, DEA agents sprang from every corner of the park. "YOU'RE UNDER ARREST FOR SELLING A THOUSAND ECSTASY PILLS," one bellowed as Mark was forced to the ground and handcuffed by another. "I was in total shock," Mark says of the arrest. "I had no idea this was going to happen. I guess you could say that I was oblivious."

After being shoved into an unmarked car, Mark was driven to a DEA holding facility in downtown Boston. "If you want to go home tonight," one agent told him, "tell us who your sources are." When Mark refused, the agent began becoming more aggressive, citing the harsh sentencing guidelines for Ecstasy-related offenses that the USSC had just instituted that spring. "You're looking at at least five years," the agent growled, "plus we have a slam dunk case against you." Mark was petrified—he had never been arrested before, let alone served time in prison. But he refused to cooperate, so the agent moved him to a federal administrative prison facility in downtown Boston, where Mark would sit waiting for a court hearing. On his ninth day in prison, Mark was brought before a magistrate judge who ruled that he could be released on approximately $1,000 bail. Though Mark was happy to be going home, he realized that he faced a grim choice: serious prison time or cooperating against his high-level distributor. Soon after arriving back at his apartment, however, Mark found out that his distributor had received word of the bust and would no longer sell him drugs, let alone take his phone calls. Snitching on his higher-ups was now out of the question.

With a loan from a friend Mark hired a criminal defense attorney in hopes that he could find a legal angle in his case that could lead to an acquittal. Instead, Mark's lawyer advised him to cooperate. He also warned Mark that "the feds really don't like people who refuse to cooperate. They will throw everything they have at you." That was all Mark needed to hear. On his lawyer's advice, he agreed to cooperate, though with his distributor out of the picture he didn't have a clue of whom he would cooperate against. Mark's attorney arranged for a meeting with the assistant U.S. attorney handling the case anyway. When Mark and his attorney arrived at the U.S. attorney's office in November 2001, he was astonished to see not only the prosecutor but a cast of DEA, FBI, and customs agents. (The feds believed—wrongly—that Mark was importing Ecstasy from Canada.) What happened next was even more surprising: the agents presented a slide show featuring surveillance photos of local drug business players and asked if he could recognize them. Mark said that he did—and then agents showed snapshots of his distributor and even his customers. Did he recognize them, too? Stunned, Mark admitted that he did. "They wanted to see if I was being truthful," Mark remembers, "so that they could move forward with the deal." After passing the test, an assistant U.S. attorney produced a cooperation agreement, which Mark signed. "A DEA agent will be contacting you next week to see what you've come up with for us," he told Mark. "You're free to go now."

Cooperation agreements are opaque: they do not specify the number of cases that need to be made by the cooperator, nor the amount of time he or she needs to work for the government. As Loyola University law professor Alexandra Natapoff puts it, "although cooperation agreements resemble contracts and formal plea bargains, they are generally vague and open-ended. . . . Snitch relationships with the government tend toward the open-ended and indefinite; they may outlast a particular charge and go on for years." Indeed, criminal defense attorney Robert Simels says that "sentencing is delayed sometimes years to keep the hammer on a witness." Though Mark's attorney was as honest with him about his cooperation deal as he could be, Mark was relieved to have signed it anyway. The agreement, after all, offered the possibility of the much sought-after 5K motion, which could result in a significant reduction in his sentence.

The weekend after his meeting with federal prosecutors, Mark and his girlfriend hit Boston's clubs in hopes of taking their minds off of their uncertain future. On the dance floor of one club, a short, stocky Asian man offered them a handful of hits of Ecstasy, which they happily accepted. As the drug took effect, Mark and his girlfriend got into an intense conversation with the dealer on the dance floor. "I'm on crystal!" he suddenly announced to Mark and his girlfriend with a sense of shamelessness that only someone on drugs could display. Mark's girlfriend nudged him in his ribs. "Get his number," she whispered. Mark didn't know why he'd want the number—he didn't do crystal meth—but he got it from the dealer anyway. When Mark and his girlfriend arrived at his apartment that night, she suggested that he turn the dealer in to the feds. Mark didn't think the feds would be interested—he was just a retail level dealer—but he decided to let his DEA handlers know about him anyway. There was little doubt in Mark's mind that it was far safer to cooperate against a low-level retail dealer than a big-time distributor.

"The next day I called one of the DEA agents handling my case," Mark remembers, "and said, 'I found a guy who sells Ecstasy *and* crystal.' The agent said, 'OK, good, see if you can get sixty grams of crystal from him.'" (The DEA agent likely asked for sixty grams of meth because fifty grams triggers a mandatory ten-year prison sentence under federal sentencing guidelines.) So Mark called the dealer and asked for the sixty grams, explaining that he was interested in such a sizeable quantity of the drug (individual doses of crystal are small, between ten and twenty-five milligrams) to supply a high-roller friend. To Mark's surprise, the dealer agreed to make the transaction even though he and Mark had just met. After the call, Mark's DEA handler suggested that he set up a preliminary meeting with the dealer to make sure that he'd come through with the drugs. Mark arranged for this meeting from the DEA's office, and his handler actually got on the phone to pose as the high-rolling, meth-buying friend in order to make the transaction seem convincing. "He was a no-nonsense talker, and he cursed a lot," Mark says of the DEA agent, "so he actually seemed credible." It was a done deal: Mark would meet the dealer at a McDonald's and would provide him with a small bag of crystal that he could "taste."

In preparation for the McDonald's meeting, DEA agents gave Mark a hollowed-out cell phone that held recording equipment. They instructed Mark to put the phone in his front shirt pocket when he arrived at the restaurant so that it would pick up his conversation with the dealer. A team of undercover DEA agents would also be scattered around the site: one would sit in McDonald's posing as a customer, while a team of about half a dozen agents would sit in unmarked cars in the parking lot. When Mark arrived at the McDonald's in November 2001, everything went as the agents had planned. In fact, it worked out better than they'd hoped because the dealer also brought his distributor along. As a team of DEA agents watched from outside, Mark and the dealer sat down at a table; after shaking hands, the dealer passed a small bag of crystal to Mark under the table. Once they completed the transaction, the dealer asked Mark if he'd like to smoke some crystal with his distributor, who was waiting in his car. Mark declined, and the dealer got into his car and drove off toward Boston. Two unmarked cars carrying DEA agents trailed close behind. When the dealer's car was finally out of sight, Mark walked over to one of the DEA agents waiting in an unmarked car and handed him the bag of crystal. He then turned around to go home, but the agent stopped him and frisked him. "You're clean," the agent said, and Mark headed for the T station.

"That was good shit." It was a few days after the McDonald's meeting, and Mark's DEA handler was talking to the dealer on the phone as Mark stood beside him. The DEA agent then quietly passed the phone to Mark, who set up another appointment for the following week. After they hung up the phone, Mark's DEA handler explained that the protocol for the takedown would be far more rigorous than the initial meet-up. One agent would drive Mark to the meeting site, the corner of a busy street in downtown Boston. Simultaneously, two separate sets of agents would be parked on the block: one near the dealer's car to prevent him from driving away, the other down the block to provide surveillance of the transaction. When the deal was completed, Mark was to stand aside and let the agents tackle the dealer. Mark would also submit to being handcuffed in order to fool the dealer into thinking that he was being arrested, too.

Just after three PM that Wednesday in late November, Mark stood on a street corner waiting for the dealer to arrive. When a minivan pulled up on the street in front of Mark a few minutes later, its windows rolled down revealing the dealer and, to Mark's surprise, his distributor. The dealer jumped out of the van, shook Mark's hand, and explained that the distributor was going to wait inside the vehicle with the drugs. Mark told the dealer that he had the cash in his car parked down the block. As they walked toward the car, Mark saw the agents begin to pile out of a minivan with darkened windows, which they had parked down the block. Remembering his handler's instructions, Mark slowly moved aside as the agents drew closer to the dealer. "Four DEA agents running at full speed tackled him," Mark recalls. "When he hit the ground, they forced me onto my knees. The dealer stared at me in shock—but I couldn't look him in the eyes. I felt so guilty." As Mark and the dealer kneeled on the cold sidewalk, a car full of DEA agents pulled in front of the distributor's minivan, blocking its exit. He was then dragged from the car and arrested. "Good job," one agent said to Mark. "We expected one, but we got two. Nice surprise." If his DEA agents were happy, Mark was thrilled.

In the months following the takedown, more agents called with the same request—"let us know what else you have." Even though he never had anything more to share, they didn't press Mark because he had already provided them with two arrests. Then, at the beginning of 2002, agents stopped calling. The DEA's apparent satisfaction with his performance was, according to Mark's attorney, a sign that he'd get a glowing 5K motion from the federal prosecutor. But during the spring of 2002, Mark's lawyer and the assistant U.S. attorney handling his case began to go over the particulars of his plea deal. The prosecutor wanted Mark to admit to having a much larger role in the drug business than he'd actually had. He also wanted Mark to take a lesser drug possession charge because agents had found drug paraphernalia in his Boston apartment after he was arrested. Mark and his attorney spurned the prosecutor's offers, and as 2002 progressed, Mark worried that he'd have to initiate another bust.

■ ■ ■

In the spring of 2002, just one year after the United States Sentencing Commission established extraordinarily punitive sentences for Ecstasy-related offenses based mostly on the research of George Ricaurte and Una McCann, a British medical journal called the *New Scientist* published a scathing critique of their work. The *New Scientist* found while some of the brains of their control subjects performed up to forty times better than the "Ecstasy brains," some of the Ecstasy brains outperformed the control brains by ten times or more. The *New Scientist* said that this represented an unacceptably high level of "scatter"—or variability—in the results. "There are no holes in the brains of ecstasy users," University of Toronto neuropathologist Stephen Kish told the *New Scientist*. "And if anyone wants a straightforward answer to whether ecstasy causes any brain damage, it's impossible to get one from these papers."

Ricaurte responded to the criticisms of his and McCann's study by claiming that "the fact that significant differences were found [between control brains and Ecstasy brains] speaks for itself." But beyond the variability issues, there was another significant problem with Ricaurte and McCann's work. Several of its participants had used Ecstasy on more than two hundred occasions over four to five years—far more than allowed by the study's protocols. In 2003, I spoke with a man—whom I'll call "Roger"—who served as a Ricaurte and McCann subject in 1998. Roger told me that he had used Ecstasy hundreds of times as well as other drugs like cocaine and ketamine. He described himself as being a hardcore "poly-drug" user when he enrolled in the Ricaurte-McCann study, and he admitted that he had done drugs just hours before he had arrived at Johns Hopkins. (He said that he had just come off of an all-night cocaine bender.) An interview with Ricaurte-McCann subjects conducted by Donald G. McNeil Jr. of the *New York Times* in 2003 found similar drug abuse patterns among the study's participants. A participant whom McNeil called "Greg M." said that when he enrolled in the study he was using Ecstasy, marijuana, LSD, cocaine, amphetamines, and heroin, and that he had used heroin just five days before he arrived at Johns Hopkins. Ricaurte called Greg M.'s heroin use "unfortunate," and he stressed that his staff administered blood and urine tests on the subjects to determine that they were clean. But Roger told me that while he was given urine tests, it would have been unlikely for the tests to come up clean. "There's no way I was clean," Roger told me. "I had been doing cocaine the entire night before the drug test."

Ricaurte's reputation was dealt another huge blow in September 2003, when *Science* retracted a 2002 study he had published in the magazine. The study claimed that a single night's use of Ecstasy could cause permanent damage. Unfortunately for Ricaurte, it was later discovered that the monkeys and baboons in the study were injected with methamphetamine, not Ecstasy. In an interview with the *New York Times*, Ricaurte said that the vials of drugs brought into his laboratory were mislabeled. "We're not chemists," he said. "We get hundreds of chemicals here. It's not customary to check them."

A spokesman for Johns Hopkins medical school admitted to the *Times* that the errors were regrettable but stated that Ricaurte was "still a faculty member in good standing whose research is solid and respected."

Responding to criticism from drug policy analysts that his work was politicized and used as a tool to buttress harsh sentencing guidelines for Ecstasy-related offenses, Ricaurte said, "We're scientists, not politicians." Similar claims of objectivity have been made by scientists whose Ecstasy research is funded by the government. During the 2001 USSC hearings on sentencing guidelines for Ecstasy-related offenses, National Institute on Drug Abuse acting director Glen Hanson said, "Never once did NIDA inflict on me any sort of suggested result to my research. They've never implied they wanted me to demonstrate neurotoxicity for a substance."

Discerning the intentions behind flawed Ecstasy research is an impossible and ultimately useless task—what matters more is that shaky science became the foundation for sentencing guidelines that makes the drug, on a per-dose basis, five times more serious to possess or sell than heroin. More importantly, no effort has been made to revise the sentencing guidelines in light of the revelations about Ricaurte's research, though editorials from medical journals such as the *New Scientist* characterized his work as "so irretrievably flawed that the scientific community risks hemorrhaging credibility if it continues to let them inform public policy." That the increased sentencing guidelines for Ecstasy-related offenses still stand today institutionalizes documented falsehoods about the drug's effects—and subjects defendants like Mark to unduly harsh punishments.

Perversely, the tough sentencing guidelines for Ecstasy and other drugs create an incentive for law enforcement to pursue not high-level distributors but retail-level dealers, like Mark and the meth dealer, who can be lured into moving more weight. In the early 1990s courts began recognizing just such scenarios as "sentencing entrapment," defined as cases where a defendant is entrapped into a large crime that he or she was not predisposed to commit. Though it is impossible to say whether or not a judge would have accepted this defense in Mark's case, his situation is the very definition of sentencing entrapment. Prior to his arrest, Mark had solely sold retail amounts of Ecstasy. His deal with the undercover DEA agent not only marked the first time he had ever dealt in weight but also triggered the greatest possible punishment under federal law, as sale or possession of eight hundred pills or more brought a sentence of at least five years in prison under the new sentencing guidelines. The meth dealer ensnared by Mark and his DEA handler as part of his cooperation deal could also have made a sentencing entrapment defense, as he had been a retail-level dealer lured into selling a much larger amount.

But even if Mark had made such a defense, the odds of its success would have been long. The sentencing entrapment defense has not been viewed favorably by judges. Indeed, the very first judge to acknowledge the concept of sentencing entrapment did not *wholly* accept it as a defense. In *United States v. Lenfesty*, the result of a yearlong undercover investigation into a methamphetamine distribution organization based in Rochester, Minnesota, more than half a dozen arrests were made, including the ringleader, Gary Lenfesty. The defendants were convicted on drug conspiracy charges but then appealed their sentences in the Eighth Circuit court. One defendant, Twila Smith, contended that an undercover agent working on the case entrapped her into "repeatedly purchasing drugs . . . [in order] to increase both the amount of drugs in the conspiracy and her sentence." In 1991 an Eighth Circuit judge affirmed Smith's sentence but opined that "where outrageous official conduct overcomes the will of an individual predisposed only to dealing in small quantities, this contention [sentencing entrapment] might bear fruit. . . . We are not prepared to say there is no such animal as 'sentencing entrapment.'" That year, another Eighth Circuit judge provided the definition of sentencing entrapment: it occurs when a defendant "although predisposed to commit a minor or lesser offense, is entrapped in committing a great offense subject to greater punishment."

Though sentencing entrapment is far from an accepted defense in federal courts, criminal defense attorneys say that it is routinely perpetrated by DEA agents, particularly in crack cocaine cases, where sentences that are vastly greater than those involving powdered cocaine can be triggered with just slight increases in drug weight. A typical sentencing entrapment scenario goes something like this: a cooperator, informant, or DEA agent makes a drug buy of powdered cocaine from a dealer. He then urges the dealer to "rock up" in order to bring the maximum sentence or, if there's a cooperator involved, the best possible 5K motion from a federal prosecutor. One criminal defense attorney told me of a case in which a cooperator purchased fifty grams of powdered cocaine from a dealer and then instructed him to "rock up" in his kitchen. When the dealer returned with the drugs, he was arrested and, under the sentencing guidelines, faced ten years' imprisonment. (He would have faced less than half that sentence if he had simply sold the fifty grams of powder cocaine to the cooperator).

Sentencing entrapment is the by-product of an increasingly punitive criminal justice system that seeks not to reform or rehabilitate defendants but to give them the longest possible prison terms. Worse, the work of cooperators like Mark—who finally received his 5K motion in 2006, which resulted in a sentence of a short period of home confinement followed by four years of supervised release—rarely make a dent at the distribution level of the drug trade. Even if retail hustlers like Mark *were* able to cooperate against their distributors, true higher ups would be untouched because, in the words of drug policy expert Jon Caulkins, "true higher ups don't sell to retail sellers." Perhaps the best result federal prosecutors can hope for from a cooperating retail seller is the lowest-level wholesaler, who then has to be convinced to turn in the second-lowest-level wholesaler. The drug business has become so multitiered—from retail dealers to the multiple levels of distributors and wholesalers to the marijuana and coca growers and manufacturers in Colombia and Mexico—that the prosecution of retail dealers has barely any impact on the drug problem. The combination of mandatory minimums and the centrality of the 5K motion in receiving a downward departure from those sentences has transformed drug enforcement into a game of tag in which small-time dealers constantly turn on one another. Under this law enforcement paradigm, minor players in the drug business—instead of their higher ups—face the steepest consequences for their actions.

Chapter Six

BROTHERHOOD OF THE BOOKSTORE

The $100,000 Informant, the Thirty-fourth Street Bomb Plot, and the Preemptive Indictment Brought by the Feds

Just as the sentencing guidelines created a cottage industry of co-operators who fabricate evidence in hopes of receiving a reduced sentence for themselves, post–9/11 terrorism investigations—which target potential terrorists based not on their capability to cause harm but on the attacks they may carry out—have given rise to fictional plots hatched by paid informants. These informants often goad gullible young Muslims into plots by stoking their anger about U.S. foreign policy. Alleged terror suspects are also indicted long before an attack is imminent (indeed, most post–9/11 terror suspects are not caught with weapons or explosives of any kind). As the *Buffalo News* wrote of the Lackawanna Six, a group of young Muslim men currently serving prison sentences for having trained at an Al Qaeda camp in Afghanistan prior to 9/11: "They never built a bomb, never hijacked an air-liner and, as far as the U.S. Justice Department can determine, never made any plans to commit terrorism." Instead of infiltrating terror plots, informants concoct them, promising suspects access to weaponry and even high-level terrorist leaders. In a recent case involving six Muslim men accused of planning an attack on soldiers at Fort Dix, the informant at the center of the investigation bragged to the suspects that he could get them sophisticated weaponry. According to the *New York Times*, "it was the informer who seemed to be pushing the idea of buying the deadliest items, startling at least one of the suspects." Worse, just as the informant/cooperator institution has sowed fear and distrust of cops among African-Americans, so too does it threaten to harm law enforcement's already fragile relationship with the Muslim community in the United States, which may result in Muslims' reluctance to come forward with information about true threats. Finally, because the mainstream media usually provides sensational, breathless coverage of terror busts, there is little scrutiny given to these indictments, which, as the story of an alleged bomb plot against New York's Thirty-fourth Street subway station proves, are often comprised of no more than fantastic tales concocted by informants.

It began with a visit to a fifty-year-old Egyptian immigrant named Osama Eldawoody (also known as Dawadi). Early in the afternoon of October 9, 2002, Eldawoody heard a loud knock on the door of his Staten Island home.

As Eldawoody rose from the couch in his living room and headed toward the doorway, he suspected that he was receiving yet another visit from the FBI. Though Eldawoody had trained as a nuclear engineer in his home country, he cobbled together a living in the United States selling clothing bought in bulk on the Internet. The constant stream of packages landing on his doorstep aroused the suspicion of neighbors, and the fact that the packages were addressed to "Osama" only heightened fears about him. So, in the year since September 11, Eldawoody had been questioned by FBI agents about the packages. Eldawoody's fears that day turned out to be somewhat justified: the caller was not an FBI agent, but an NYPD detective named Stephen Andrews from the department's Intelligence Division. Like the FBI agent who had visited before, Detective Andrews was there to inquire about the UPS shipments.

While most would chafe at such scrutiny from law enforcement, Eldawoody took the questioning with patience and grace, even inviting the detective into his home to inspect his closets. Detective Andrews declined, since the boxes clustered in his living room were open and clearly contained only clothing. "He was extremely helpful and gracious," Detective Andrews remembered later. But as the detective headed toward the door, Eldawoody's patient facade suddenly slipped. "Why the discrimination?" he blurted out. Detective Andrews was, naturally, taken aback by the question, as Eldawoody had been so cooperative. He asked Eldawoody to explain. Eldawoody said that he'd already been visited by the FBI, and that soon afterward he told his wife he was sure they'd come back. Detective Andrews was sympathetic. He explained to Mr. Eldawoody that because of "the strange state of things," unfortunately "this is the climate that exists," and he "apologized for having come to his home and having to investigate such a matter." Eldawoody seemed pleased by the detective's thoughtful reply, and just as Detective Andrews opened the front door to leave, Eldawoody pulled him aside and offered to assist the detective and the NYPD in "any way, shape, or form, at any time." All Detective Andrews had to do was call.

Nine months after the visit, Detective Andrews took him up on his offer. On July 22, 2003, he phoned Eldawoody and asked to meet him near a police precinct in Staten Island to discuss his offer of assistance. "The nature of the interview was to see if Mr. Eldawoody was still interested in assisting the department," Detective Andrews said later, "and how much time he would be able to devote towards being an informant, and if he had any knowledge of any sort of criminal activity." When Eldawoody met Detective Andrews that afternoon, he explained that while he didn't have any knowledge of criminal activity in the Muslim community, he would be able to assist the NYPD in tracking down people involved in the sale of fraudulent ID cards to illegal immigrants. Detective Andrews wasn't interested, but suggested that Eldawoody could serve as the NYPD's "eyes and ears" in the Muslim community. Eldawoody agreed to the idea. A few days later, after a background check that came up clean, Eldawoody received his first assignment: he was to attend services at the Masjid-al-Noor Mosque in Staten Island and "keep his eyes and ears open" for the department.

Unfortunately, the NYPD's instructions to Eldawoody were vague and open to interpretation. Soon after his first visit to al-Noor in July, he surprised his handlers at the police department by providing them with a long list of license plate numbers from the mosque's parking lot. When Detective Andrews asked Eldawoody if he'd simply copied the license plate numbers of *every* car in the lot, Eldawoody admitted that he had done just that. "I instructed him that's not his position to do," Detective Andrews remembered. He then told Eldawoody that he should take down license plate numbers from vehicles only "if he had good reason to do so." Eldawoody kept his handler's new instructions in mind when he began worshipping at the Islamic Society of Bay Ridge, a religious complex in a working-class section of Brooklyn, which boasts a mosque, a community center, and a nursery school. Just down the street from the Islamic Society is Islamic Books and Tapes, a bookstore where young Muslim men from the area congregate to talk about religion and politics. Eldawoody found that he could blend in easily with the patrons and customers of Islamic Books and Tapes because he had a strong grasp of current events—specifically the Iraq war and the Israel/Palestine conflict—as well as Koranic verse. "When he heard the call for prayer, he would start to cry," the Islamic Society's Zein Rimawi said of Eldawoody in a 2004 interview. "When someone would read the Koran, he would start to cry. He was a very good actor."

Indeed he was. Shahawar Matin Siraj, a twenty-two-year-old Pakistani immigrant who worked at Islamic Books and Tapes, was completely taken by Eldawoody. Siraj's life had been marked by failure: he didn't make it past the tenth grade in high school in Karachi, and when he came to America from Pakistan in 1999—illegally—he could only manage to find work at a series of low-paying jobs at places like Blimpie's and a 99 Cent shop near his apartment in Queens. Though he had several close family members living in New York—his father worked at Islamic Books and Tapes, and his uncle owned the bookstore—Siraj seemed lost in his adopted city. But Siraj's life changed forever on 9/11. That morning, as he stood on the corner of Second Street and Third Avenue in the East Village, he was frozen with fear as he watched the jets slam into the World Trade Center. At first, Siraj reacted to the terrorist attacks with strong feelings of empathy for his fellow New Yorkers. Just after the towers collapsed, he told his relatives that he wanted to donate blood. But by the end of 2001 he had become radicalized (and more religious) by the war in Afghanistan. Siraj began worshipping regularly at the Islamic Society, a few steps away from his uncle's bookstore. By early 2002, he became a near-constant presence there.

With so much of his time devoted to praying at the Islamic Society, Siraj took a job at Islamic Books and Tapes in June 2002. Though it was a low-level position—Siraj sold prayer rugs and religious photos and paintings—he enjoyed being so close to the mosque. Siraj also savored the debates about the Middle East that took place at the bookstore. He had only a rudimentary understanding of the issues affecting the region, but he was always a good listener. By the late summer of 2003, Islamic Books and Tapes was a hotspot for Bay Ridge's Muslims looking to discuss the most controversial issues of the day, from Palestinian statehood to the legitimacy of Osama Bin Laden's jihad against the West.

That summer, a newcomer to the scene named Osama Eldawoody managed to impress its spirited and intelligent denizens with his expertise on not just Koranic verse but the most minute details of 9/11 conspiracy theories. Even more impressively, Eldawoody claimed to be descended from a family of Islamic scholars and said that his father was a well-known author of Islamic books and a "big sheikh" in Egypt. Eldawoody even suggested to Siraj that they go into business together selling Islamic literature because his father owned a printing press in Egypt. His father's press, he explained, would sell books to them at a lower cost, and they could pass that discount on to customers in the United States.

The book distribution venture never happened, but Eldawoody and Siraj became close friends anyway. The politically savvy Eldawoody had a fatherly relationship with Siraj, who found that he could barely keep up with the debates about the Middle East at the bookstore. Siraj, once described by his attorney as "not the brightest bulb in the chandelier," listened raptly as Eldawoody explained how the beams of the Twin Towers couldn't have melted from the heat of the jet fuel that flowed over them on 9/11. Eldawoody insisted that the World Trade Center *had* to have been dynamited by the U.S. government; after all, he said, the government pulled off a similar ruse with the bombing of the Alfred P. Murrah building in Oklahoma City in April 1995. Coming from anyone else, this would have seemed like crackpot stuff, even to an impressionable young immigrant like Siraj. But because Elda-woody boasted of his background in nuclear engineering, his rants about 9/11 and Oklahoma City seemed convincing. When Siraj questioned him about why he wasn't working as a nuclear scientist, Eldawoody explained that he had a liver problem that prevented him from working.

But Eldawoody *was* working—as an informant for the NYPD. As Eldawoody schooled Siraj on 9/11 conspiracy theories and the West's war on Islam, he was being compensated about $300 a week by the NYPD. Eldawoody made for a convincing informant. With each passing week, he ratcheted up his heated rhetoric about U.S. foreign policy. To Siraj, Eldawoody was an angry man—angry about the Iraq war, angry about the treatment of Muslims after 9/11. "He used to come to the store to say, 'I don't want to die like that,'" Siraj remembered later. "'I want to do something.'"

While the Iraq war and 9/11 inflamed the passions of the patrons of Islamic Books and Tapes, there was still a sense of restraint permeating their debates. Siraj, for example, offered only qualified support for suicide bombings, arguing that while he could understand how Palestinians might resort to terrorism given the conditions they lived in, he didn't feel it was right to murder innocents. But when revelations about the abuse of Iraqi prisoners at Abu Ghraib surfaced in the early spring of 2004, Siraj and the customers of Islamic Books and Tapes were instantaneously radicalized. Eldawoody smartly seized on the dark, angry moment by showing graphic photos of abuse at Abu Ghraib to Siraj and his friend James Elshafay, another young Muslim. When Eldawoody showed Siraj and Elshafay a photo of a dog menacing a cowering female Iraqi prisoner, Siraj ranted about how the young woman would never be able to erase the memory of what had happened at Abu Ghraib even during the happiest moments of her life, like her wedding. "We have to do something," Siraj said furiously, repeating what

Eldawoody had said to him just a few months earlier when the men discussed the 9/11 attacks. "*We have to do something,*" he said again. Eldawoody silently nodded his head in agreement. "*Insha'Allah* [God willing]," he then said soothingly to Siraj. "*Insha'Allah.*"

Eldawoody told Siraj and Elshafay that he could do more than just offer the comfort of a father figure: he would assist the pair in conducting an attack on U.S. soil. More importantly, he had connections to a shadowy terror network called "The Brotherhood," which could serve as a second family to the men. The Brotherhood was everywhere, said Eldawoody—Europe, the United States, Pakistan—and they took care of their own. As generous as the Brotherhood could be, though, they could also be astoundingly brutal if members displayed any disloyalty. "After going into the Brotherhood and accepting them as your brother," Eldawoody told Siraj, "[if you] hurt them, they can hurt your family and they can hurt you, too." This was not an empty threat: Eldawoody said that the Brotherhood was connected to Sheikh Omar Abdel-Rahman, the blind Egyptian cleric who masterminded the 1993 bombing of the World Trade Center. Since Eldawoody had once boasted that his father was an Islamic scholar in Egypt, the notion that he knew Sheikh Abdel-Rahman did not seem at all far-fetched. And Eldawoody's claims about the Brotherhood were all the more convincing because he could name the organization's point man in New York: Abdel Hakim.

The timing of Eldawoody's revelation about the Brotherhood could not have been more fortuitous for the two young Muslims. Since 9/11, James Elshafay had been drawing crude, schematic maps of police stations and bridges like the Verrazano-Narrows, all with the vague idea of mounting a terror attack on them. At the same time, Siraj was so distressed and angry about the Abu Ghraib scandal—he later admitted that photos of abuse at the prison made his blood boil—that he felt compelled to retaliate against the United States. So Siraj showed Elshafay's maps to Eldawoody in hopes that they might be of use to the Brotherhood in a terrorist attack. Eldawoody was pleased. He told the young men that he would take the maps to Abdel Hakim and outline the plan to the Brotherhood. Unsurprisingly, Elshafay's amateurish maps were deemed useless, so it fell to Siraj to devise a new plan. In the early summer of 2004, Siraj suggested that they mount an attack on the Thirty-fourth Street subway station in Manhattan. Siraj targeted the station because he was familiar with its layout: he transferred there from a Queens train when coming to work at the bookstore. He also surmised that because of its location below Penn Station, an attack on the Thirty-fourth Street stop could cause great economic harm. Siraj told Eldawoody to take care, however, to avoid the mass casualties that resulted from Al Qaeda's bombing of a Madrid train station earlier that year.

But as the summer months passed, Siraj became increasingly uncomfortable with the plan that he had hatched. It had grown to frightening dimensions, with Eldawoody even suggesting that they obtain nuclear material from his contact in the Russian mafia. Siraj fretted over every detail of the plan, right down to the fate of the homeless people who slept in the Thirty-fourth Street station. Siraj pleaded with Eldawoody to try to save them. Eldawoody told Siraj not to worry, and reassured him that they were ultimately going to save the lives of Muslims in Iraq. Siraj still felt uneasy about the attack, though, and on August 23, 2004, just a few days after they had cased the station, he told Eldawoody that he wanted to call the plot off. Furious, Eldawoody threatened to inform Abdel Hakim about Siraj's change of heart. Still, Siraj insisted that they not go forward with the bombing. "I don't want to do it," Siraj told him.

That Siraj backed away from the bomb plot—and that he did not obtain or even attempt to obtain explosives of any kind—did not matter to law enforcement. Eldawoody had been wearing a wire during his months of conversations with Siraj and Elshafay—and the NYPD, joined by investigators working with the U.S. attorney for the Eastern District of New York—were ready to close in on them. On August 28, 2004, soon after Siraj arrived for work at Islamic Books and Tapes, he received a call from the cops summoning him to a police precinct in Bay Ridge. The caller explained that a misdemeanor assault charge stemming from a fight he'd gotten into was about to be dropped. They asked Siraj if he could come by and fill out some paperwork so they could dismiss the case. So Siraj closed up shop and began the short walk to the precinct, only to be seized on the street and arrested. Meanwhile, in Staten Island, James Elshafay was arrested by cops as he sat on the steps of the al-Noor mosque, the place where Eldawoody began his career as an informant. The pair were charged by the feds with four counts of bombing conspiracy: they "did knowingly and intentionally conspire to maliciously damage and destroy, by means of an explosive, a building, vehicle and other real property: to wit: the 34th Street subway station at Herald Square in New York, New York."

The charges against Siraj and Elshafay were deadly serious—they could result in life imprisonment—but the operation that brought them down was marked by a near-comic absurdity. It turned out that the Brotherhood was a fictional terrorist organization created by Eldawoody. The network's point man—Abdel Hakim—was also Eldawoody's invention: indeed, he later admitted that "Abdel Hakim" was a code name he made up for his NYPD handler Detective Andrews. Eldawoody had no connections to the Russian mob or terrorist leader Sheikh Omar Abdel-Rahman, nor did he have the means to acquire nuclear material or any other types of explosives.

If Eldawoody's terrorist plot was a flimsy fantasy, it would also be hard to find a pair of would-be terrorists more bumbling than Siraj and Elshafay. Siraj could barely hold down a minimum wage job, let alone conduct a sophisticated terror plot. He was once recorded on an NYPD surveillance videotape admitting, "Everyone thinks I'm stupid." Similarly, Elshafay had long been plagued by psychological problems, was on anxiety medication, and had only the foggiest idea of how to execute a terror strike. His renderings of the Verrazano-Narrows Bridge and New York police precincts were no more sophisticated than doodlings on a napkin. Like Siraj, Elshafay possessed an intelligence that can only be described as far below average.

Yet the arrests of Siraj and Elshafay merited praise for NYPD's Intel unit from the mainstream media and right-wing bloggers. In a 2004 special terrorism-themed issue of *New York* magazine, the NYPD's work in the Siraj case was cited among the reasons for "Why They Haven't Hit Us Again." "These kinds of homegrown, lone-wolf incidents start way below the level the federal government would focus on," David Cohen, the NYPD's deputy commissioner for intelligence, told *New York*'s Craig Horowitz. "If we weren't doing it, nobody would be." Accompanying the article about Siraj was a laundry list of explanations for "Why They Haven't Hit Us Again," among them "#6: We have informants everywhere." Conservative bloggers, unsurprisingly, also commended the NYPD's work in the case and offered hysterical characterizations of Siraj and Elshafay's alleged terror plot. Just before Siraj went to trial in the spring of 2006, ultraconservative blogger Michelle Malkin—best known for authoring a book defending the internment of U.S. citizens of Japanese descent during World War II—wrote a post about the case titled "Brooklyn Bridge Is Falling Down." Meanwhile, a lesser known right-wing blogger who calls himself "The Bay Ridge Conservative" linked to an article about Siraj in the conservative newspaper the *New York Sun* as a response to the question "Why do I take terrorism seriously?"

• • •

The fevered atmosphere fomented by the media and the right-wing blogosphere surrounding terrorism indictments—particularly when they involve foiled terror plots—often brings guilty verdicts for defendants even when the basis for the charges are reed-thin. "In this climate, juries are not making the best decisions," says Juliette Kayyem, a former Department of Justice official who was named Undersecretary of Homeland Security for Massachusetts in 2007. "So, out of fear, a lot of these guys will plead out." Indeed, that's precisely what happened in Elshafay's case: he pleaded out to a much less serious arson charge. Siraj would not be so fortunate. Following a trial in which his attorney, Martin Stolar, mounted a risky entrapment defense, Siraj was convicted and subsequently sentenced to thirty years' imprisonment.

The entrapment defense often requires that the accused take the stand, and the none-too-bright Siraj withered under cross-examination by Assistant U.S. Attorney Todd Harrison. On the witness stand, Siraj wavered on the question of whether he supported suicide bombings in Israel and Osama Bin Laden's jihad against the West. He also frequently contradicted himself about the dates of specific conversations that took place at Islamic Books and Tapes. After the trial, one juror, speaking anonymously to the *New York Times*, said that there wasn't sufficient evidence to support the entrapment defense even though Stolar presented proof that Eldawoody's payments from the NYPD more than doubled when the terror plot was hatched during the spring of 2004; that the escalation in Siraj's rhetoric began when Eldawoody showed him Abu Ghraib photos; and that Eldawoody was paid nearly $100,000 by the NYPD for his work. "I believe it could have been entrapment," the juror said, "but the defense didn't come up with the evidence—sad but true. The final thing was that we couldn't put our finger on any evidence."

Yet few journalists cast any doubt about the legitimacy of the guilty verdict, even after it was revealed that the entire terror plot was the fictional creation of a police informant—and that Siraj could hardly be considered a terrorist. "Anyone who still disputes that cameras deter criminals and terrorists—ACLU, that would be you!—should read the testimony of the Pakistani immigrant convicted in May of plotting to blow up New York's Herald Square subway station," scolded Heather MacDonald in the conservative *City Journal*. Massachusetts Homeland Security official Kayyem, however, is much more critical of informant-driven terrorism cases brought by the Justice Department. "In the same way that we were sold a war by Ahmed Chalabi," Kayyem says, "we are sold guilt by informants willing to put out their hands for money."

Incredibly, Eldawoody acknowledged his financial motivations in the case in a letter to Senator Hillary Clinton. In this letter, he identified himself as an NYPD informant working with Detective Steven Andrews and outlined his connection to the Thirty-fourth Street plot.

I worked as an informant for NYPD on a terrorism case which is "Plot to bomb Herald Sq. station" bet. Aug. 03 to Aug/04. The defendant was convicted in May/06.

While I was working on the case, when it became very serious in April/04, I met the Detective more than 5 times to make sure how my life is going to be after the cas [sic] is over, he promised me the greatest life financially and securing our life and not to release my name to the media.

After Aug./04 and until 6/6/05 we were in a sad financial situation. During that period of time I get a job as an Intepreter [sic] for US Army in Iraq, but they stopped me from having that job. And all the promises were gone.

Not only that, but my name, photo and video were released to the media. Now my family receiving all kinds of threats and our life become [sic] in danger and financially we became [sic] in debt because of the case.

The Honorable Senator, I really need to wipe my 10 year old daughter's tears. The great honorable Senator, would you help us.

During the fall of 2006, Eldawoody also lamented his plight to CBS News journalist Armen Keteyian, who, in an "exclusive" report on the network's evening news, portrayed the informant as an American hero who had suffered mistreatment at the hands of the NYPD and the feds. "As a paid confidential informant for the New York Police Department," Keteyian said, "Eldawoody helped the government derail a post–9/11 plot that would have been one of the city's worst nightmares: an attack on its subway system." Though Keteyian noted that Eldawoody *continued* to be paid by the NYPD and that his "$1,200-a-month stipend . . . has grown to $3,200," he neglected to mention that the informant concocted just about every aspect of the terror plot. To Keteyian and nearly all of the reporters covering the case, Elshafay's plea deal and Siraj's guilty verdict implicitly proved their guilt.

The informant-driven approach of the Siraj case—and the practice of bringing indictments in terrorism cases in which evidence consists of little more than vague talk of terror plots—is typical of the manner in which the feds conduct such investigations. In June 2006, the U.S. attorney for the Southern District of Florida broke up an alleged terror plot targeting Chicago's Sears Tower and FBI buildings in Miami, New York, Los Angeles, Chicago, and Washington, DC. The sting, which occurred in a dingy warehouse in the Liberty City section of Miami, was kick-started by an informant who told the defendants that he was an Al Qaeda member, but just as in the Siraj case, no explosives or weapons were seized from the alleged plotters. Similarly, the seven Miami defendants—who belonged to a bizarre cult called "Seas of David"—seemed not only incapable of pulling off a terror strike but also mentally incompetent. Seas of David leader Narseal

Batiste refers to himself as "Prince Manna" and was known in his Liberty City neighborhood for wandering the streets in a bathrobe. And when Seas of David member "Brother Corey" gave an interview to CNN in June 2006, he offered rambling non se- quiturs about the cult. "We are Seas of David," Brother Corey pro- claimed as he stood outside the Miami warehouse that served as the organization's base. "I know my brother has not been treated right in the system. . . . We're trying to build up a restaurant here. . . . We are not no terrorists." When the CNN interviewer confronted Brother Corey with rumors that the Seas of David members were homeless men, he shot back, "We are not no homeless—this is not no homeless shelter for a terrorist attack. You hear me?"

Though the feds charged Batiste and several of his underlings with seditious conspiracy and providing material support to ter- rorists, the Seas of David case was not the strangest, most specu- lative terrorism indictment brought by the federal government in 2006. That designation should go to the December 2006 indict- ment by U.S. Attorney Patrick Fitzgerald of a twenty-two-year- old Illinois man named Derrick Shareef, who was charged with "use of certain weapons of mass destruction" for allegedly plot- ting to set off hand grenades at a Chicago shopping mall and thus "disrupt Christmas." According to the indictment, Shareef told an undercover FBI agent that he wanted to blow up malls and public buildings that he had found by "doing MapQuest." Like Siraj and the Seas of David members, Shareef was indicted for his *intentions*, not his actions, and just like Siraj and Elshafay, he never possessed explosives or weaponry of any kind. He was ar- rested after trading stereo speakers for four nonfunctioning gre- nades given to him by an undercover agent. To Fitzgerald's credit, he acknowledged soon after Shareef's arrest that "while these are very serious charges at no time was the public in any imminent peril as a result of the defendant's activities. He didn't come with a prearranged plan to attack the mall. He didn't come with pre-arranged financing."

It's hard not to sympathize with a Justice Department that, since 9/11, has been charged with preventing terror attacks as opposed to investigating incidents that have already occurred. But divining intent among potential terrorists is an "inevitably speculative en-deavor," as David Cole, a professor at Georgetown University Law Center, told the *Atlantic Monthly*. To quote *Atlantic Monthly* writer Amy Waldman's apt metaphor, prosecuting bank robberies and drug deals requires training "in the classic art of whodunit—collecting fingerprints, interviewing bank tellers after a robbery, trying the purported robber," while agents involved in terrorism investigations in the post–9/11 era must find out "who *will* do it." It's no surprise, then, that preemptive indictments often involve informants and FBI agents concocting terror plots that wouldn't have otherwise existed. "In the context of post–9/11 terrorism," Siraj's attorney Stolar says, "it's a sham that we conduct terrorism investigations by having informants create fictional terror plots." Massachusetts Homeland Security official Kayyem adds that these indictments represent a dangerously distorted interpretation of "imminency" (the notion of how close a terrorist plot is to its exe-cution) among law enforcement, all fed by informants fabricating tales of terror strikes. "Informants drive imminency in a very un-helpful way," Kayyem explains. "There's no reason you can't wait to see if there is something more out there. National security is un-dermined when you go after people too soon. It's prosecution by press conference." Kayyem says that the result of such prosecutorial practices is simple: "Juries get swayed—and informants get paid."

Chapter Seven

JONATHAN LUNA'S LAST DAYS

The Rap Label, the Rogue Cooperator, and the Murdered Prosecutor

EARLY ON THE MORNING OF DECEMBER 1, 2003, THE GOVERNMENT BEGAN ITS opening arguments in the drug conspiracy case against Walter Oriley Poindexter and Deon Lionnel Smith, a pair of Baltimore men charged with using the offices of their record label, Stash House, as a front for heroin trafficking. It should have been a typical case for Assistant U.S. Attorney Jonathan Luna: Baltimore has one of the most severe heroin abuse problems in the country, with nearly 45,000 of its residents addicted to the drug. In his four years as a federal prosecutor, the thirty-eight-year-old Luna had faced far more daunting prosecutions than Stash House, including an online sex sting that netted a Navy physicist accused of soliciting sex from an undercover FBI agent posing as a teenage cheerleader. Yet Luna's case against Poindexter and Smith was beset by seemingly insurmountable hurdles from the very beginning: a pair of veteran criminal defense attorneys who shook Luna's calm, deliberate courtroom style and, more troublingly, a suddenly uncooperative cooperator named Warren Grace. After being indicted in 2002 on charges of possession with intent to distribute more than a hundred grams of heroin, Grace agreed to cooperate in the Stash House investigation in the hopes of receiving a downward departure from the sentencing guidelines for heroin-related offenses. So, in the weeks before the Stash House trial began in late 2003, Grace was cooperative when Luna visited him several times at the Philadelphia area prison where he was incarcerated in order to prep him for his testimony.

But despite Grace's motivation to cooperate, the federal prosecutor—who rose from a childhood of poverty in the South Bronx to take a prestigious job at the Maryland U.S. Attorney's Office—failed to elicit meaningful testimony from Grace when the trial began in December, throwing the case into a tailspin. "History," says Andrew White, a former federal prosecutor who worked closely with Luna, "is full of cooperating witnesses who spin federal prosecutors. When they get on the stand, they'll fight a prosecutor when the prosecutor doesn't expect it. That's what was happening with Jonathan." White may have been understating the case: in just the first few hours of the Stash House trial, Luna became so frustrated by Grace's combativeness and purposefully vague testimony that he began offering leading questions, which brought a stern rebuke from U.S. District Judge William Quarles. Quarles suggested that Luna remind Grace of "his incentives to cooperate"—namely the possibility of a 5K motion from the U.S. attorney—which often "worked wonders in getting witnesses who were recalcitrant, or didn't want to be there" to be more helpful.

By the second day of the trial, Luna's direct examination of Grace had all the testiness of a defense attorney conducting a cross. "How do you know how much heroin Mr. Poindexter would get at the studio?" Luna asked. Grace gave an incoherent non-answer: "He would tell me when we come home." Confused, Luna asked again, and Grace simply repeated himself. Luna continued his attempt to have Grace provide the jury with the precise amount of drugs sold by Poindexter and Smith. "Can you give the members of the jury an example of how much heroin you would get, that Mr. Poindexter would get?" he tried. Grace remained steadfastly nonspecific. "One occasion, it might be forty grams," he said; "one occasion it might be twenty." Luna then made one last attempt at achieving even the slightest sense of clarity from his combative cooperator: Could he recall Poindexter and Smith receiving wholesale amounts of heroin at *any* time during the alleged conspiracy? "I don't remember the date," Grace said.

Grace's credibility was then further called into question when he admitted that, after being indicted in 2002, he violated the terms of his house arrest by escaping from an electronic bracelet. He also revealed that on a day when he made drug buys from Poindexter and Smith for the FBI, heroin was seized from his black Ford Excursion SUV. But instead of being embarrassed by the revelations, Grace pointed to his bad behavior as a necessity in the cooperation game. "Upon my cooperation," Grace helpfully explained, "I had to make it appear like I was constantly in the street." The drug stash in the Ford Excursion, Grace continued, was meant to "build my credibility back up."

Judge Quarles was unconvinced. He upbraided both Luna and Grace's FBI handler Steven Skinner—who was also testifying in the trial that day—for their cooperator's misdeeds. "It is difficult for me to conceive," Judge Quarles said, "that the government would actually seize drugs from a cooperator and then, on that same day, send him to work a case. That is just—well, that is difficult for me to reconcile." Even more damaging to the government was the revelation that Grace sold heroin and shot at a rival while cooperating with—and being paid by—the FBI. Defense attorneys Kenneth

Ravenell and Arcangelo Tuminelli compounded the blow to the prosecution's case by arguing that the Maryland U.S. Attorney's Office had not disclosed Grace's numerous incidents before trial, as required by law. "Today was the first time we have heard that this man had been out on the street," Ravenell complained bitterly to Judge Quarles, "taken off his bracelet, gone out on the streets doing whatever he was supposedly doing." Ravenell then motioned for a mistrial.

During court proceedings early the next day, which got off to a late start because Luna was tending to his sick young son, Ravenell withdrew his mistrial motion. But when FBI agent Skinner admitted on the stand that the FBI had paid for Grace's cell phone and rent bills as well as his car payments, Ravenell revived his concerns about the government's Brady violations in even stronger terms. "I just wanted to bring to your attention, your honor, that this is again information that has not been disclosed to us, of the informant being paid," Ravenell protested. "I mean, this is just unbelievable." Then Tuminelli dropped a bombshell about Grace that would overshadow all of the earlier discoveries about the cooperator: Grace had escaped his FBI handlers during a visit with his wife, Robin, and was out of their observation for a total of four hours. "We don't know what happened for the four hours while he was in the room. . . . Was there a way to exit the room and be out on the streets?" he asked. Citing the FBI's lapse in monitoring, Tuminelli asked Judge Quarles to assign new handlers to transport Grace from the Philadelphia area prison where he was incarcerated to the Baltimore courthouse. But Judge Quarles rejected the request because the report of Grace's escape from his FBI handlers stemmed from an anonymous phone call. Still, Quarles chided the Maryland U.S. Attorney's Office for its "kid gloves treatment of Mr. Grace" and pointedly remarked that "all of these matters raise troubling concerns about how the government gets into bed with its witnesses."

A few hours later, with the foundation of the Stash House case growing shaky, Luna announced that he'd struck a plea deal with the defense. As Quarles adjourned for the day to allow Luna to begin to draft the plea agreement, Luna publicly apologized for arriving late that morning. "I just wanted to express that . . ." Luna stammered, "that I meant no disrespect to the court. That's all I wanted to say." Quarles was forgiving—though earlier that day he had taken the rare step of fining Luna $25 for his lateness. The combination of the cooperator's catastrophic performance and Luna's tardiness made for the most calamitous day of a disastrous trial. Luna also faced the wrath of his boss, Maryland U.S. Attorney Thomas DiBiagio, who was openly displeased with his performance, according to Luna's friends and coworkers.

That night, by phone from his modest home in Elkridge, Maryland, Luna hashed out the details of the plea agreement with defense attorney Tuminelli. Under the terms of the deal, Poindexter would plead guilty to three counts of heroin distribution, while Smith would plead to one count of heroin distribution and to possessing a firearm. Eager to put the excruciating trial behind him, Luna drove back to his office at the courthouse. Luna spent the next two hours conferencing by phone with defense attorneys Tuminelli and Ravenell about the plea deal, pausing only to quickly check in with his obstetrician wife, Angela.

Then, just after eleven thirty, Luna suddenly left the courthouse without informing friends, family, or coworkers. "The only thing that can bring you out of the office at that time of night," says Andrew White, "is either the point of a gun or the equivalent thereof." Leaving his cell phone and eyeglasses on his desk, he drove his silver 1999 Honda Accord into the night. Luna's route was baffling: instead of returning to Elkridge, he made his way north on I–95 toward Philadelphia, where Grace was incarcerated. But Luna never stopped at the prison. Records indicate that he withdrew $200 from an ATM in Newark, Delaware, and headed west over the Delaware River two hours later, onto the Pennsylvania Turnpike. The toll plaza surveillance video is grainy, but whoever was behind the wheel got a paper ticket even though the car was equipped with an E-Z Pass—suggesting that either the driver was unfamiliar with the vehicle or Luna was being directed against his will. After more than an hour on the turnpike, the car pulled off at Exit 286 near Denver, Pennsylvania, a small town of three thousand located deep in Amish country.

An hour and a half later, Luna's Accord was found tipped into a shallow creek on the wooded property of Sensenig & Weaver Well Drilling in Denver, about a mile from the highway. An employee of Sensenig & Weaver called 911 when he noticed that there was a car half in the creek, half on the ground—and that there was blood on the door. When Pennsylvania State Police arrived at the scene moments later, they found blood smeared on the open driver's side door, cash strewn around the car's interior, and Luna's body, still dressed in an overcoat and business suit. His U.S. Attorney's Office ID was discovered in a nearby field. The killer worked quickly—not even pausing to turn off the car's engine—and with a primal rage, stabbing Luna thirty-six times with the prosecutor's own penknife. There was no indication that he had been tied up, but the large amount of blood in the backseat and the shallow, pinprick cuts all over his body suggested both an extremely violent struggle and the possibility that Luna could have been forced into submission, made to lie down in the back—right next to his young son's car seat—and driven out to this desolate area to be dumped. At 8:05 AM, he was pronounced dead by the Lancaster County Coroner, the victim of "fresh water drowning" and "multiple stab wounds."

. . .

That the life of Jonathan Luna should end in a shallow creek in a desolate part of Pennsylvania is particularly perverse. Luna had ascended to the rarified world of corporate law firms and U.S. attorney's offices against the longest of odds. Raised in a housing project in the Mott Haven section of the South Bronx—a bleak neighborhood dominated by wide swaths of public housing and empty warehouses—he developed a fierce sense of pride about his heritage (his father is Filipino, and his mother is African-American). As a teenager, Luna devoured books about John F. Kennedy and was known in the neighborhood for collecting copies of GQ and saving up for overcoats, neckties, and penny loafers instead of jeans and high-tops. When the *New York Times* profiled the area in a 1991 series, "Life at the Bottom," Luna responded with an excoriating letter to the editor: "Contrary to the images in the news media and in popular literature like Tom Wolfe's *Bonfire of the Vanities*, there is much hope and promise in Mott Haven."

Luna's resolve propelled him through Fordham University in New York and on to law school at the University of North Carolina at Chapel Hill, where he thrived thanks to his friendships with a tight-knit group of idealistic law students. "Jonathan stood out because he was so easygoing and likeable," says Reginald Shuford, a former UNC classmate and now an ACLU staff attorney. Shuford had grown up in a North Carolina housing project, and he and Luna bonded over their similar backgrounds. "We never felt the need to make a lot of money," Shuford says. "We felt fortunate to go beyond our circumstances and give back to the people who did not have a similar opportunity."

Swayed by his empathetic manner and good looks, Luna's law school peers elected him class president during his third year at UNC. His striking eyes and warm smile earned him comparisons to Tiger Woods, and he sometimes joked that he was the golf superstar's long-lost brother, "Lion Woods." That spring, while working for a federal judge in North Carolina, Luna met medical student Angela Hopkins, whom he married a year later. After graduating in 1992, Luna took a job with Arnold & Porter, a white-shoe law firm in Washington, DC. Senior partner James Sandman recalls Luna's loyalty to his parents—particularly his father, who fell ill with cancer. "Jonathan made regular trips to New York to check on him," Sandman says. "I was impressed by that." (In fact, just before his death, Luna had bought plane tickets for himself and his father to visit his native Philippines.)

Luna lasted just one year at Arnold & Porter, partly because there were so few minorities at the firm. "I can't say personally that there's been any overt racism here," Luna told the *Legal Times* in 1994. "However, black attorneys feel a little more isolated than their white counterparts." But Luna's friends say that it was his long-held desire to serve others, not racism, that drove him from Arnold & Porter and into a series of public sector jobs beginning in the mid-1990s, ultimately joining the Brooklyn District Attorney's office in 1997. According to former homicide prosecutor Robert Reuland, Luna's low-key demeanor, quietly wry sense of humor, and devotion to his wife and kids stood in stark contrast to the "high testosterone environment" of the Brooklyn D.A.'s office, in which heavy drinking, womanizing, and office hookups were commonplace. Luna was also somewhat alienated from his colleagues by his status as a "lateral"—someone hired individually rather than with others from the same law school class.

It wasn't until 1999, when Luna was hired as an assistant U.S. attorney at the Maryland U.S. Attorney's Office, that Luna found his niche. Baltimore was every bit the East Coast crime capital portrayed on HBO's *The Wire*, and he prosecuted Ecstasy dealers, pedophiles, and the Old York and Cator Boys, one of the city's most violent crack crews. The caseload consumed him—he often stayed at the office past ten PM—but was more rewarding than he had ever imagined. And though he was one of only a few African-Americans out of roughly fifty assistant U.S. attorneys in the criminal division, he easily befriended his colleagues, spending nights chatting over beers at the Hopkins Bar and Grill across the street from the courthouse. "Jonathan was very adept at putting together investigations," remembers Andrew White. "If you ever met him or listened to him talk about a case, he had a complete lack of guile. Jonathan had the ability to convince."

But if Luna's prosecutions went smoothly, his relationship with his boss, U.S. Attorney Thomas DiBiagio—a heat-seeking trial lawyer-turned-federal-prosecutor—was shaky from the start. "Tom hated Jonathan," says a former assistant U.S. attorney. "He was putting the screws to him in the office." The two men were polar opposites. While DiBiagio was an aggressive, elbow-throwing prosecutor who conducted controversial, politically charged investigations of Democratic politicians, Luna racked up more traditional, clean-up-the-streets indictments. By the fall of 2003, just months before Luna's death, his friends and coworkers say that he was thinking about leaving the U.S. Attorney's Office to start a firm of his own.

■ ■ ■

Two hours after Luna was pronounced dead in Pennsylvania, the Stash House trial in Baltimore entered its fourth and final day. The young federal prosecutor was missing. Assistant U.S. Attorney James Warwick, who was representing the government in Luna's place, had no idea what had befallen Luna. "I don't know where he is at the moment. We are trying to locate him and trying to locate the final agreement." Because Luna had been late the previous day, Judge Quarles seemed unconcerned by his absence.

Instead, Judge Quarles focused on the unfinished plea agreements for Stash House's Poindexter and Smith. "Generally, what's the deal?" he asked impatiently. Warwick explained that Poindexter would plead guilty to three counts of heroin distribution, while Smith would plead guilty to one count of heroin distribution as well as a weapons charge. In exchange for Poindexter and Smith's guilty pleas, the government would drop the more serious drug conspiracy charges against the pair.

After a brief recess called to accelerate the plea process, concern for the missing Luna began to creep into the proceedings. "Your honor, we called his house, and we didn't get an answer," said Warren Grace's FBI handler Steven Skinner. "Mr. Tuminelli spoke with him last night, and he was supposed to fax down the plea agreement. It was still in his computer up in his office, and we have paged him. His cell phone and glasses are in his office. We are probably going to go over to the parking garage . . . and just look for his car." Defense attorney Ravenell also expressed concern. Judge Quarles then suggested that Skinner search for Luna while Warwick complete the plea deals.

Late that afternoon, just after the plea deals were entered, Quarles concluded proceedings without offering any concern for Luna. He congratulated the defense team ("It was fun. . . . You are both extraordinarily good lawyers"), wished Tuminelli and his wife well on an upcoming vacation to Hawaii, and told Warwick that he was going to discipline Luna when he arrived back at court. "Tell him I'm not going to yell at him or chew him out, but I do have some fatherly words for him," he said sternly. "Tell him, 'No yelling, no problem, just some concern,'" he added in a manner more befitting a parent than a judge. Warwick agreed to relay the message.

Late that evening, news of Luna's death finally reached his family and colleagues. The rare murder of a federal prosecutor—like the killing of a cop or an FBI agent—usually generates an around-the-clock investigation until law enforcement gets their man. Indeed, Luna's boss U.S. Attorney DiBiagio publicly vowed to track down the killer. "We will find out who did this, and we are dedicated to bringing the persons responsible for this tragedy to justice," he proclaimed. "That's a commitment from me. That's a commitment from every law enforcement officer in the state of Maryland." But in the wake of Luna's murder, the fiery vows of justice from DiBiagio and then–Attorney General John Ashcroft—as well as wall-to-wall coverage of the killing in the *Washington Post* and the *Baltimore Sun*—instead gave way to an onslaught of finger-pointing, bureaucratic incompetence, and dubious suicide theories promoted by the feds. Ironically, his own death is exactly the type of case in which Luna, were he still alive, might have delivered swift justice. But as of this writing four years later, the crime is still unsolved. "This is a monumental failure on the part of the feds," says Robert Reuland, a former homicide investigator with the Brooklyn District Attorney's office. "They can't solve the murder of one of their own. They can't even give a credible cause of death."

From the very beginning the FBI and the Maryland U.S. Attorney's Office (which were initially charged with handling the investigation) offered every possible theory for the slaying—from suicide to a soured personal relationship—yet ignored Luna's combustible relationship with cooperator Grace. Incredibly, not a week after Luna's body was discovered, an anonymous tip from a "law enforcement official" to the *Baltimore Sun* hinted that Luna's murder was already close to being solved—and that it was not connected to Luna's job but rather a consequence of his personal behavior. As such, it was expected to be handled as a state murder case by the local prosecutor in Lancaster County and not as a case of federal kidnapping or murder of a federal law enforcement officer. Another series of leaks to the media about Luna's personal life soon followed, also from anonymous law enforcement sources, claiming that authorities were investigating messages posted in 1997 on an Internet dating site by someone using the name Jonathan Luna. The author of the messages allegedly described himself as a "discreet 31-year-old married, professional black male seeking a white female sexual partner."

But Luna's case never went to the Lancaster County District Attorney—it is being investigated by the U.S. attorney for the Eastern District of Pennsylvania—and the Internet postings allegedly made by Luna were never authenticated. The mischaracterization of the motives for Luna's murder as "highly personal" stemmed from more than mere misjudgment: a source close to Luna told me that the leaker was not an ill-informed, low-level law enforcement official, but U.S. Attorney Thomas DiBiagio himself. The source says that DiBiagio was motivated by both a personal dislike of Luna and professional interest in preventing Luna's case from taking media attention away from DiBiagio's forthcoming high-profile indictment of Maryland State Police Superintendent Edward T. Norris. "This is pretty ironic," DiBiagio told me when I confronted him with the allegation that he was the *Sun* leaker. "Somebody leaked disparaging personal things about Jonathan's personal life and professional life while I, on the other hand, went on the record for saying he was a good person." But in 2004 the *Sun* reported that DiBiagio admitted to his staffers that he lied about his shaky relationship with Luna in the wake of the prosecutor's murder. DiBiagio acknowledged to me that he did not tell the truth back then, but he said that his intentions for doing so were good—he sought to protect the slain prosecutor's family. He added that he's angry that he has been criticized for his positive public pronouncements about Luna following his death.

In late 2004, DiBiagio left the U.S. Attorney's Office for a position at DC-based law firm Beveridge and Diamond, citing personal reasons, though DiBiagio's troubled tenure as Maryland U.S. attorney—marked by allegations of misconduct from both his superiors and his own staffers—suggests otherwise. In 2004, DiBiagio sent a series of e-mails to his staff instructing them to produce at least three "front page" indictments for public corruption or white collar crimes. After the e-mails were leaked to the media, the *Washington Post* editorial board blasted them as "astonishingly inappropriate," and Deputy Attorney General James B. Comey instructed DiBiagio to submit any proposed indictments relating to public corruption to his office for review. Justice Department officials said later that DiBiagio was forced out of the job for performance and morale issues; they also cited DiBiagio's false public statements about Luna after his murder as evidence that he had problems with candor.

Meanwhile, the FBI office investigating Luna's murder has been dogged by similar allegations of misconduct. In June 2005, Justice Department Inspector General Glenn A. Fine charged that Jennifer Smith-Love, the acting special agent in charge of the FBI's Baltimore field office handling the case, approved an illegal search of the computer used by a female agent who was wrongly accused of having an affair with Luna. Though Smith-Love called the allegations "false and malicious," the inspector general concluded that there was "credible evidence" of wrongdoing on her part. Smith-Love later received a promotion to a counterterrorism position in early 2005 while the allegations against her were still pending, prompting the Senate Judiciary Committee to open an investigation. At a May 2006 Judiciary Committee hearing, Senator Chuck Grassley asked FBI Director Robert Mueller III why he had approved this promotion "while an investigation was still being conducted of her involvement in possible misconduct related to her handling of the investigation of the death of federal prosecutor Jonathan Luna." But Mueller refused to answer Grassley's questions, nor would he provide a copy of a report from the FBI's Office of Professional Responsibility (OPR) about the Smith-Love matter. During a hearing later that year, Grassley submitted the same questions about Smith-Love but again received no response from Mueller. In March 2007, Mueller privately addressed Grassley's concerns; the senator's spokesperson, however, characterized Mueller's response as "nonanswers." In response, Mike Kortan, an FBI spokesperson, told me that the findings of Inspector General Fine were referred to the Office of Professional Responsibility and as a result "the actions of several employees were examined, and while no misconduct was found, performance issues were identified and for the on-board employees, remedial action was taken."

Law enforcement's many missteps in the Luna case are now being scrutinized by the Senate Judiciary Committee. Citing the FBI's OPR report, Vermont Senator Patrick Leahy said that FBI agents assigned to the Luna investigation offered "conflicting stories during interviews with agents of the FBI's Internal Investigations Section." Judiciary Committee members also asked for a final copy of the OPR report, which the FBI refused to provide. "The main problem here is that the FBI refuses to provide us with a final copy of the Office of Professional Responsibility report," Senator Grassley told me. "They aren't cooperating because they're embarrassed." I asked Grassley what specifically the FBI might be embarrassed about in the Luna case. "I don't know," he said. "But if the FBI does what they're good at doing, which is conducting investigations, they're fine. But when they try to cover something up, they end up with egg on their face."

A cover up is exactly what appears to be happening in the Luna case, because from the very beginning the FBI and the Maryland U.S. Attorney's Office offered every possible theory for the slaying yet ignored Luna's relationship with combustible cooperator Grace. Indeed, Inspector General Fine's memo implicitly confirms that the FBI focused far too narrowly on Luna's personal life at the earliest—and most important—stage of the investigation. The focus by investigators on Luna's personal life—and the incessant leaks about everything from his alleged Internet postings to credit card debt—have also long obscured the slain prosecutor's combustible relationship with Grace. While it is true that, as Stash House attorney Tuminelli told the *Sun*, his clients had "every incentive to want to see Jonathan Luna show up" in the courtroom because they had just struck a favorable plea deal, Luna's relationship with Warren Grace was far more adversarial and much more dangerous. And while many cooperators engage in illegal activity while they are working for the government, Grace's misdeeds were far worse than most. "It's commonplace for cooperators to be involved in petty drug deals or domestic violence incidents," says New York–based criminal defense attorney Renato Stabile. "But shootings and big drug deals—that's pretty shocking." In Baltimore's Park Heights neighborhood, Grace had a reputation as a singularly bloodthirsty thug. One man in the *Stop Fucking Snitching, Vol. 1* DVD described Grace as a "nigga who will snitch on you—and kill you." When I spoke with Stash House's Walter Oriley Poindexter by phone from a prison in Fort Dix, New Jersey, he told me that on Baltimore's streets, Grace was considered so dangerous that few suspected he was cooperating with the government. "I'd hoped that the things that Warren did while he was cooperating would have affected the outcome of my case," Poindexter told me. "I was wrong." (Poindexter is rightly bitter: Grace will be released in 2009, while he will come home in 2014). Grace also had connections to one of the city's most notorious hit men: Eric Hall, who faced the death penalty for a series of alleged murders for hire he committed from 1996 to 2003. Grace's attorney, Joseph Balter, refuses to comment on his client's case.

The fact that Warren Grace—who is currently incarcerated in a federal prison in Kentucky—had turned on Luna and was chummy with a trigger-happy enforcer should have raised red flags among law enforcement. Yet neither the FBI nor the Maryland U.S. Attorney's Office ever connected the dots. DiBiagio admitted to me that he was unaware of Grace's connection to Eric Hall. He explained that the feds did not scrutinize any of the players in the Stash House case because "the defendants got a very favorable deal, and no one ever mentioned to me that the cooperator was unhappy with him [Luna]."

Law enforcement's inability to examine Luna's contentious relationship with his dangerous cooperator casts doubt on the investigation into the young prosecutor's murder. "Due to its problems with its Confidential Informant in this case," wrote Pennsylvania State Representative Mark Cohen in a 2005 letter to Inspector General Fine, "how can the public be assured that this case is being properly investigated by the FBI?" Cohen told me that he urged Fine to open a new investigation into Luna's murder because "the FBI tended to favor explanations for Luna's murder that focused on *everything* but his job as a prosecutor. More than three years later, there is still no evidence that a personal relationship led to his death nor is there any evidence that he committed suicide." Indeed, Lancaster County Coroner Gary Kirchner has said that he is "at least 98 percent certain" it was a homicide.

The FBI's refusal to cooperate with a Senate Judiciary Committee investigation, the allegations of misconduct against DiBiagio and Smith-Love, law enforcement's promulgation of bogus murder theories, and the total lack of scrutiny of Luna's relationship with cooperator Grace all point to a cover-up by the feds. "It looks like the murder was committed by someone who knew they weren't going to get flak for it," former federal investigator William A. Sewell says, "and they didn't." Similarly, Ed Martino, a private investigator hired at the behest of a friend of Luna's, told me that "Jonathan Luna was a good prosecutor who got nailed for what he knew. He knew things that could cost him his job—he saw federal agents committing crimes. That's my opinion, and I'm prepared to back it up."

In February 2007, Martino and Pennsylvania attorney Jim Clymer petitioned the Lancaster County Court to force County Coroner Kirchner to hold an inquest into Luna's death (the autopsy on the slain prosecutor has still not been released). In an interview with the *Lancaster County News*, Martino explained that they could solve Luna's murder if only the feds would cooperate. "We have enough evidence. . . . We'll bring that out at the inquest. But we have to force these agents to testify." Given the Senate Judiciary Committee's struggles with FBI Director Mueller, that is unlikely to happen anytime soon. In the interim, Luna's friends and coworkers hope that law enforcement will refocus the investigation to where it should have been all along: the Baltimore drug players—and the rogue cooperator—he prosecuted until his untimely death. "Everybody was saying afterward that it made no sense for the defendants to kill him because the case was going to plead to an acceptable amount of time," says Andrew White. "That presumes that the defendants ordered it. But this could be a witness who doesn't like being put in that position—and then opportunity strikes."

Chapter Eight

KILLER COOPERATORS

The Harvey Family and St. Guillen Murders

"SHOW US YOUR HANDS!" IT WAS A LATE JANUARY AFTERNOON IN PHILADELPHIA, and Ricky Javon Gray was cornered in the dank basement of a decrepit rowhouse on the city's south side. Though the twenty-eight-year-old career criminal was unsuccessfully trying to conceal himself behind a water heater, he refused to comply with the cops' request. "Show us your hands!" the cops shouted again. Gray's response was to slowly step out from behind the water heater and throw a punch at one of the officers. Gray missed his mark, and he was subdued and handcuffed. As he stumbled into the light, the officers could see his heavily bruised and deeply scarred face and a scraggly, unkempt beard and Afro. Gray looked every bit as weary as one would expect from someone whose hideout from a massive manhunt was nothing more than a piece of plumbing.

After being extricated from the rowhouse, Gray was driven to Philadelphia police headquarters, nicknamed the "Roundhouse" by local cops. At six thirty that evening Gray sat down at a conference room table in the Roundhouse directly across from

Philadelphia Police Detective Howard Peterman, a twenty-nine-year veteran of the force. "Ricky asked me if a person named Ray Dandridge was in the building," Peterman remembered later. When Peterman said that Dandridge—Gray's nephew and long-time partner in crime—was indeed incarcerated at the Round-house, Gray asked, "Did you talk to him?" Peterman said that he had. "Do you know the truth?" Gray continued. "I know the truth according to Ray Dandridge," Peterman said. "I want you to hear it from me," Gray blurted out.

After an escorted trip to the men's room, Peterman walked Gray back to the conference room and advised him of his right to have a lawyer present during their interview.

Gray waived his rights and began his confession.

On the previous Sunday or Monday, Gray said, "one of the two. I think it was New Year's Day," Gray, his twenty-one-year-old girl-friend, Ashley Baskerville, and Dandridge were driving around in Gray's van in the Wooodland Heights neighborhood of Rich-mond, Virginia. They were looking for a house to rob. At the cor-ner of West Thirty-first and Chesterfield streets in Woodland Heights, the trio spotted a house with its door slightly ajar. As Baskerville waited in the van, Gray and Dandridge approached the house, where inside Bryan Harvey, his wife, Kathryn, and their daughter Ruby had just begun preparing a New Year's Day party for their friends. "We went up there," Gray remembered. "The white lady was in the kitchen. The dude was in the living room, and the daughter was in the bedroom." When Gray and Dandridge entered the Harvey residence, Ruby was the only Har-vey daughter present; the family was waiting for their other daughter, Stella, to return from a New Year's Eve sleepover at a friend's home.

The men forced the Harveys downstairs and split up into teams; Gray was in charge of binding them with extension cord and duct tape, while Dandridge scoured the house for valuables. But as Gray cinched Bryan's hands with an extension cord, Kathryn cautioned that a girlfriend would soon be dropping Stella off at the house. Moments later, just as Kathryn said, the doorbell rang; it was family friend Kiersten Perkinson, her daughter Grace Lynn, and Stella Harvey.

"Hello!" Stella shouted through the open door. "I'm home." Silence. After a few minutes passed, Kiersten heard the sound of someone coming up the basement stairs. It was Kathryn, who looked pale and ashen. "I'm not feeling well today," Kathryn explained. Kiersten assumed Kathryn was stricken with a stomach flu that had struck their circle of friends that winter. "Is there anything I can do for you?" Kiersten said. "No," Kathryn replied listlessly. "Just come back at two PM" for the party. Kathryn waved good-bye to the Perkinsons, took Stella by the hand, and led her toward the basement. Gray had threatened to take her life if she had done otherwise.

"That was weird," Kiersten said to Grace Lynn as they walked toward their car. "Where was Ruby?" Mother and daughter guessed that Ruby was in the basement with Bryan readying for the party. Still, something about the encounter bothered Kiersten. "I felt like she wanted me to leave," Kiersten remembered. Not wanting to frighten her daughter, Kiersten said soothingly, "It's OK. We'll be back later."

As Kiersten and Grace Lynn headed home, Gray returned to the work of corralling the Harveys. Now that he had yet another victim to handle, Gray redoubled his efforts to subdue them. When he tried—and then failed—to duct tape the hands of the Harveys, Gray "had a conversation with them" reminding them that he couldn't leave if they weren't tied up. Gray's insistence that they be bound terrified the Harveys, so they calmly stretched out their arms to be taped.

Then, for reasons Gray still cannot explain, he began to slice
the Harveys' throats with a long butcher knife. But the Harveys
did not die immediately—"they kept gettin' up, and they was
scaring me," Gray remembered—so he swung wildly at their
heads with a claw hammer. Gray struck Kathryn the most severely; she was hit with the hammer twelve times. "It was a real
nasty scene," Gray recalled, and one that needed to be covered
up. So, Gray tipped over an artist's easel, broke open two bottles
of wine on a basement table, and set everything on fire with
matches before escaping upstairs. "All I know is," Gray explained, "nobody was moving when I left out there." Dandridge,
meanwhile, had managed to snatch a few stray items—Bryan's
laptop, cookies Kathryn had baked for the party—and joined
Gray in fleeing the burning Harvey home.

■ ■ ■

"I have one!" Richmond firefighter Raymond Neville shouted as
he crawled on his hands and knees through the dense smoke that
filled the Harvey basement. The Richmond Fire Department had
been called to the scene by Harvey family friend Johnny Hott,
who had arrived for their New Year's Day party only to find the
home engulfed in fire and smoke. When the firefighters arrived at
West Thirty-first Street, they found thick black smoke pouring
out the front door; inside, visibility was near zero. Neville was
forced to blindly run his left hand against the wall of the basement in hopes that he would find a victim; sure enough, his hand
soon passed through the hair—and then face—of Kathryn Harvey. "I have one!" Neville shouted again. Believing that they
could save a victim who would be suffering from smoke inhalation
at worst, Neville and another firefighter carried her toward the
front porch. But when Neville lay Kathryn next to a flowerbox

outside, he noticed that her eyes were covered in bruises. Fire-fighter Hallie Tilton, who helped Neville lift Kathryn's body out of the basement, then made an equally grim discovery: Kathryn's duct-taped legs. It was now obvious that the Harvey home was not the site of a typical house fire but a gruesome murder scene. When Richmond Police Detective Jeff Dwyer arrived at the Harveys' that afternoon, he recovered the tools used in the brutal killings: extension cords, two claw hammers, knives, two broken wine bottles, and even a scarf covered with blood.

Unfortunately for the killers, they had chosen one of the most beloved Richmond families as their marks: Bryan Harvey worked in technology in the Henrico County school system and also fronted a local band called House of Freaks, which briefly achieved alternative rock star status in the 1990s, even appearing on the MTV show *120 Minutes*; Kathryn was the half-sister of *Desperate Housewives* actor Steven Culp. Kathryn also owned World of Mirth, a sprawling, 3,400-square-foot toy and novelty store on West Cary Street in Richmond's trendy Carytown district. The store was hugely popular among adults and kids alike because of its unusual items, like an Edgar Allan Poe action figure. Many Richmond residents had an emotional bond with World of Mirth—it was a store where one could always find inspired presents for Christmas or a birthday. And just one year before her murder, the *Richmond Times Dispatch* had named Kathryn one of the city's business innovators. The brutal murder of the Harveys was mourned as a tragedy for the entire city. Two candlelight vigils held after their deaths brought thousands of mourners; during the second vigil, which was held on January 3, 2006, outside the Harvey home, Richmond Commonwealth Attorney Michael N. Herring addressed the crowd.

"This is a challenging scene and it's going to require your patience," Herring said. "I know you want answers. The police department—your police department, our police department—is working diligently to give you answers." Yet though Gray and Dandridge had performed the sloppiest of cover-ups of their crime, the Richmond Police Department had no suspects in its aftermath.

As Herring spoke to the Harvey mourners in Richmond, Gray and Dandridge struck again. Only two days later, Gray, Dandridge, and Baskerville stopped at the home of Bonnie Goolsby on Hollywood Drive in nearby Chesterfield County, Virginia. After pretending to ask for directions they burst inside. During the home invasion, they grabbed a computer, a TV, and a DVD player from the room of Goolsby's daughter Brandy (who had been killed in September 2005 by a drunk driver) and then threatened to tie up Bonnie, her husband, her sister, and her brother-in-law, all of whom resided at the Hollywood Drive home. "By the time you call someone," Gray growled at Bonnie, "we'll be out of the area." Bonnie's husband attempted to convince Gray, Dandridge, and Baskerville to leave them unharmed. Remarkably, they did just that—and then fled the scene in their van. But while Bonnie gave a detailed description of the incident to police that same night— Baskerville's face remained particularly fresh in her mind—Gray and Dandridge's rampage was still not complete.

Just after seven PM on Friday, January 6, Gray and Dandridge broke into the Richmond home of their accomplice, Ashley Baskerville. When Gray and Dandridge swung open the door using a key Gray had taken from Ashley, they found Ashley and her parents, Percyell Tucker and Mary Baskerville-Tucker, at home. Just as they had done with the Harveys, Gray and Dandridge bound the Tuckers. First, they stuffed a stocking in Ashley's mouth and then wrapped her head, mouth, nose, and one eye in silver duct tape, placing a bag over her head when they were finished. Then they turned to Mary, stuffed a sock into her mouth, and wrapped what a medical examiner would later describe as a "virtual mask" of duct tape around her head, all while her curlers were still in her hair. Finally, Gray and Dandridge covered Percyell's head in duct tape, used a white sock to gag him, and then covered his eyes, nose, and mouth with strips of duct tape.

As the family sat bound and gagged, Gray and Dandridge picked the house clean, snatching even small items like hair clippers and a cheap men's watch. But Gray and Dandridge worried about leaving the family alive, so Gray stabbed Mary once in the chest and neck and Percyell in the neck five times with "a little knife I got from the house." Gray then headed to the bedroom where girlfriend Ashley was sitting bound in duct tape and strangled her. To Gray's surprise, the Tuckers, like the Harveys before them, survived his initial attack (though they would die hours later from suffocation). "Something so simple," Gray recalled, "became so complicated." Gray called out to Dandridge, and the pair fled in Percyell's Chevrolet, heading for Philadelphia.

By the time Gray and Dandridge reached Pennsylvania, however, both the Richmond and Philadelphia police departments were on their trail. The description of Ashley Baskerville that Bonnie Goolsby provided to the cops was a crucial lead, as her relationship with both Gray and Dandridge was well-known among her family and friends; that she and her parents were murdered in a manner so similar to the Harveys sealed Gray and Dandridge's fate. So, early in the morning of Saturday, January 7, after receiving a tip that a Chevrolet Blazer bearing Virginia license plates was parked in front of a rowhouse on Wanamaker Street in Philadelphia, homicide detective Joe Bamberski set up surveillance outside the building. When Bamberski spotted Gray and Dandridge, a search warrant was prepared, and later a team of cops stormed the rowhouse—finding the frightened killer of seven crouched behind a water heater.

Sitting with Detective Howard Peterman at the Roundhouse later that day, Gray confessed to the murders of the Harvey and Tucker families in emotionless, undescriptive, and largely unremorseful language. "I know I wasn't in control of myself," Gray said of his murders of the Tuckers, "and I'm sorry they died. Nothin' can bring them back, so I can't see why I should be spared." A Richmond jury agreed: that August, Gray was sentenced to death for the murders of Stella and Ruby Harvey. He was given life sentences for the slayings of Bryan and Kathryn; after the trial, prosecutors said that they would not seek indictments in the slayings of Ashley Baskerville and her parents. Dandridge, meanwhile, pleaded guilty during his trial that September to three counts of capital murder. As part of a deal with prosecutors, he received three life sentences for the killings of the Baskerville-Tucker family.

Given the gruesome and high-profile nature of the crime, Gray's trial was a remarkably uneventful affair. Gray did not present any evidence during the guilt phase of the trial, and his defense attorney, Jeffrey Everhart, could do little more than acknowledge his client's culpability and plead for mercy by saying that Gray was sexually abused as a child and had been addicted to drugs since he was twelve. (As if to corroborate his attorney's claim, Gray claimed that he was high on PCP when he murdered the Harveys). Though the courtroom was packed with Harvey family members and their many friends, the proceedings had all the emptiness of Gray's confessions at the Roundhouse. The prosecution presented their witnesses in a mechanistic manner, with little in the way of cross-examination or rebuttal from the defense. Gray himself seemed dulled by the proceedings, even when it became abundantly clear that the jury would likely sentence him to death. One day during the trial, I sat directly behind Gray to see if I could detect any signs of life—to no avail. Gray, who was dressed in a crisp white dress shirt and a yellow tie, distractedly tapped his left leg and blankly shuffled papers back and forth on the wooden desk in front of him as the Richmond prosecutor presented his case. Gray's only striking feature were his fingernails, which were so inexplicably long and unmanicured that they resembled tiny daggers.

Toward the end of the trial, Richmond prosecutor Learned Barry attempted to summon up a biblical rage during his closing statements—"for God's sake," he thundered, "you give him death for killing those two children!"—but the effort seemed to have little effect on the jury or on anyone else in the courtroom. Instead, it was Richmond Circuit Judge Beverly Snukals who best captured the grim mood after the verdict was read. "This is probably the most difficult thing you've ever done," she told the jury, "probably for me, too." The sheer meaninglessness and cruelty of the crime—coupled with the spiritual blankness of Gray, for whom punishment did not seem to matter—lent the trial a sense of hopelessness and despair. Unsurprisingly, after the verdict was read, Harvey family members sounded less than relieved; instead they seemed to be consumed with the very meaninglessness of Gray's acts. "I had a hard time imagining any human being was capable of what he did," Kathryn's sister Shelly Link told reporters outside the courtroom.

Though the Harvey murders dominated Richmond headlines throughout 2006 and were even the subject of a *Dateline NBC* segment, one question surrounding the horrible tale of Ricky Javon Gray remains unasked: Why was a killer like him on the streets in the first place? The answer, unfortunately, is simple: in June 2000, after being charged with conspiring to distribute fifty grams or more of crack cocaine, Gray cooperated in a drug conspiracy case and received a 5K motion from a federal prosecutor in Virginia about one year later. The recognition of Gray's "substantial assistance" by a federal prosecutor helped convince U.S. District Judge T. S. Ellis III to make a significant downward departure from the sentencing guidelines: Gray received 60 months in prison instead of 120.

That a 5K motion was made on Gray's behalf was difficult to reconcile even before the murders he committed. In the mid-1990s Gray and nephew Dandridge pleaded guilty in Alexandria Circuit Court to a series of crimes—including a stick-up of college students in the Georgetown neighborhood of Washington, DC, and three robberies in Alexandria, Virginia—that were similar (though not nearly as violent) to the home invasion and murder spree he would later commit in Richmond. In the Alexandria Circuit Court case, Dandridge was sentenced to eleven years in state prison on charges of robbery and use of a firearm in a felony. He was released from prison in October 2005 after serving ten years. Just one month later Gray bludgeoned his wife, Treva, to death with a lead pipe. Meanwhile, Gray was sentenced to a maximum of four years and was released after three. In the crack distribution case in which he received a downward departure from the sentencing guidelines because of his "substantial assistance," Gray did not even serve out the full term of his sixty-month sentence; he spent the last four months of his term in a halfway house.

It's not hyperbole, then, to say that two entire families—the Harveys and the Baskerville-Tuckers, as well as Gray's wife, Treva—would be alive today had Gray not been the beneficiary of the 5K motion and therefore been forced to serve out his full 120-month sentence. Under the sentencing guidelines, Gray would have been incarcerated until late 2011. Both Morris Parker Jr., the assistant U.S. attorney with the U.S. attorney for the Eastern District of Virginia who made the 5K motion in Gray's case, and Denise Tassi, the Virginia-based attorney who represented Gray in his federal case, have repeatedly refused to comment. Indeed, when I called Parker, he said, "Uh-oh," and hung up the phone.

■ ■ ■

Since no one involved in Gray's case seemed interested in talking about him, a few weeks after his trial concluded in Richmond I returned to New York to talk to Joseph Tacopina about an eerily similar case of a cooperator-turned-killer. Tacopina is a criminal defense attorney representing the family of Imette St. Guillen, a twenty-four-year-old graduate student at John Jay College of Criminal Justice whose murder in February 2006 was just as gruesome as the slaying of the Harveys. St. Guillen was allegedly killed by Darryl Littlejohn, a parolee illegally working as a bouncer at The Falls, a Soho bar where St. Guillen was partying the night she was killed.

Brooklyn District Attorney Charles Hynes charges that Littlejohn lured St. Guillen into his van, strangled and raped her, and then shoved a sock down her throat, wrapped packing tape around her head, cinched plastic ties around her wrists, and cut off her hair. Littlejohn, like Ricky Javon Gray, had once been a cooperator in a federal case. And just as in the Gray case, the media offered feverish coverage of the St. Guillen slaying ("Cops Spread Net in Torture Slay!"), but failed to uncover Littlejohn's role as a cooperator in an armed robbery case in the 1990s. Instead, news coverage focused on Littlejohn's illegal employment at The Falls bar, which inspired the New York City Council to draft "Imette's Law" requiring that bouncers be licensed and bars have one bouncer for every seventy-five patrons. The bouncer panic even influenced the New York State Liquor Authority decision in the fall of 2006 to refuse to issue new liquor licenses to bars and clubs in certain areas of Manhattan.

When I met with Tacopina in his Madison Avenue office during the late summer of 2006, Imette's Law had just been signed by New York Mayor Michael Bloomberg, so the cell phones and pages scattered all over his desk rang and buzzed constantly. Soon after sitting down with Tacopina in his twenty-fifth-floor office, which is decorated with courtroom sketches of his famous clients (including Michael Jackson), he apologetically explained that he had no choice but to answer his phones because he was expecting a call about St. Guillen from New York Governor George Pataki sometime later that day.

Though Tacopina was understandably distracted, he was alarmed to hear that in 1997 Littlejohn worked as an informant for the Nassau County District Attorney's Office after being charged with a series of armed robberies there. By striking a deal with prosecutors, Littlejohn (who had a long criminal record that included numerous robberies) had avoided a fourteen-year prison sentence. I also told Tacopina that after Littlejohn was hit with federal armed robbery charges in 1998, he cooperated with the U.S. attorney for the Eastern District of New York in their indictment of former associates of Southeast Queens drug kingpin Lorenzo "Fat Cat" Nichols. Littlejohn—who was raised in the same building on Guy Brewer Boulevard in South Jamaica, Queens, that Kenneth "Supreme" McGriff used as a home base during the 1980s—told prosecutors that he was a member of the Nichols-affiliated crew. But according to a source close to the case, Littlejohn was nothing more than a gangster wannabe: he was never part of Nichols's crew, and Southeast Queens hustlers dismissively nicknamed him "Nazi" because he strode the streets in head-to-toe camouflage gear. "Fatty doesn't even know who the hell this guy is," the source close to the case says. Littlejohn's lack of connections to the crew didn't stop him from claiming that Nichols's onetime associates Charles Thomas and Luc Stephen committed a series of armed robberies across Long Island during the early and mid-1990s, including a 1995 heist at NatWest Bank in South Farmingdale. Littlejohn's testimony helped bring about the indictment of Stephen and Thomas on federal armed robbery charges. But according to the source close to the case, the crew Littlejohn gave up was a *drug* crew, not a robbery crew, and prosecutors had little evidence implicating Stephen and Thomas other than Littlejohn's testimony. In fact, the U.S. attorney's case against Stephen and Thomas ended in a dismissal of most of the charges against them.

While the wisdom of cutting a cooperator deal with a violent career criminal like Littlejohn is debatable, there is no doubt that he provided inconsistent information to cops and prosecutors in the Stephen and Thomas cases, resulting in what was probably a wrongful indictment. According to handwritten notes taken by cops and FBI agents during interviews with Littlejohn, it's clear that he provided contradictory answers to law enforcement about the identities of those involved in the armed robbery crew. In one interview Littlejohn included himself in the crew along with the names "Scrooge, Rick, Bryant, Anthony, and Mel." In another, Littlejohn again identified himself as one of the robbers but then claimed that "Luke [Luc Stephen], Rolando, O'Quinn, Chucky" comprised the remainder of the crew. But what really should have set off alarm bells among agents was an interview in which Little-john admitted that "Chucky, Luke and Rolando are connected through Fat Cat and drugs. We are not really robbers." Perhaps because he knew he was being untruthful, Littlejohn was incredibly reluctant about cooperating. During the trial, Littlejohn acknowledged on the witness stand that after being charged with the NatWest robbery and realizing that he would face more than a decade in prison, he had a family member contact the Department of Justice on his behalf about cooperating.

Upon hearing the news of Littlejohn's long history as an informant, Tacopina seemed angry but not surprised. "It goes to show that the system is seriously addicted to informants," Tacopina said. "Is Darryl Littlejohn worth giving a break to because he had some other information? It's better to keep Littlejohn in jail for the length of his sentence so he can't go out there and do something horrific as opposed to giving him a reduced sentence simply because he will say something about someone else. Prosecutors need to start looking at a bigger picture: they need to look at what's not just good for a particular case, but what's good for society as a whole." With our informant- and cooperator-coddling justice system, Tacopina continued, "what you get is not justice—but Darryl Littlejohns."

Littlejohn's savvy in staying on the streets was also abetted by probation and parole officers who made numerous mistakes in handling his case. "He was on federal probation, and they lost his file," Tacopina said. "He got arrested in state court, and they thought it was going to be transferred to state court, and it wasn't. And when he was on parole in the state system, they didn't monitor him at all. He literally slipped through the cracks." To make the job of tracking him more difficult, Littlejohn used aliases such as "Johnny Handsome" when he was arrested. Littlejohn pulled off a similar ruse when he was indicted by the feds: he used the name "Jonathan Blaze," taken from a motorcycle-riding Marvel comic book character Johnny Blaze, also known as the "Ghost Rider." Incredibly, Littlejohn was known as "Jonathan Blaze" throughout his proceedings with the feds and testified against Luc Stephen and Charles Thomas under that name; when I looked up his case in federal court records, it was still filed under the alias. When asked if it would be possible for a defendant to be indicted in the federal system even under a painfully obvious alias such as "Spider Man," Tacopina answered that indeed it was. "They'd go ahead and indict you under 'Spider Man,'" he explained, "and then if you were fingerprinted and turned out to be someone else, you would be indicted under that name, too."

The St. Guillen family is refusing to allow the numerous mistakes made by law enforcement in Littlejohn's case to go unpunished: in the late spring of 2006, Tacopina filed notice of intent to sue New York State for $100 million on behalf of St. Guillen's mother, Maureen. Tacopina's notice on behalf of St. Guillen cites three New York state agencies—the Division of Parole, the Board of Parole, and the Department of Correctional Services—and accuses them of "gross negligence" in their handling of Littlejohn. Tacopina says that the St. Guillen family is also pushing for funds to be allocated to lessen the caseloads of New York state parole officers and to develop a more sophisticated computer database linking state and federal agencies in order for parole records to be shared.

Darryl Littlejohn and Ricky Javon Gray may be particularly egregious examples of informants and cooperators run amok, but they are, as Tacopina points out, by no means the worst of the bunch.

Gambino crime family underboss-turned-snitch Sammy Gravano, Tacopina says, killed nineteen people but was given a "great deal" because he cooperated against John Gotti. "And you know, in the end, they didn't really need him because they had such an overwhelming case against Gotti," Tacopina adds. Gravano's behavior *after* entering the Witness Protection Program in the mid-1990s was nearly as outrageous as his mob days: when he and his family moved to Arizona, they started a drug trafficking ring that moved wholesale amounts of crystal methamphetamine and Ecstasy using members of a local neo-Nazi gang called the Devil Dogs as enforcers. (In 2000, Gravano was indicted on drug conspiracy charges; two years later he was convicted and sentenced to nineteen years in prison.)

The mafia informant perhaps second only to Gravano in infamy—Henry Hill, the "goodfella" who ratted out storied made men Paul Vario and Jimmy Burke and as a result had five A1 felony indictments against him dismissed—followed a similar downward spiral. Just nine months after relocating to Nebraska, Hill was thrown out of the Witness Protection Program when he caught a series of narcotics charges. "Informants get up on the stand and say 'I'm a changed man,'" Tacopina explains, "but when they're done with their testimony they say things like 'I got over on the system.' They mock the deal. And as soon as someone looks at them funny, they call their handler." This was true of Henry Hill. Though Hill has been arrested countless times on narcotics charges ever since being booted from the Witness Protection Program during the 1980s—most recently in January 2005, when he was charged with felony cocaine possession—he's nonetheless been bailed out repeatedly for more than twenty-five years by the FBI, according to his former attorney Robert Simels.

While FBI agents often go to great lengths in order to protect their informants and cooperators, the latter are treated as pariahs in their own neighborhoods by criminals and noncriminals alike. Former friends and street associates of Littlejohn's say that while they are not fully convinced of Littlejohn's guilt in the St. Guillen case, he has long been a toxic presence in Queens because of his role as a cooperator and his penchant for fabricating evidence. Littlejohn's former Queens associates add that while Littlejohn was routinely portrayed in the media as a strange outcast—*Dateline NBC* described him as a "short-tempered loner who dressed like a cop"—none of the reporters bothered to find out why he was so estranged from his neighborhood. Interestingly, Littlejohn's is a case in which social taboos against snitching had positive benefits, namely, isolating a career criminal from the community around him. But that was not enough to keep Littlejohn off the streets, and his enablers in law enforcement are at least partly to blame. When Littlejohn was indicted for St. Guillen's murder during the spring of 2006, Brooklyn District Attorney Hynes boasted that "I think someday this case is going to be taught at law school as a particularly special example of forensic testimony." It would be more beneficial, though, if the tragic cases of Darryl Littlejohn and Ricky Javon Gray could be held up as examples of a criminal justice system with a deadly addiction to cooperators.

Chapter Nine

STOP SNITCHING

The Barber, the Corrupt Cops, and the Prosecutor on the Frontlines of the Battle over Witness Intimidation in Baltimore

ON A COLD, BLUSTERY DAY IN MID-OCTOBER 2006, RONNIE THOMAS WAS led by cops from a holding cell at 111 North Calvert Street in downtown Baltimore to a wood-paneled courtroom upstairs for a pretrial hearing. Standing at over six foot five and possessing a lithe, lean build, Thomas was once such a promising street basketball player that friends from his West Baltimore neighborhood swore he'd make it to the NBA. But as Thomas walked to the courtroom, he moved with a slow, laborious gait because handcuffs were locked tightly around his wrists while heavy shackles held his legs together. "Rodney Thomas? Rodney Thomas?" the judge called out, not realizing that she had gotten his name wrong. Thomas's attorney Allan H. Rombro rushed from the back of the courtroom—where he was chatting with a handful of journalists, including a reporter from the *Atlantic Monthly*—to correct the judge. "*Ronnie* is still in lock up," Rombro said. "He'll be here shortly." Moments later, Thomas appeared in front of the judge dressed in grey sweatpants and a grey Roc-A-Wear T-shirt that clung to his lanky, string bean–like frame. Though there were no more than a dozen people in the courtroom, Thomas avoided any eye contact with the onlookers, preferring instead to stare sullenly at the floor. "Calling the State of Maryland versus Ronnie Thomas," the Baltimore prosecutor shouted. "We are ready for trial." Rombro turned to Thomas and explained that under Maryland law he had a right to be tried within 180 days. Did he understand that? Thomas murmured that he did. The judge then ordered the prosecution and defense teams to go across the street to the Clarence Mitchell Courthouse to attend an administrative hearing to schedule a trial date for Thomas. "Would you like to attend the hearing?" the judge asked Thomas. He shook his head. "Mr. Thomas waives his appearance in administrative court," Rombro announced. A bailiff then stepped in and led Thomas away; the pair disappeared through a door behind the judge.

To the small group of criminal defense attorneys and family members of defendants gathered in the courtroom on that October day, Ronnie Thomas—who was charged with assaulting and robbing a female acquaintance—probably seemed like just another defendant in Baltimore's sprawling criminal justice system. But Thomas was no ordinary defendant. Just two years earlier, Thomas had become an outsized street icon on Baltimore's streets and a foe to the city's police department thanks to a straight-to-DVD documentary he starred in called *Stop Fucking Snitching, Vol. 1*. In the DVD Thomas (whose street name is "Skinny Suge") serves as guide to Baltimore's inner-city neighborhoods, introducing viewers to its gun-toting, marijuana-smoking denizens who angrily lament the prevalence of informants and cooperators in their communities and threaten the "rats," "bitches," and "snitches" with violent retribution. In one early scene, Thomas stares at the camera and warns, "To all you rats and snitches lucky enough to cop one of these DVDs, I hope you catch AIDS in your mouth and your lips are the first thing to die." The meandering, 108-minute documentary is packed with threats against informants and, more boldly, the naming of cooperators such as Stash House hustler Warren Grace and Tyree "Blackie" Stewart, a drug kingpin-turned-witness in a murder-for-hire case involving Solothal "Itchy Man" Thomas, a street legend once dubbed "one of the most violent inhabitants of the city."

The most notorious scene in *Stop Fucking Snitching, Vol. 1*—better known as simply *Stop Snitching*—features Denver Nuggets forward Carmelo Anthony, who stands on Monroe Street in Baltimore surrounded by a group of friends laughing as they threaten Tyree Stewart. At one point the joking becomes serious, and Anthony says that he'd like to put "money on his motherfucking brains." Unsurprisingly, Anthony's appearance in the DVD caused a huge uproar in the NBA, and in an interview with the *Baltimore Sun* soon after its release in the fall of 2004, Anthony tried to cast his role in the project in a more innocent light. "I understand that everybody is on there talking about killing and doing this and that," he explained, "but it's not like I'm on there with guns." Sensing that Anthony's appearance in the documentary might land him in legal trouble, his agent, Calvin Andrews, told the *Sun*, "He's not involved in any sort of activity or committing any sort of crime."

But Anthony's justifications for appearing in *Stop Snitching*—"I was back on my block, chillin', . . . going back to show love to everybody"—did not lessen the law enforcement furor over the DVD. To cops and prosecutors, *Stop Snitching* was a witness intimidation tool meant to put cooperators and informants in the crosshairs of criminals. "Think how bold criminals must be to make a DVD," Baltimore Circuit Judge John M. Glynn said of *Stop Snitching*. "It shows that threatening snitches has become mainstream—so much so that they make a DVD joking about it." In a *Sun* piece that fall, law enforcement officials even claimed that the boastful threats of *Stop Snitching* (which the newspaper characterized as a "witness intimidation DVD") were in fact *all* aimed directly at Tyree Stewart, the cooperator whose testimony would later be crucial in bringing about a conviction in the federal murder-for-hire case against Solothal "Itchy Man" Thomas in the late fall of 2006, (Thomas was sentenced to life imprisonment for carrying out a hit on a thirty-three-year-old Baltimore man named Jesse Williams on October 2, 2001.)

That the DVD spread virus-like through the city's streets only infuriated law enforcement further. Enterprising employees at Changes, a clothing shop in Baltimore's Mondawmin Mall, began selling T-shirts featuring a stop sign with the words "STOP SNITCHING" superimposed on it, and within weeks of the DVD's release, the T-shirts were selling faster than Changes could keep them in stock. Soon afterward, pirated copies of the DVD were auctioned off on eBay for over $100, and bootleggers around the country were moving pirated copies by the thousands, some of which landed in the hands of street-credible hip-hoppers like the Diplomats.

Inspired by the DVD's message—which is not witness intimidation but a nostalgic call for a restoration of "old-school" street values, meaning that hustlers do the prison time they're faced with instead of "talking" their way out of their legal bind—rappers began sporting "Stop Snitching" T-shirts in their music videos and promotional DVDs. On an early summer day in 2005, just months after *Stop Snitching* hit the streets, the Diplomats descended on an abandoned lot in the East New York section of Brooklyn for a video shoot. Nearly everyone present that day—stylists, production assistants, even preteen nieces and nephews of the Diplomats—sported "Stop Snitching" T-shirts, creating a sea of red stop signs in the lot. It was a fashion craze that, for a brief moment, made urban clothing lines from Roc-A-Wear and Sean John seem passé. In the span of a few months, "Stop Snitching" became an authentic cultural phenomenon that brought the DVD's unlikely coproducer, a thirty-three-year-old West Baltimore barber named Rodney Bethea, feelings of elation and dread in equal measure.

■ ■ ■

At just over five foot nine with soft brown eyes, a neatly trimmed beard, and smart fashion sense (he often sports sweatshirts from the trendy Japanese clothing line A Bathing Ape) Rodney Bethea hardly conforms to the caricature of a fearsome hustler brandishing a "witness intimidation" DVD so menacing it could cow major drug business players and everyday citizens alike. When I met Bethea in Baltimore during the late fall of 2006, there was little about him that seemed stereotypically "street"; he criticized hustlers and rappers alike for dressing "bummy" and, to my surprise, embraced the politics of both the Black Panthers and Bill Cosby. "Bill's right," Bethea says of Cosby's recent controversial rants about the state of black America. "There is a ridiculous level of ignorance in our communities. It's to the point where everything is backwards—everything you shouldn't be doing *is* the thing that is cool and slick. It's cool to look bummy. It's cool not to go to school."

Bethea's involvement in *Stop Snitching* began to make sense when he told me about his rough upbringing in Philadelphia. He was raised on Seventeenth and Susquehanna streets on the city's north side—a dangerous block that once swarmed with hustlers— and by his early teens had been arrested several times on drug and robbery charges. Fortunately for Bethea, just before he entered his senior year, he and his mother—a retail worker who raised him by herself—moved to suburban Bucks County, Pennsylvania, about twenty-five miles away from Philadelphia. The transition was a rough one for Bethea—"I went from an all-black high school to a school where you could count the blacks on one hand," he says—but being an outsider in Bucks County had the unintended effect of giving him a fresh perspective on the profoundly destructive direction his life had been taking on the streets of Philadelphia. "I'm seeing kids whose parents have nice cars and houses," Bethea explains, "and I realized that I didn't need to sell drugs and commit crimes to get those things. I started to understand that on the streets, everything is set up for me to fail. I was selling drugs, but at the end of the day I was still broke. Plus, it was so easy for me to get in trouble and go to jail—but if I ever got caught up in something serious, it would be hard for me to get out."

So Bethea refocused his attention from the streets to high school and upon graduation set his sights on barber school. In 1995, Bethea moved to Baltimore to attend barber school and be closer to his father, who was living in the city at the time. "I thought it might be a chance for us to get to know each other better," Bethea remembers, "but that didn't work out." Barber school, however, did work out for Bethea, and he found that he made fast friends in his adopted hometown. Though he hung out with hustlers like Ronnie "Skinny Suge" Thomas—so named because he was an aspiring rapper and hip-hop executive who wanted to distinguish himself from the portly Los Angeles hip-hop impresario Marion "Suge" Knight—he steered clear of the drug business, which had the unintended effect of earning him admiration on the streets. "Suge and the street guys liked me because they knew that I had a head on my shoulders," Bethea explained. "They looked at me like, 'Damn, maybe he can help us get out [of the 'hood].' Really, everybody wants to get out. People talk about the 'hood life and try and glorify it, but, man, no one likes it. It's bullshit. If they had another track to jump on, they'd jump on it quick."

Bethea's stock on the streets skyrocketed when he launched a clothing line called "One Love" in the late 1990s. Because the One Love operation was such a homegrown success—Bethea went from selling shirts and jeans from the back of a van to operating his own storefront on Pennsylvania Avenue in West Baltimore in a matter of months—he began to attract a group of hangers-on. But Bethea's business was still modest enough that he had to cut hair to make a living, so he could do little but offer his street friends (who wanted to break into a legitimate hustle like hip-hop or the fashion industry) advice from a savvier, non-street perspective. At the beginning of 2003, Bethea concocted a plan to help the likes of Ronnie "Skinny Suge" Thomas realize their hip-hop dreams: he'd videotape their freestyle rhymes and compile them on a DVD, which he'd give out to One Love's customers for free with every purchase. "All my friends were trying to be rappers," Bethea remembers, "and I wanted to come up with a way to indirectly market my clothing line. So the idea of a One Love DVD was perfect."

Bethea's instincts about the project turned out to be spot-on: the first installment, produced under the One Love Films banner and dubbed *One Love Freestyle Battles*, sold out instantly thanks to an appearance by the charismatic Thomas, whom Bethea hails as a "Snoop Dogg mixed with Dave Chappelle—but with street cred through the roof." Six more volumes of *One Love Freestyles* followed in quick succession, all of which were as successful as the first (Bethea won't say exactly how many DVDs he sold, but he estimates he moved several hundred copies of each volume). The popularity of the series also strengthened the growing bond between Bethea and Thomas; Thomas's cartoonishly over-the-top commentaries and freestyle rhymes about Baltimore street life—which law enforcement would later find so menacing on *Stop Snitching*—worked as a perfect counterbalance to Bethea's calm, cool, entrepreneurial style.

Soon after releasing the seventh volume of *One Love Freestyles* in the summer of 2004, Bethea and Thomas decided to tackle a new, distinctly different DVD project. Armed with cheap camcorders, the pair would travel to Thomas's old stomping grounds on Emerson Avenue (sometimes nicknamed "EA") in West Baltimore and record local hustlers freestyle rapping or just riffing about what was happening in the 'hood. The DVD was to be an homage to Thomas's neighborhood, with an appropriately simple title: *EA: All Day in the Hood*. But when Bethea and Thomas began shooting that July, they soon found that EA's street guys weren't interested in rapping or reminiscing about the old days in the neighborhood. "All they wanted to talk about was snitching, snitching, snitching," Bethea remembers. "That's all we heard. So I said to Suge, 'Listen, we need to change the title to *Stop Snitching*. And Suge said 'Let's do it.'"

The DVD's title was deliberately provocative—"If we would have called it *Don't Be a Fool; Stay in School* no one would have cared," Bethea points out—and the footage taken in West Baltimore lived up to its controversy-creating name in every way. In one scene, one hustler says of an informant, "We gon' lynch his ass if he ever come here," as Denver Nugget Carmelo Anthony watches and laughs. In another, a street guy sitting on a stoop in front of a rowhouse takes a break from eating chicken wings to rant that "snitches should get wet up [shot] once a day; as a matter of fact, once an hour, twice a *second*. That's how it's supposed it be." A few moments later a hustler clad in a white T-shirt pulls a bullet from the chamber of a gun with a dramatic flourish and proudly displays it for Bethea's cameraman.

Bethea says that he knew that such scenes guaranteed that *Stop Snitching* would provoke strong reactions from law enforcement—"we thought that this would be the punch in the mouth to get our messages through the door"—but he adds with evident frustration that its message has been universally misinterpreted. "It was never made to intimidate people from calling the cops," Bethea explains, "and it was never directed at what they call 'civilians.' If your grandmother calls the cops on people who are selling drugs on her block, she's *supposed* to do that because she's not living this lifestyle. When people say 'Stop snitching' on the DVD, they are referring to *criminals* who lead a criminal life who make profit from criminal activities. But when the curtain comes down, they want to rat on other guys that they have been hanging with to get out of their situation. What we're saying is that you gotta know how to take responsibility for your actions. If you're out here on the streets, you gotta know that you're gonna end up dead or in jail. You gotta know that that is part of the package. So when it comes time for you to pay, don't *not* want to pay because that is part of what you knew you were getting into in the first place. *Stop Snitching* is about taking it back to old-school street values, old-school street rules."

Ironically, when *Stop Snitching* hit the streets that fall, Baltimore law enforcement interpreted the DVD's success as a sign that old-school street rules were already reigning over the city's streets. Baltimore had in recent years been wracked by a series of dramatic, gruesomely violent incidents involving witness intimidation, which to the cops was powerful evidence that *Stop Snitching* was documenting a deadly phenomenon. Three years previously, the home of Baltimore anti-drug activist Angela Dawson was fire-bombed, leaving Dawson and her five children dead. Dawson had called the cops numerous times on drug dealers in her East Baltimore neighborhood, and her killing was an astonishingly bold act of cruelty that shrouded a jaded city in an apocalyptic mood. One *Sun* columnist referred to the slain activist as "Angel Dawson" and proclaimed that she "died a martyr for that future Baltimore in which we are asked to believe, free of the drug dealing and the intimidation, the violence and the wasted lives that mark the city's past quarter-century." But Bethea maintains that, like the Dawson incident, *Stop Snitching* was a wake-up call about just how violent and corrupt Baltimore had become in recent years.

Against the backdrop of the countless slayings of witnesses in the city, local politicians and cops were in no mood for such a lesson. Maryland Congressman Elijah Cummings, who represents the district where much of *Stop Snitching* was shot, called on the Denver Nuggets to "take immediate action to formally condemn any association by its players with activities that promote the illegal drug trade." Baltimore city police, meanwhile, vowed to arrest all of the DVD's participants, and surveillance was set up near a West Baltimore bar featured in the DVD. "I want them to keep making these DVDs," Anthony Barksdale, acting chief of the police department's organized crime division, told the *Sun.* "Go to volume 50 because we're making cases off these."

■ ■ ■

For all of Barksdale's tough talk, the participants in *Stop Snitching* could not be arrested merely for their threatening words or even their actions (like waving guns in the air), a simple fact that Baltimore State's Attorney Patricia C. Jessamy immediately recognized. "The first thing people wanted to know was 'Are we gonna charge people in the video?'" Jessamy told me. "But if you got someone in the video with a gun, you don't know if the gun is real. If they're smoking what they say is marijuana, you don't really know what it is. And though they might be talking about committing a crime, they have a constitutional right to say almost anything that they want to say. We need real evidence. So we made the determination that we're not prosecuting anybody." Instead of issuing empty threats against the hustlers in *Stop Snitching*, Jessamy, who has been Baltimore's top prosecutor since 1995, said that the DVD proved that legislation needed to be passed in Maryland increasing the punishment for witness intimidation from five years to twenty. Jessamy also sought to add a "forfeiture by wrongdoing exception" to the bill, allowing for statements to be admitted from a witness who did not show up in court if it could be proven that he or she had been threatened. A similar provision allowing for "forfeiture wrongdoing exception" already exists in the federal system, but it is most often applied to child abuse cases at the state level. Long before the release of *Stop Snitching*, Jessamy had been pushing for just such a bill in the Maryland House of Delegates—but with little success. She says that in early 2004, she and Maryland's then-governor, Robert L. Ehrlich Jr., a Republican, brought a witness intimidation bill before the heavily Democratic Maryland House only to have it "fail miserably." "It did not come out of committee," she told me with evident frustration. "It was viewed as an administration bill, a partisan effort. We went down and testified, and we didn't get any traction."

Stop Snitching, then, presented a rare opportunity for Jessamy to revive her long-dormant legislation. "We got lemons," she says with a knowing laugh, "which is people on the streets talking about the horrible things they're gonna do to people who tell. And we decided we're gonna make lemonade!" Jessamy made for an unusually savvy opponent for the *Stop Snitching* crew. A tenacious fifty-seven-year-old black prosecutor whose downtown Baltimore office is adorned with framed photographs of civil rights leaders such as Coretta Scott King, she is profoundly resistant to law enforcement stereotypes—which is perhaps more important than usual in a race- and class-charged battle such as this one. Jessamy also smartly rejected the confrontational style of the Baltimore city police—who made a DVD of their own called *Keep Talking*—in favor of a quieter, more strategic approach. "We're not going to get into the DVD business," she says dismissively. "That's for the Baltimore police." Instead, soon after Jessamy's office received a copy of *Stop Snitching* from a local TV news reporter, she invited a group of local legislators to her office for a breakfast screening of the DVD. When Jessamy played a two-minute clip at the breakfast, the legislators "sat there with their mouths open," she remembers. Jessamy's apocalyptic view of the state of Baltimore's streets—in which drug business players brazenly threatened anyone who dared to testify against them—played out right there on the TV screen. To ensure that the lawmakers wouldn't forget what they had just seen, Jessamy handed each of them a copy of the DVD.

Soon after the breakfast screening at Jessamy's office, the political fortunes of her witness intimidation bill seemingly reversed. "Now, instead of having no traction on our bill, suddenly we have people who want to cosponsor it across party lines," Jessamy remembers. "Which is the way it should have been because it's not a Democratic or Republican issue; it's a public safety issue. We had about eighty delegates sign on, and we had a number of senators sign on with no changes." The passage of the bill seemed assured when Jessamy went before the Maryland House Judiciary Committee and provided dramatic testimony about witness intimidation in Baltimore. "We estimate that at least 25 percent of nonfatal shooting cases are dismissed due to witness issues," Jessamy explained, adding that the vast majority of unsuccessful homicide prosecutions involved some form of witness intimidation. Then, addressing *Stop Snitching* directly, she said, "Many of you have asked, 'Is this DVD real? Is this really happening on our streets?" The answer is yes, the DVD is an accurate picture of what prosecutors see, hear, and witness every day in courthouses across our city." But in a repeat of the bill's earlier failure, it stalled in the House Judiciary Committee, requiring yet another public relations push from Jessamy to prod lawmakers into action. Finally, in April 2005, the bill became law in Maryland but with extensive restrictions on the kinds of cases in which the "forfeiture by wrongdoing exception" could be applied. "They limited it to certain crimes," Jessamy explains. "It could not, for example, be applied to child abuse cases. So we were not happy. We called it a toothless tiger. It threatens you, it makes you shiver in your boots, but when it opens its mouth, it has no teeth."

■ ■ ■

The passage of a neutered witness intimidation bill during the spring of 2005 may have been something of a pyrrhic victory for Jessamy, but Baltimore law enforcement was about to suffer a setback that would far overshadow the powerful prosecutor's legislative challenges. On May 11, 2005, Baltimore city police officers William A. King and Antonio L. Murray were hit with a five-count indictment from the Maryland U.S. attorney, charging them with crimes ranging from drug conspiracy to robbery. By November the indictment increased to thirty-three counts. Prosecutors alleged that King and Murray ran a lucrative shakedown operation on the streets of West Baltimore—the very area that served as a backdrop for *Stop Snitching*—in which they would rob hustlers of their drugs and then resell them to addicts or give them to their favored informants. Even to crime- and corruption-plagued Baltimore it was a shocking case—King and Murray were like real-life versions of the crooked cops in the Denzel Washington movie *Training Day*, who justified their involvement in the drug business with the memorable phrase, "Sometimes you gotta have a little dirt on you for anybody to trust you." But the embarrassment the indictment caused cops was compounded by the fact that King and Murray's activities were described in *Stop Snitching*.

"Word is they work for King and Murray," one hustler complained of West Baltimore drug dealers on the DVD. "Now if you don't know, you gotta be from here to understand who King and Murray is. King and Murray is two police officers on narcotics. They say that everybody work for King and Murray. Don't nobody go to trial . . . but everybody catch cases." This characterization of the Baltimore cops, made months before they were indicted by the Maryland U.S. Attorney's Office, turned out to be stunningly prescient: prosecutors alleged that King and Murray would grab hustlers off the street, take their drugs in the privacy of their unmarked car, and return them to the street corners on which they plied their trade without arresting them. The hustlers on *Stop Snitching* were also dead-on in their complaints about infamous Stash House cooperator-run-amok Warren Grace. On the DVD, one hustler laments that Grace "told on Deon [Deon Lionnel Smith] and Fella [Walter Oriley Poindexter], and then he be out here shootin' niggas. Here's a guy who will snitch on you—and kill you!"

Rodney Bethea says that the King and Murray case proved what he had been saying about *Stop Snitching* all along: namely, that "what the DVD was doing was airing out a lot of dirty laundry. From the mayor to local officials on down, they're doing a lot of cruddy shit." Bethea also maintains that it was the act of exposing dirty cops and rogue informants on *Stop Snitching*—not the threats against snitches—that provoked such strong reactions from Baltimore cops and prosecutors in the first place. "They tried to blame the DVD for everything in the city that went wrong," Bethea explains. "The attitude was 'Hold up—we can't have these young niggers talking on this DVD about shit that's going on when we're trying to make it look like we're reducing crime.' They needed to make *Stop Snitching* look like witness intimidation so people would ignore the issues we brought up on the DVD."

When asked if local law enforcement were concerned about the sections in the DVD concerning King and Murray, Jessamy says, "We didn't scrutinize the DVD to that extent. It's hard to listen to the DVD; it's a tough listen. You can only take so much of it. . . . The cursing, the slang, the accents." Jessamy does seem genuinely furious about the ramifications of King and Murray's behavior—"it has done a lot of damage to the public's perception of the Baltimore city's police"—but Bethea is right to point out that scrutiny of the corrupt cops by the media and law enforcement paled in comparison to the overwhelming amount of attention *Stop Snitching* received. "They talked about it for a day or two and then they swept it under the rug," Bethea says of King and Murray, "and that was one of the main things in our DVD." In August 2005, nearly one year after the release of *Stop Snitching*, *Sun* columnist Gregory Kane acknowledged (albeit in a back-handed fashion) that Bethea and Ronnie "Skinny Suge" Thomas "may have performed a public service" by exposing the likes of Warren Grace and King and Murray. "The emphasis is on that word 'may,'" Kane continued. "If the snitching about King and Murray turns out to be true, then the 'Stop Snitching' DVD—as bad as it is—will have done some good after all."

The "snitching" about King and Murray on *Stop Snitching* turned out to be more accurate than even West Baltimore denizens like Bethea—who told me that "people who didn't even *live* the life knew they were dirty cops"—could have imagined. When King and Murray went to trial at U.S. District Court in downtown Baltimore during the spring of 2006, a stunning picture of police corruption emerged from government witnesses and even from King and Murray themselves. In a profoundly ill-advised move, the cops took the witness stand in an attempt to convince the jury that while they had routinely violated police department protocol, they did so after training by NYPD detectives in drug-enforcement tactics.

■ ■ ■

"King is working!" In the fall of 2004, Officer William King suddenly discovered that whenever he'd head out on patrol in West Baltimore, a shout would rise from the streets: "King is working!" Once the alarm about King was sounded, entire West Baltimore drug blocks would be shut down for the day, and as King would remember at his trial later, "if they see me, people getting on their cell phones and contact *everybody* in the city saying I'm working." In his twelve years on the force, King, thirty-five, had never encountered such strong resistance to his work, even though he had served with a number of high-profile Baltimore City Police Department units, from FAST (Firearms Apprehension Strike Team) to OCD (Organized Crime Division). West Baltimore hustlers had a sixth sense about his presence on the streets; he couldn't step onto the block without catcalls of "King is working!" ringing throughout the area. "It was very hard," King remembered. "I couldn't go out in an area and work and do the police work and do drug enforcement at all. My partners were complaining."

One day, during a routine traffic stop, he unexpectedly discovered the source of his troubles. "We stopped a car for a possible narcotics violation," King explained, "and the occupant had a handgun in the car. While we were searching the vehicle to make sure there was nothing else in the vehicle, we found a video called *Stop Snitching*." When King watched it at home later that afternoon, he was stunned to hear his and partner Antonio L. Murray's police work described in intricate detail. "After I heard my name in the video, I gave the video to my sergeant," King explained. While King remembered that "no one in the police department knew about the video at the time," that would soon change, as "my sergeant gave the video to the lieutenant, lieutenant gave it to the major, major gave it to the commissioner, Commissioner gave to Patricia Jessamy. I believe Patricia Jessamy gave it to the mayor." (Jessamy denies that she received a copy of *Stop Snitching* via King or any of his superiors.) "Because of the video I had to adjust the way I worked," King explained. "I no longer can do police work or do narcotics enforcement, because as soon as the dealers see me, they all disappear. They don't come back out. You would think that would be a good thing, but it's not because I can't get any numbers."

Stop Snitching may have changed how King operated on the streets of Baltimore—he had to switch unmarked cars almost constantly in order to avoid that call of "King is working!" from being issued—but it did not bring about a shift in his and his partner's unorthodox, often illegal police tactics. King and Murray had long utilized an informant named Antonio Mosby, a heroin addict desperate for cash who helpfully pointed out West Baltimore drug dealers for them. It was a typical informant-cop relationship, except that King and Murray defied police protocol by giving Mosby $40 to $60 in cash per day, funds they later acknowledged were seized from other drug dealers in West Baltimore. Occasionally, the pair would even give Mosby cash out of their own pockets. "The police department did not have money to just give $40, $50, $60 to an informant," Murray explained. "You had to come up with resources out there yourself to help with your investigation." But by the fall of 2004, Mosby's heroin addiction had become so severe that King and Murray felt that they had to supply him drugs to keep him working. "Initially, I tried to just give him money," Murray said, "but he had a ten pill a day habit [heroin is often packaged in clear capsules]. So if I didn't give him any drugs, I didn't give him anything that would constitute him running out getting arrested, working for somebody else, double dipping." "Double dipping"—street slang for working for the cops *and* hustlers—is a common practice among many opportunistic informants, an outcome that King and Murray said they worked hard to avoid with Mosby. "I didn't want him to go work for one of these shops [drug operations] that make $30,000 a day," Murray explained. "That could have easily been done. I didn't want him doing that. So I wanted him to work for us."

Eventually, by the end of 2004, King and Murray began attracting attention from the feds—not because of their cash payments to Mosby, but because of large cash deposits they were making in their bank accounts. Murray had a total of four bank accounts—with Nations Bank, Wachovia, and MECU, the Municipal Employees Credit Union—and he would make cash deposits of several thousand dollars at a time. Murray said that the source of his income was legitimate—he claimed that he ran "a store in the office in which we sold sodas, juice, candy, because we didn't have any convenience machines down there" and that he was "the family treasurer of my family reunion," charged with collecting cash from relatives for a trip to Disney World in Florida. Law enforcement's suspicions about King and Murray were confirmed when informant Mosby told them plainly, "I can buy drugs from a police officer in Baltimore City." Mosby's stunning admission was followed by his indictment on drug conspiracy charges by the Maryland U.S. Attorney's Office and a subsequent plea agreement in which he agreed to cooperate in the investigation into King and Murray. That Mosby would cooperate against the very cops who helped kick-start his career as an informant in the first place perfectly illustrated the double- and triple-dealing that characterizes the drug game.

The first operation in the federal sting of King and Murray began with Mosby. During the late fall of 2004, just as King was dealing with those "King is working!" catcalls, he received a call on his cell phone from Mosby about a stash of crack left in a West Baltimore alleyway. Though King wasn't aware of it at the time, the crack was actually placed in the alley by a special agent with the FBI. King quickly picked up the drugs and handed them over to Mosby to resell. A few months later, King gave Mosby 140 ziplock bags of marijuana he found while searching a car, instructing Mosby to "move it." Instead of selling the drugs, though, Mosby went back to his handlers at the FBI and picked up cash, which he then gave to King in order to deceive him into thinking that he had found a buyer for the stash. About two weeks later, on February 17, King phoned Mosby and asked him to meet him in a parking lot on the corner of Martin Luther King and Saratoga streets, just outside a building where the Baltimore city police's Housing Unit is based. Mosby arrived at the meeting wearing a body wire, and when he climbed into King's Chevy Lumina, King was recorded offering 116 vials of crack to him. With yet another drug sale from King documented, the FBI and the Maryland U.S. Attorney's Office obtained a court-ordered wiretap on his Nextel cell phone. "It became clear in those phone calls," federal prosecutor A. David Copperthite said later, "that there was a relationship between William King, Antonio Murray, and Antonio Mosby."

After a wiretap of Murray's cell phone was authorized, the extent of the officers' corruption became clear. "When we began listening to those phone calls, you could see this relationship between the three of them and see how they operate," Copperthite explained of the officers and their informant. "And from there, it became obvious that what they were doing is putting people in the car or accosting people in and around the car." Investigators suspected that King and Murray were using their Chevy Lumina to sell drugs to Mosby *and* to shake down hustlers in private. So federal investigators bugged the cops' unmarked car that King used on patrol in Baltimore's housing projects in order to avoid those "King is working!" warnings.

Thanks to Mosby's body wire and the bugged Lumina, federal investigators got a detailed picture of King and Murray's methods. Mosby would locate "hitters"—the drug business workers who actually hold and distribute the drugs—and then provide a description of them to King and Murray. "King and Murray would then go into the area, locate the person, basically stop him, tell them they've seen them dealing drugs," Copperthite explained. "Then they get drugs and money off the person, and then they put them in the police car." Once inside the Lumina, King and Murray would "basically tell the person, 'Look, here's what we're going to do. We're not going to charge you, we're going to hold these, and you're going to call us tomorrow or call us back on Monday, and you're going to tell us where there are more drugs. If you don't, we're going to put these drugs on you, and you're going to be charged with these drugs.' And they would act like they were arresting the person. And they didn't arrest the person." When King and Murray did arrest dealers, according to Copperthite, they would charge them with a minor offense like "hindering" (interfering with an arrest) without seizing drugs or cash. An examination of the officers' paperwork by federal investigators revealed that while they appeared to be busy enough making misdemeanor arrests, they rarely turned in any drugs or money. These they kept for themselves. "You can hear them taking the money and drugs right off the person in the car. You can hear them counting," says Copperthite. The Lumina and Mosby wires as well as the taps of King and Murray's cell phones caught not only the counting of drugs and cash but its subsequent divvying up as well.

As federal investigators observed King and Murray's actions through wiretaps and body wires, they began to realize that the cops had more than just Mosby in their employ. "King was trying to create sort of an army of people out there like Antonio Mosby," Copperthite explained, "spotting drug dealers, spotting targets for them to rob, take the drugs, take the money." On April 21, 2005, King and Murray apprehended a hustler named Dion Snipe only to have King tell him to keep his eyes open for drug stashes—and that if he saw any, he could call King, and they could split it. On other occasions, King and Murray would instruct a hustler to sell most of his "pack" (supply of drugs), take the proceeds, and then arrest him for the remaining drugs. "They want to get down to one or two pills versus selling the drugs so then they can have something to hold over them," Copperthite said. Then King and Murray would take the remainders and hand them over to Mosby to sell. This cycle was repeated throughout the spring of 2005, as the two cops trolled the streets daily looking for targets—though King and Murray, like the dealers they exploited so ruthlessly, had their off days. "I didn't get any cake at all," King said one day when a cop picked up a West Baltimore hustler before he could get his hands on his drug supply.

■ ■ ■

For the Baltimore City Police Department, it would be hard to exceed the embarrassment of the mid-May day in 2005 when the feds issued arrest warrants for two of its seasoned veterans. But one year after the indictment, the department did manage to come out looking even worse when King and Murray went to trial in U.S.

District Court in downtown Baltimore. Though Assistant U.S. Attorney Copperthite told jurors in his opening statement that the case was "not about some widespread police corruption," the picture that emerged from the proceedings—King and Murray shaking down dealers and informants alike inside the Lumina, threatening to "fuck up" arrestees, complaining about days in which they didn't make any "cake," and, perhaps most disturbingly, during the hundreds of hours of wiretaps evincing little interest in actually taking drugs or law-breakers off the streets—was one of a police department that is just as menacing (or perhaps even more so) than West Baltimore hustlers themselves. That both King and Murray had worked their way up from the lowest ranks of the Baltimore Police Department—both had patrolled Baltimore's Central District from the early to the late 1990s and then moved onto specialized units such as FAST, OCD, and CENTAC (the Central Technical Unit)—only confirmed fears that the cops were not wayward rookies but savvy senior officers who had perfected the art of gaming West Baltimore's lucrative drug business. The sole sympathetic spots in their biographies—King served in the military in the first Iraq war, and Murray was shot while on duty in the mid-1990s—were overshadowed by their own unconvincing and occasionally clueless testimony on the witness stand.

Neither King nor Murray appeared contrite about their behavior, and their rationale for their tactics was implausible: they said that when they were working with the OCD, "we was [sic] taught how to sell drugs" by New York City cops who were training members of the Baltimore City Police Department in the more proactive policing that had helped bring down crime rates in their hometown during the 1990s. The purpose of the training from the NYPD, Murray explained, was to change the Baltimore City Police Department's "philosophies" from "just getting guns and getting numbers to basically doing more investigative work."

The cops also defended their practice of giving drugs and cash to Mosby as a necessity to maintain their stable of informants. "Now, these informants, you know, they are a necessary evil," Murray explained. "You need them. They are a very essential part of what you need to do. You have to, you have to keep them happy. You *have* to keep them happy. You have to satisfy them. They are not going to sit out there and work all day for $20 and just do everything that you want them to do. They're just not going to do that. . . . They going to be in the trade either way. Either way they going to be in this game."

Under cross-examination from Copperthite, Murray sounded more like a street hustler than a cop when he complained that he'd been hit with drug conspiracy charges for giving small amounts of heroin to an informant. "Eight pills within eight months and I'm here in a federal distribution case," Murray groused. "Where do you draw the line?" He claimed that his policing methods were for Baltimore's "better good," which prompted a testy exchange between him and Copperthite:

COPPERTHITE: Whose better good is that?
MURRAY: You going to let me finish, sir?
COPPERTHITE: Go ahead.
MURRAY: I said the better good.
COPPERTHITE: Whose better good?
MURRAY: The city.
COPPERTHITE: Is this like if you and King are the only
    drug dealers, then there won't be any more drug dealers
    on the street?

To no one's surprise, a Baltimore jury delivered a guilty verdict on nearly all of the more than two dozen counts of robbery, drug conspiracy, and drug distribution against King and Murray. The sentences for both cops, however, stunned even judges accustomed to the punitive punishments regularly meted out in the federal criminal justice system: King received 315 years and one month in prison, while Murray was given 139 years behind bars. "There is something fundamentally wrong with this sentence," U.S. District Judge J. Frederick Motz said at King's sentencing, adding that the prison term was "absolutely disproportionate to the wrong that was committed, although the wrong that was committed was a very serious one." In an interview with the *Sun* after the verdict, Assistant U.S. Attorney Charles Peters defended King's sentence by arguing that the indictment provided merely a "small snapshot of what Mr. King and Mr. Murray were doing on the street." Baltimore City Police Commissioner Leonard D. Hamm also defended the cops' punishment by declaring that "people like William King have no place in the Baltimore Police Department and never will. Thanks to the tireless efforts of the Police Department internal affairs section and the United States attorney's office, justice was served."

In contrast, nonprofit organizations committed to sentencing reform like the November Coalition sprang to King and Murray's defense, pointing to their extraordinary punishment as proof that the sentencing guidelines desperately needed to be reformed. King and Murray were even featured on the November Coalition's website, along with other defendants who received long prison terms under the sentencing guidelines, such as Euka Wadlington. In Baltimore the cops' sentences even inspired a public debate about the sentencing guidelines, with Maryland U.S. Attorney Rod J. Rosenstein telling the *Sun* that "Congress is always free to review" them.

To Rodney Bethea, the guilty verdicts for King and Murray merely reinforced the issues he'd raised in *Stop Snitching*: namely, that police corruption and an erosion of integrity on the streets were the result of the increasing pervasiveness of informants. "The game is over," Bethea declares. "Now all the big-time drug dealers are working for the cops. That's why guys were naming names on the DVD. It was like, 'Damn, *they* working with the feds?'" Still, Bethea worries that with the arrest of several of the DVD's participants as well as Carmelo Anthony's refusal to take on its critics, the most opportune moment to address the controversial ideas of *Stop Snitching* may have already passed. "When [Congressman] Elijah Cummings issued that statement, he [Anthony] should have said, 'OK, you say you want to meet me and talk about it; let's meet on Emerson Avenue,'" Bethea says, his voice rising with anger. "'Let's meet in Murphy Homes [a notorious Baltimore housing project]. Let's meet right in the heart of these communities. As a matter of fact let's meet right on Monroe Street, where I taped the DVD. Let's walk these blocks, and let me show you what's really going on out here. Let me show you how bad it is, and then you tell me why you weren't doing anything about it. Because a person in your position has the power in your hands to address the situation and make a change. When you do that, I'll tell you why I was on the DVD.'"

But Bethea holds out hope that with a slew of recent corruption scandals—soon after we met in the fall of 2006, it was revealed that a pair of Baltimore drug kingpins made financial contributions to local politicians—and with some in Baltimore coming to understand what he set out to accomplish with *Stop Snitching* in the first place, he is engaging in a much more constructive debate with the local politicians, prosecutors, and Baltimore cops about their crime-plagued city. "If you really want things to change, come to us," Bethea says. "We'll tell you what's really going on and what needs to be done. That is, if you *really* want things to change." He clears his throat. "If not," Bethea continues, pointing out that he has enough material for several more installments of *Stop Snitching*, "we gonna keep airing out your shit."

Chapter Ten

A SESSION WITH SESSIONS

Sentencing Reform and Snitching Solutions

"THE TRUTH IS, GENTLEMEN, THAT THE UNITED STATES CONGRESS DOES NOT trust you to sentence." It's just after eleven AM on a late November day in 2006, and Alabama Republican Senator Jeff Sessions is sitting in his spacious third-floor office in the Russell Building on Capitol Hill remembering with evident relish what a congressman—he will not say who—said to a federal judge just after the sentencing guidelines were enacted by Congress in the mid-1980s. "Congress, you see, was fed up with the disparity in sentencing by federal judges, who had total discretion in what sentences they handed out," Sessions continues. "You would try someone on a drug charge, and one judge would give them probation, and another one would give them fifteen years. . . . It was a revolving door system, and some people even doubted that incarceration had any effect on deterrence. But after the sentencing guidelines passed, the crime rate, murder rate, all went down dramatically. Of course, the inmate population surged soon afterward. So you heard people say, 'Oh, we got too many people in jail.' Well, we got a lot of people alive today because *murderers* are in jail, you understand me?"

Senator Sessions's forceful style has—for better and worse—defined his tenure both as a federal prosecutor during the mid-1980s and early 1990s and later as a senator. When he was the U.S. attorney for the Southern District of Alabama, he infuriated minority groups and civil liberties watchdogs by indicting three civil rights workers—including Albert Turner, a former aide to Martin Luther King Jr.—on voter fraud charges in an Alabama state election. Sessions's investigation yielded a mere fourteen allegedly tampered ballots out of more than 1.7 million cast. The trio were acquitted on all of the charges against them. Soon after the verdict came down, a Justice Department employee named J. Gerald Hebert testified in front of the Senate that Sessions called the National Association for the Advancement of Colored People (NAACP) and the American Civil Liberties Union (ACLU) "un-American" and "Communist-inspired" groups who "forced civil rights down the throats of people." This shaky civil rights record has earned Sessions the label "The Senator Who's Worse Than [Trent] Lott" from the *New Republic*.

So it is all the more surprising that Sessions is now leading the charge to overhaul the federal sentencing guidelines, legislation that some judges and drug policy experts compare to the Jim Crow laws of the South because of the disparity in incarceration rates for whites compared to blacks. It is Sessions's involvement in the sentencing reform movement that brings me to his Senate office. Sessions is a slight man physically: he's not much taller than five foot five, has a tiny, pinkish, almost pinched face, and the perfectly coiffed gray hair of an anchorman. He is so genteel, so corn-pone Southern in his manner—"Come into my *parlorrrr*," he practically purred at me when opening the door of his Senate office—that it seems like a put-on. But when he discusses the sentencing guidelines, his face becomes stern, and his voice booms with a preacherly passion; it's a change in tone that brings his aides to rapt, silent attention.

Though Sessions remains a firm believer in the philosophical foundation of 1984's Sentencing Reform Act—the notion that sentencing in federal courts needed to be uniform, particularly at a time when violent crime and drug use were sharply on the rise—he has since become one of the most vociferous critics of the twin Anti-Drug Abuse Acts that followed in its wake in 1986 and 1988, specifically the notorious 100:1 sentencing disparity between crack cocaine– and powder cocaine–related offenses.

In July 2006 Sessions and a group of legislators he dubs "the Generals" (former state attorneys general–turned-senators John Cornyn, Mark L. Pryor, and Ken Salazar) introduced the Drug Sentencing Reform Act of 2006, which proposes an increase in the amount of crack cocaine necessary to trigger a mandatory minimum of ten years in prison from fifty grams to two hundred grams while slightly lowering the amount of powder cocaine necessary to trigger the ten-year mandatory minimum from five kilograms to four. "With regards to crack, the sentences are too heavy," Sessions explains. "It comes down awfully hard on people. A lot of African-Americans are concerned about it—and I can't disagree with them."

Like Eric Sterling, the former counsel to the Senate Judiciary Committee who was instrumental in drafting the Sentencing Reform Act but who has come to criticize the omnibus bills that followed in the late 1980s and early 1990s, Sessions believes that legislators thoughtlessly created steep prison sentences for the sale of insignificant amounts of crack because of the hysteria surrounding the drug. "I don't think anybody gave a lot of thought to the disparity between powder cocaine and crack when the sentencing guidelines were passed," Sessions told me. "We passed a mandatory of five years for five grams of crack. A *nickel* weighs five grams." He turns to his aides for a fact-check. "Is that right?" They nod their heads in agreement. "A *nickel* weighs five grams! So, you know, I've concluded that there are valid criticisms of the sentencing guidelines. There's too big a gap between powder cocaine and crack. Why don't we fix it?"

Why, indeed? The long history of failed attempts to reform the sentencing guidelines—which dates back more than a decade—provides an answer to Sessions's question. Soon after President Clinton's Violent Crime Control and Law Enforcement Act passed in 1994, the United States Sentencing Commission (USSC) issued a report that found that crack dealers were being sentenced more severely than powder cocaine suppliers and that, while the 100:1 ratio in sentencing between the drugs was not motivated by racism, minorities nonetheless bore the brunt of higher sentences. In the wake of the report's release in February 1995, the USSC proposed a revision to the sentencing guidelines that would eliminate the 100:1 disparity. Under the USSC proposal, the term "cocaine" would be redefined to include *all* forms of the drug. But not all of the USSC members supported the proposal: three of its seven members dissented from the recommendation, arguing that crack and cocaine presented distinct harms and therefore needed to be treated differently under the sentencing guidelines. Nonetheless, the proposed changes to the guidelines were set to go into effect that fall unless Congress modified them—or rejected them.

When Congress held hearings on the USSC's report on October 30, 1995, they rejected its findings, arguing that "the sentence imposed for trafficking in a quantity of crack cocaine should generally exceed the sentence for trafficking in a like quantity of powder cocaine." Congress's disapproval of the USSC's proposal was even codified into law, namely S. 1254, "a bill to disapprove of amendments to the Federal Sentencing Guidelines relating to lowering of crack sentences." Upon signing the legislation that fall, President Clinton acknowledged the "substantial disparity" between sentences for the two forms of cocaine but argued that it was inappropriate to reduce penalties related to crack given the "devastating impact" it had on communities across America.

Two years later, yet another showdown between the USSC and Congress took place when the commission issued yet another report, this time a direct response to the lawmakers' rejection of their earlier proposals. The USSC recommended that the amount of crack necessary to trigger a five-year mandatory minimum be raised from 5 grams to between 25 and 75 grams while *decreasing* the quantity of powder cocaine needed to bring a five-year mandatory minimum from 500 grams to somewhere between 125 and 375 grams. Under the new USSC proposal, the sentencing disparity between crack and powder cocaine decreased from 100:1 to a much more reasonable 5:1. Congress was urged by the USSC to adopt its recommendations "as soon as possible," and to add to the sense of urgency the USSC said that they wouldn't allow legislators the option of rejecting their findings. But while the USSC's 1997 report did inspire the introduction of bills in Congress that aimed to reduce the 100:1 disparity between crack and powder cocaine, no legislation passed that year.

This pattern—the introduction of bills meant to amend the sentencing guidelines followed by legislative inaction—has occurred with a mechanistic regularity since the USSC's 1997 report. In 2000, Michigan Republican Senator Spencer Abraham introduced legislation that would lower the 100:1 sentencing disparity between crack and powder cocaine to 10:1, which passed in the Senate by one vote—but was never enacted. Just one year later, Senator Sessions and his Republican Senate colleague Orrin Hatch introduced the Drug Sentencing Reform Act of 2001, which recommended lowering the sentencing disparity between the drugs from 100:1 to 20:1. "The 100:1 disparity in sentencing between crack cocaine and powder cocaine, which falls the hardest to African-Americans, is not justifiable," Sessions said then. In an acknowledgment of the legislative inaction that stymied attempts to reform the sentencing guidelines, Sessions implored his fellow lawmakers "to cast aside the politics of the Left and the Right and to support this bill on the merits as a matter of plain, simple justice." But the Drug Sentencing Reform Act of 2001 ended up sharing the fate of its predecessors on the Hill: the bill was referred to Senate committee but not voted upon.

Frustrated by his legislative failure, Senator Hatch wrote the USSC to ask for yet another report on the penalty structure for crack and powder cocaine offenses. The USSC complied by issuing a 2002 report containing some of the sharpest criticism of the sentencing guidelines yet. "The current federal cocaine sentencing policy is unjustified," the USSC wrote, "and fails to meet the sentencing objectives set forth by Congress in both the Sentencing Reform Act and the 1986 Act [the Anti-Drug Abuse Act of 1986]." Echoing the conclusions of its earlier reports about the sentencing guidelines, the USSC found that the laws punish low-level dealers most severely and that the disparity between crack cocaine and powder sentences leads to a perception of "improper racial disparity." Most significantly, the USSC found that policymakers' claims about crack cocaine—ranging from its addictiveness to the propensity of young people to use the drug—could no longer be supported by evidence.

In its conclusion, the USSC recommended the creation of sentencing enhancements to target the small percentage of offenders who engage in the most harmful conduct (such as drug-related murders); an increase in the quantity of crack needed to trigger a mandatory minimum of five years from five grams to twenty-five grams (while preserving the current sentencing structure for powder cocaine related offenses); and a repeal of the provision mandating a five-year prison sentence for simple possession of crack. Inspired by the USSC's new report, New York Democratic Congressman Charles Rangel—the very lawmaker who urged the passing of the twin Anti-Drug Abuse Acts of the mid- to late 1980s—introduced the Crack-Cocaine Equitable Sentencing Act of 2003 in late March of that year. The bill would eliminate the mandatory mini-mums for crack-related offenses entirely. But the bill fell into the same legislative black hole as its predecessors: it was referred to nu-merous House subcommittees but never enacted. Two years later, Rangel revived nearly identical legislation under a similar sounding name—the Crack-Cocaine Equitable Sentencing Act of 2005—only to see it once again languish in House subcommittees.

As sentencing reform stood at a standstill in both houses of Congress, the U.S. Supreme Court handed down a decision in Jan-uary 2005 that seemed to have historic implications for the sen-tencing guidelines. In *United States v. Booker*, defendant Freddie Booker was convicted of possession with the intent to distribute 50 grams of crack, which under the sentencing guidelines should have earned him almost twenty-two years behind bars. Instead, he was sentenced to thirty years to life. Booker's higher sentence came from a posttrial proceeding in which it was discovered that he had both obstructed justice and possessed an additional 566 grams of crack. Booker's codefendant Duncan Fanfan faced a similar fate in federal court. Fanfan was convicted of possession with intent to distribute 500 grams of powder cocaine, which would have brought a sentence of five to six years under the sentencing guide-lines, but because in a posttrial hearing the court found that Fan-fan had distributed an additional 2.5 kilograms of powder cocaine and 261.6 grams of crack, he was hit with a sentence of fifteen to sixteen years. When the U.S. Supreme Court heard Booker's ap-peal in early 2005, it issued a two-part decision, each decided by a different 5-to-4 majority, in which it ruled that the sentencing guidelines violated defendants' Sixth Amendment right to trial by jury by giving judges, instead of juries, the power to make factual findings that determined the sentence within the range provided by the guidelines. "The jury never heard any evidence of the additional drug quantity," wrote Justice John Paul Stevens. The court then ruled that the guidelines should become "advisory" in order to avoid running afoul of the Sixth Amendment. "If the Guidelines . . . could be read as merely *advisory* provisions that recommended, rather than required, the selection of particular sentences in response to differing sets of facts," Justice Stevens wrote, "their use would not implicate the Sixth Amendment." The court also ruled that sentences could be upheld on appeal as long as they were not "unreasonable."

Though *Booker* represented a historic moment in the history of the sentencing guidelines, its practical effects in U.S. district courts are still not completely clear. In August 2006, Larry Schwartztol, a fellow at Yale Law School's Arthur Liman Public Interest Fellowship and Fund, estimated that since *Booker*, "about two dozen district courts have issued sentences below the ranges in the sentencing guidelines at least in part because the crack penalties were too harsh." More significantly, because the Supreme Court ruled somewhat vaguely in *Booker* that sentences must not be "unreasonable," it is open to interpretation what exactly constitutes an "unreasonable" sentence. Indeed, in his dissenting opinion in *Booker*, Supreme Court Justice Antonin Scalia warned that "a discordant symphony" of interpretations of what constitutes an "unreasonable" sentence "varying from court to court and judge to judge" would follow. Scalia's prediction has turned out to be prescient. Post-*Booker*, the more conservative Fourth, Fifth, Sixth, Seventh, Eighth, and Tenth Circuits have held that the sentencing guidelines themselves are "presumptively reasonable," while the Third Circuit has held that they are "more likely" to be reasonable. The Ninth and Eleventh Circuits, conversely, ruled that while sentencing court must consider the guideline range, it must not "presume" the appropriate sentence to be within that range. Finally, the Eleventh Circuit held "that a district court may determine, on a case-by-case basis, the weight to give the Guidelines."

Because of the widely varying interpretations of the reasonableness presumption, Schwartztol argues that "the maneuvering room eagerly claimed by many district courts [in the wake of the *Booker* decision] may be disappearing." Indeed, defense attorneys complain that in the two years since *Booker*, the decision has had little or no effect on sentencing. "The Guidelines continue in practice to exert much the same force as before," the National Association of Criminal Defense Lawyers said in February 2007. "District judges are imposing Guideline sentences at nearly the same rate they did when the unconstitutional system was in place."

The case of Juan Castillo, a defendant who pled guilty in federal court in Brooklyn on crack conspiracy charges in the spring of 2004, is a strong example of the often contradictory interpretations of *Booker* by federal judges. At Castillo's sentencing in 2005, his attorney argued that in the wake of *Booker* the U.S. District Court was "now free to ignore the harsher penalties imposed under the Guidelines for cases involving 'crack' cocaine as opposed to cocaine, and find the appropriate guideline by treating the sentences with equal severity, as there was never any rational reason to treat the substances differently." U.S. District Judge Robert Sweet concurred and set Castillo's sentence based on a 20:1 crack to powder cocaine ratio instead of the 100:1 ratio mandated by the sentencing guidelines. "Since *Booker*," Sweet explained in his decision, "a number of courts, concerned by the disparity between crack and powder cocaine sentences imposed under the Guidelines, have imposed non-Guideline sentences in cases involving crack." Sweet recommended a sentence of 87 months' imprisonment, a drastic reduction from the guidelines range of 135–168 months. The government appealed Sweet's decision, and in the fall of 2006, Robert A. Katzmann, a judge for the U.S. Court of Appeals for the Second Circuit, vacated Castillo's sentence and rebuked Sweet's interpretation of *Booker*. "Nothing in *Booker* specifically authorizes district judges to re-write different Guidelines with which they generally disagree," Katzmann wrote, "which is effectively what district judges do when they calculate a sentence with a 20:1 or 10:1 ratio instead of the 100:1 ratio in the sentencing table."

In February 2007 the debate about the guidelines once again reached the U.S. Supreme Court. In *United States v. Rita* a former Marine and veteran of the Vietnam and first Gulf wars, Victor A. Rita Jr., was convicted of giving false testimony to a grand jury and obstructing justice in an investigation of illegal gun trafficking. Rita was convicted on five of the counts against him, and under the sentencing guidelines, he was sentenced to thirty-three months in prison. When Rita appealed, the Fourth Circuit Court upheld his sentence, as it was within the range of the guidelines. But in a brief with the U.S. Supreme Court, Rita's attorney, Thomas N. Cochran, argued that the "reasonableness" presumption adopted by the Fourth Circuit (and applied in Rita's case) "simply resurrects the system rejected in *Booker*." In another case heard by the Supreme Court earlier this spring, *Claiborne v. United States*, a twenty-year-old Missouri man named Mario Claiborne pled guilty to possession with intent to distribute five grams or more of crack cocaine. Though Claiborne faced thirty-seven to forty-six months in prison under the sentencing guidelines, the U.S. district judge imposed a sentence of only fifteen months, telling Claiborne that the higher guideline sentence "would be tantamount to throwing you away." The government appealed, and an Eighth Circuit appeals judge ruled that a lower sentence could only be justified by "extraordinary" circumstances, which he believed were not present in Claiborne's case. Claiborne's attorney appealed to the U.S. Supreme Court, and in a writ of certiorari filed with the court by the New York Council of Defense Lawyers it was noted that appeals courts "have reversed nearly all of the below-guidelines sentences appealed by the government." (Claiborne's case was dismissed in June after he was shot to death in St. Louis.) So the *Claiborne* and *Rita* cases—in which the guidelines are reaffirmed as reasonable and appeals courts reverse sentences when a judge finds that a lower sentence is reasonable—signify the lack of "maneuvering room" with the sentencing guidelines promised by *Booker*.

Sentencing reform must be undertaken by Congress. Both appeals court judges and U.S. Supreme Court justices alike have said as much. In the *Castillo* case, Judge Katzmann said that the merits of the disparity between crack and powder cocaine–related sentences should be decided by the legislative branch. And, as Justice Stephen Breyer wrote in *Booker*, "the ball now lies in Congress's court."

■ ■ ■

The legislative branch is exactly where the debate about the 100:1 disparity between crack and powder cocaine sentences— and the sentencing guidelines themselves—has returned. When I met with Senator Sessions in the fall of 2006, he was just beginning the legislative push for his Drug Sentencing Reform Act of 2006. Though his previous efforts at sentencing reform have failed, Sessions was optimistic about the bill's chances because it is backed by law-and-order Republican legislators. "Surely they won't think *we* are soft on drugs," Sessions says of himself and the bill's cosponsors. "I think we can get some momentum on this. I think that I've come up with a bill that everybody can support, even the Department of Justice."

Yet that same week, the USSC held hearings in Washington about the disparity between sentences for crack and powder cocaine offenses in which the Justice Department simply reiterated their hard-line stance on the guidelines. "We . . . believe the current federal cocaine sentencing policy is properly calibrated," U.S. Attorney R. Alexander Acosta said during the hearings, "and advances the law enforcement response to crack cocaine in a fair and just manner. We continue to believe higher penalties for crack cocaine offenses appropriately reflect the greater harm posed by crack cocaine." Acosta also defended the sentencing guidelines on the grounds that they are a critical tool in inducing defendants to enter into cooperation agreements. "Simply put, if these drug defendants are not facing significant prison time," Acosta said, "they will simply not cooperate in the investigation." It's not surprising that while Sessions disagrees with Acosta on the issue of sentences for crack, he, like the DOJ, recognizes the importance of the sentencing guidelines in bringing about cooperation among defendants.

"Twenty years ago defendants were expected by their criminal associates to take their medicine and keep their mouths shut," Sessions says. "Now sentences are so strong they all know that when they get caught they're gonna talk, their buddies are gonna talk—*everyone* is gonna talk. There is no more honor among thieves. And that is progress for law enforcement."

There's no doubt that the sentencing guidelines have, in criminal defense attorney Gerald Shargel's apt description, created a "cottage industry of cooperators," which in turn has made it much easier for law enforcement to make drug cases. But justice—and the public good—is not served by the hammering of defendants into cooperators through the harsh sentencing guidelines. Coercive prosecutions made possible by the sentencing guidelines—and specifically section 5K1.1—merely reinforce an unjust system rather than serving justice. That the sentencing guidelines disproportionately affect low-level drug dealers has already been well-established by the USSC and drug policy analysts. It is also true that the harsh sentencing guidelines for drug-related offenses have done little to affect the price or availability of drugs. "Because crack is no longer a big news story, people mistakenly believe our anti-cocaine policy has worked," Eric Sterling wrote in a November 2006 *Los Angeles Times* op-ed the week the USSC held hearings on the disparity between crack and powder cocaine sentences. "Not so. There is no scarcity of cocaine. Since 1986, the price of cocaine has fallen and the quality is better. Cocaine deaths have increased. The number of crack users is basically unchanged." In the op-ed, Sterling suggested raising the quantity triggers for all drugs (not just cocaine), which would effectively target high-level traffickers and require the U.S. attorney general to approve the prosecution of cases involving less than fifty kilos of cocaine. Sterling also pointed to Sessions's Drug Sentencing Reform Act of 2006 as a "good sign that a political fix [to the sentencing guidelines] is viable."

The passage of Sessions's bill would be a long overdue start in reforming the sentencing guidelines. But as Sessions admitted to me, his bill—if successful—should merely be the first step in a massive overhaul of the sentencing guidelines that have created a skyrocketing federal prison population, an increasing percentage of whom are serving decades or even life behind bars. When U.S. District Judge Reggie B. Walton testified at the USSC's hearings in November 2006, he noted the "tremendous increase in the number of inmates in federal prisons" as well as a prison population comprised of "poor people of color (namely young black and Latino males) charged or convicted for committing crack cocaine distribution related offenses." The burden of this ever-expanding prison system falls heavily on taxpayers: federal expenditures for corrections stood at more than $60 billion per year in 2004, a staggering 585 percent increase from 1982, according to Bureau of Justice Statistics. In the not too distant future, the rapidly aging prison population—about one of every twenty-three inmates in prison today is age fifty-five or older, an 85 percent increase since 1995—will only become more expensive to care for. "There are quite a few people serving life for drug offenses," Sessions admits, "so I think Congress needs to study sentencing a lot more. Is the public good served by,.say, having someone serve twenty-two years in prison instead of fifteen? That's seven years we're paying for. A case can be made that a number of people are serving longer prison terms than they should. I also think we need to get out of this mentality that when a problem shows up we just run out and increase the guidelines. We tend to raise them when what we need to do is come back and examine them."

It is also critical that the USSC reexamine section 5K1.1 of the guidelines. Oversight and accountability are close to nonexistent under the 5K provision: prosecutors have near-total discretion about the kind of 5K motions they make, and downward departures from the sentencing guidelines granted by judges vary widely from district to district. Worse, there are usually no legal consequences for cooperators who lie to a grand jury or commit perjury on the witness stand. "Time and time again cooperators are caught lying," criminal defense attorney Joseph Tacopina told me, "and I've never once seen a 5K agreement ripped up by a prosecutor. It's unbelievable how forgiving the government is when it comes to *their* people." In addition, "the line-'em-up-and-indict-

'em" style of federal prosecutions yields guilty verdicts even when cooperators clearly do not tell the truth on the witness stand. "It's a quantitative effect," Tacopina explains. "The jury thinks, 'How could seven of them be lying?'"

Ultimately, however, a revision of section 5K1.1 can only be effective in restoring faith in the federal criminal justice system if it's accompanied by the sentencing guideline reform proposed by Senator Sessions along with a much stronger effort by the Justice Department to enforce guidelines governing the use of informants as well as the establishment of serious legal penalties for untruthful cooperators.

Some criminal justice experts—like Loyola University's Alexandra Natapoff—believe that section 5K1.1 is so fundamentally flawed that it needs to be eliminated altogether. It's a compelling argument, particularly when one considers the injustices that have flourished under the cooperator institution, from 5K beneficiaries like Ricky Javon Gray to unjust cases such as Euka Wadlington's. There is perhaps no stronger example of the perils of 5K agreements than the case of Harlem hit man–turned-cooperator Emanuel Mosley. When drug kingpin Kenneth "Supreme" McGriff went to trial in January 2007 on numerous counts of drug conspiracy and murder, Mosley (nicknamed "Dog") cooperated in the case after being charged with committing a series of murders-for-hire for McGriff in 2001. Incredibly, Mosley's involvement in these killings came *after* he received a 5K motion in a separate drug conspiracy case in Pennsylvania in the 1990s.

Mosley's cooperation deal with the U.S. attorney for the Middle District of Pennsylvania—in which he had a number of drug conspiracy charges against him dismissed and had his sentence reduced from twenty years to a mere eighty-five months as a result—allowed him to return to New York City's streets and commit the execution-style murders of aspiring rapper Eric "E Money

Bags" Smith and Southeast Queens hustler Troy Singleton. The killings of Smith and Singleton were particularly brutal; Smith was cut down in a hail of gunfire from assassins—ten bullets in all struck him—as he sat in his Lincoln Navigator near his Queens Village home; Singleton was shot just after he stepped outside a sports bar on Liberty Avenue in Jamaica, Queens. But when Mosley was indicted by the feds in the spring of 2006 on charges related to the Smith and Singleton murders, he entered into yet another cooperation agreement with prosecutors, this time in the McGriff case. Soon after Mosley signed his cooperation deal, federal prosecutors withdrew their "death notice"—a letter of intent to seek the death penalty—against Mosley while McGriff still faced the death penalty. That a defendant who allegedly committed murders *after* being the beneficiary of a 5K motion would be permitted yet another cooperation agreement is astonishing.

"He plays the 5K game," McGriff attorney David Ruhnke said of Mosley during his summation in McGriff's trial, "and he learned something really important. If you cooperate with the government, they take care of you in return. Instead of a 620-month mandatory minimum to life sentence, he got 85 months. That's seven years and one month, and he was back on the streets of New York, dealing drugs from the time he hit the bricks. Right back at it. And he's back again looking for the 5K. He faced the death penalty at one point. At one point our government believed that the only way fairness and justice could be served was to execute Emanuel Mosley. And then never mind: they took the death penalty off the table. And now fairness and justice have been redefined. It's now okay to eventually put Emanuel Mosley back on the streets. And he will be back on the streets. Mosley is a graduate of 5KU: 5K University. "

■ ■ ■

"Everything Secret Degenerates" was the title of a 2004 report by the House Committee on Government Reform on the FBI's use of murderers as informants. The study focused on the more egregious examples of the FBI's mishandling of informants (such as James "Whitey" Bulger), but the title resonates in our cooperator-centric federal criminal justice system in which just about everything is kept secret, from the number of cooperators to the identity of the cooperator to the 5K deals themselves. "In 5K agreements very little information about informant activities becomes public," wrote law professor Alexandra Natapoff in her study "Snitching: The Institutional and Communal Consequences." "Salient details of the cooperation may or may not be provided to the court; if they are, such proceedings are routinely sealed. The full extent of an informant's activities is almost never shared: the respective parties provide the court merely with enough information to support their respective sentencing recommendations. The limits on information-sharing flow from the circumscribed purpose of the proceeding: the 5K provision is not designed to permit the court to evaluate the use of the informant per se, but only to determine the extent to which that informant should benefit from his cooperation." As Natapoff notes, 5K motions are models of transparency compared to off-the-record cooperation deals that are often made at the moment of arrest. "The scope and methodology of those negotiations . . . depend on the idiosyncrasies of the particular officer," Natapoff writes, "making the process remarkable for its lack of rules or uniformity. As one prosecutor described it, 'the black hole of corroboration is the time that cooperators and agents spend alone.'"

The discretion prosecutors have in making cooperation deals and the stiff sentencing guidelines might help federal prosecutors make cases, but ultimately do not serve justice and the public good. Though Sessions and I disagree about the merits of section

5K1.1, he nonetheless expresses interest in exploring an overhaul of the sentencing guidelines that goes far beyond the disparity between crack cocaine and powder cocaine sentences. "This will be the first time we have analyzed the drug problem and re-trenched," Sessions declares. "And it doesn't mean we can't come back [and address the sentencing guidelines] again. A case can be made that a number of people are serving longer than they should, longer than's in the public interest."

Unfortunately, there's a near-total lack of bipartisan support for Sessions's Drug Sentencing Reform Act of 2006: its cosponsors are Republicans, and previous efforts at sentencing reform have also been led by the party. It's a worrisome political reality that has in the past caused similar bills to languish in subcommittee. "Let me tell you something," Sessions says angrily. "I have not been happy with the Democrats. I've been stuck out here for four or five years. I can't get any of them to sign on to any of these bills." Sessions suspects that Democrats shy away from sentencing reform because they fear being perceived as soft on crime. He's probably correct: since the Willie Horton days, Democrats have seemed unable to portray themselves as tough (and credible) on criminal justice is-sues. When President Clinton and the Democratic-majority Con-gress pushed the Violent Crime Control and Law Enforcement Act of 1994 just before the midterm elections that year, they were still hammered by conservative talk radio hosts for larding the bill with typically "liberal" programs like midnight basketball leagues. Of course, the legislation *was* an uncomfortable mix of punitive policies (such as a federal three strikes provision) and set-asides for social programs, but it was still very much in the law-and-order mold of the omnibus crime bills of the late 1980s. It's also worth noting that the first President Bush supported midnight basketball leagues as part of his "1,000 Points of Light" program. Even today, Democratic involvement in the passage of the omnibus crime bills—beginning with Senator Edward Kennedy crafting the Sentencing Reform Act—goes unnoticed by political pundits. Just after the midterm election in 2006, former *Washington Post* senior political reporter Thomas Edsall wrote an op-ed in the *New York Times* in which he pointed to the Violent Crime Control and Law Enforcement Act of 1994 as a prime example of what can happen "when Democrats bend to the will of liberal interest groups, even in pursuit of laudable goals." The bill was so "liberal," according to Edsall, that it led to the Republican revolution of 1994. No matter that it was a punitive piece of legislation in the mold of its predecessors, the Anti-Drug Abuse Acts of 1986 and 1988 (both of which were backed by top Democratic legislators like Joe Biden). Edsall also neglected to mention that the provisions of the omnibus bills are currently being criticized by the reddest of red-state Republicans as overly harsh and ultimately unjust.

Though Democrats have long faced framing from political pundits and Republican politicians alike that makes them appear to be "soft" on crime regardless of what kind of specific policies they pursue, it is crucial that they join Republicans like Sessions and Hatch in their sentencing reform efforts. Sessions is right to frame his critiques of the sentencing guidelines in politically appealing language: they target low-level drug dealers while creating a prison system that is profoundly expensive to taxpayers. Democrats might even take a page from the late Republican strategist and Willie Horton maestro Lee Atwater and turn Ricky Javon Gray into a national symbol of failed sentencing policies and the 5K institution. Such a move may seem morally suspect, but it is true that, unlike Willie Horton (who was falsely portrayed as a symbol of a "revolving door" prison system), Gray is typical of a cooperator-coddling justice system that sets sociopaths free to commit some of the most gruesome murders imaginable.

EPILOGUE

Case Closed? Are *Stop Snitching* and Witness Intimidation Leading to Low Clearance Rates and a Return to the "Bad Old Days" of the 1980s?

IN THE HALLS OF BALTIMORE'S CLARENCE MITCHELL COURTHOUSE, WITNESSES testifying in murder cases often come face-to-face with defendants who greet them with throat-slitting motions as they make their way to the courtroom. Such bold acts of intimidation even occur when a witness is being escorted through the building by a Baltimore cop assigned to guard them as part of the city's Witness Assistance Program. "We have deputies escorting witnesses to appointments," Baltimore prosecutor Patricia Jessamy told me, "and we can offer witnesses twenty-four-hour protection on a short-term basis, but often even that is not enough to protect them." Jessamy says that witness intimidation has become such a huge problem in Baltimore that about 30 percent of homicide cases investigated by the city's F.I.V.E. Unit (Firearms Investigation Violence Enforcement) cannot proceed because of intimidation of—or noncooperation by—witnesses.

I was reminded of Jessamy's comments about the Baltimore City police's difficulty with closing cases when the FBI released its crime statistics for January through June 2006. The numbers suggest that after the declines of the 1990s, crime might be making a comeback, particularly in midsize cities such as Baltimore. The FBI reported that in the first half of 2006:

- The volume of reported robbery offenses was up in all of the nation's city population groupings when compared to the 2005 reported data. The largest increase, 12.8 percent, occurred in cities with populations of 10,000 to 24,999.
- Reported robbery offenses also increased in the nation's metropolitan counties, up 8.4 percent.
- In the metropolitan counties, reported murder offenses were up 3.1 percent.
- Cities with populations of 500,000 to 999,999 had the most marked increase in reported murder offenses, up 8.4 percent.

Though criminologists cannot say for certain if the spike in 2006 portends a return to the "bad old days" of the crack-era 1980s—criminologist Franklin Zimring is on record saying, "Our leading indicators stink"—2007 was nonetheless ushered in with spectacular violence in cities like New Orleans and Baltimore. In February alone, seventeen people were murdered in Baltimore. During a two-week period from late December to early January, ten people were slain in New Orleans, including Dinerral Shavers, a member of the city's legendary Hot 8 Brass Band, who was featured in Spike Lee's Katrina documentary, *When the Levees Broke*. New Orleans has now eclipsed Compton as the murder capital of the United States, according to University of New Orleans criminologist Peter Scharf. "Now matter how you parse it, we are murder city," Scharf told the *Times-Picayune*. "But forget it, let's move on.

The second issue is that we have an ascending murder rate. It's going up. That's more worrisome."

Unfortunately, New Orleans and Baltimore have a lot more in common than just high murder rates: police departments in both cities have enormous difficulty closing cases. A study released by the *Baltimore Examiner* in March found that of the city's forty-five homicides from January through March 2, just nine had been solved. (Though clearance rates have fallen in major cities since the 1950s, New York's clearance rate for homicides is still well above 50 percent). Though it is unreasonable to expect Baltimore City police to have solved homicides that occurred so early in the year, a department spokesperson admitted that they lagged behind other major cities in closing cases. "Obviously, we'd like the clearance rate to be higher than it is right now," Baltimore City police spokesman Matt Jablow said in March 2007. "But we're confident that it will increase to our normal 60 to 65 percent clearance rate, which is normally at or near the national average."

Similarly, in March 2007 New Orleans District Attorney Eddie Jordan admitted that in January alone, 580 suspects were released from the city's jails under Article 701 of the Louisiana Code of Criminal Procedure, which allows for the automatic release of suspects if the DA's office fails to file charges within sixty days (in comparison, Jordan said that in January 2005, 187 suspects were released under Article 701 during the eight-month period in 2005 pre-Katrina. Incredibly, there were approximately 3,000 Article 701 releases during all of 2006). Though the lack of closure in cases in New Orleans can be attributed to post-Katrina disarray in the city's police department and in the district attorney's office, Jordan admitted that "these problems go back long before the chief and I; we knew some of the problems we have on a day-to-day basis really plagued the Police Department and district attorney relationship for many years." Indeed, criminologist Scharf told me that the NOPD has long failed to adequately perform case processing. "A few years ago, a police report about a quadruple homicide was a total of three pages," Scharf says.

Certainly, an unwillingness on the part of witnesses to come forward and offer information to cops plays a significant role in the low clearance rates in cities like New Orleans and Baltimore. Law enforcement points to declining clearance rates in midsize cities—45 percent in the 1990s to just below 35 percent in 2005 according to FBI statistics—as proof that witness intimidation is a growing menace that's having a profound effect on the ability of cops and prosecutors to close cases. In New Orleans, fear of reprisals from criminals runs so deep that in the spring of 2007 NOPD Chief Warren Riley suggested that residents fearful of dialing 911 should instead call the department's nonemergency number so that cops can take information over the phone (with 911, cops are compelled to visit the caller, even if he or she requests otherwise, resulting in witnesses being exposed). The vulnerability of witnesses in Baltimore and New Orleans can also be attributed to a lack of law enforcement resources. While Baltimore can set up a witness assistance program, it lacks the funds to create anything remotely resembling the federal Witness Protection Program in which witnesses are relocated and often given new identities; nor do state and local law enforcement have blunt tools like the federal sentencing guidelines that can easily hammer defendants into cooperators.

Yet it would be dishonest to blame the city's low clearance rates on witness intimidation alone; dysfunctional police departments and district attorney's offices are also key factors. In New Orleans, former mayoral candidate Leo Watermeier told me that he witnessed a savage beating in the French Quarter and not only reported the incident to the cops but also helped officers track the attacker down after he fled on foot. It was an ideal arrest: the NOPD captured the suspect just minutes after the beating, and, more importantly, the New Orleans district attorney's office had a willing (and highly credible) witness in the onetime candidate for mayor. But a little more than one month later, the attacker was back on the streets. "The DA's office rejected the case," Watermeier told me, "so the judge released him for time served. After that happened, I sent an e-mail to all of my friends saying, 'You can assault somebody viciously in the French Quarter and be out on the streets thirty-four days later.'"

Unfortunately, a freed French Quarter mugger was far from the most dramatic illustration of the problems the New Orleans District Attorney's Office has in handling witnesses. In late June 2007, DA Eddie Jordan dropped all charges against David Bonds, the alleged killer of Hot 8 Brass Band drummer Dinerral Shavers, because the sole witness in the case refused to testify. But in a July 8 op-ed in the *Times-Picayune*, Ken Foster, a founder of the New Orleans–based anticrime group Silence Is Violence who worked closely with Shavers's sister Nakita in pursuing the case, wrote that the DA's office had bungled several key aspects of the murder investigation. Foster wrote:

A ballistics test on the gun—found beneath a nearby house two days later—showed it was definitely the gun used to kill Dinerral, but there were no fingerprints on it or any other way to link the gun to the suspect. No one else at the scene was being called as a witness, for reasons that are unclear. While there were some key players who offered Nakita support—New Orleans Police Chief Warren Riley and Councilman James Carter, to name two—the overall sense was one of chaos. Other players in the case gave contradictory information, including reports that there were, in fact, no ballistics back on the gun. In the end, it seemed as if the prosecution was working with less than it had started with, so it was easy to understand why the young witness might feel reluctant to put herself and her family on the line.

In late July, Jordan dropped charges in yet *another* major murder case—the slaying of five Central City teenagers in June 2006—because, he claimed, his office could not locate the witness. Yet just one day later the NOPD produced the witness, prompting a protest march in iconic Jackson Square and calls for Jordan's resignation. Jordan resisted the demands for his removal, proclaiming during a July city council meeting, "You are scapegoating me. You are making me solely responsible for all the ills of the criminal justice system for the past 30, 40, 50 years—who knows how long." In August, the outcry prompted Jordan to re-indict the suspects in the Shavers case and the quintuple murder case.

In Detroit, a city that like New Orleans has had historically low clearance rates for violent crime, the police department long had a practice of detaining witnesses in homicide cases and holding them for questioning for days without filing criminal charges or obtaining a court order. In 1999, the Detroit Police Department reported 1,152 arrests in 415 murder cases, while that same year, New York had 748 arrests in 664 cases. (The practice was ended after witnesses filed countless lawsuits claiming false arrest.) The Detroit PD's "dragnet" approach to witnesses, though, did little to change the city's low clearance rate for violent crime and in fact may have provided a huge disincentive for witnesses to come forward in the first place.

When cops aren't simply tossing witnesses in jail, they're mishandling them. In an extraordinary March 18, 2007, column in the *Times-Picayune* called "Can I Get a Witness?" several members of the NOPD told journalist Jarvis DeBerry that the department often grossly mishandled potential witnesses, therefore putting them in peril. "I've heard the complaint from other law enforcement officers that New Orleans police seem incapable of interviewing their witnesses without creating a sideshow," De-Berry wrote. "Whereas the FBI might send a cab to an old lady's house and make sure she returns home carrying a bag of groceries, New Orleans police—or so went the allegation—make conspicuous visits that discourage future witnesses of crime from getting involved." Witnesses in New Orleans murder cases are rarely prepped by prosecutors and police. New Orleans District Attorney Jordan even admitted that preparation of witnesses sometimes "takes place the morning of trial."

The bungling of witnesses and the poor performance of DA's offices makes the enormous hue and cry over *Stop Snitching*, which reached a feverish pitch with the spring 2007 *60 Minutes* report, seem like little more than a distraction from law enforcement failures. After all, if witnesses are to be comfortable coming forward with information, they need to feel protected and, perhaps more importantly, believe their testimony will result in a conviction. In New Orleans, Detroit, and Baltimore, witnesses are aware that neither is the case. Indeed, in New Orleans prosecutors successfully prosecuted just one of the 162 homicides committed in 2006.

The crime surge in small to midsize cities from New Orleans to Baltimore also casts the explanations of the crime declines of the 1990s in a new, very different light. Supporters of harsh sentencing guidelines have long argued that putting more people in prison for longer periods of time was a major factor in driving down crime during the 1990s. But now that we're experiencing high incarceration rates accompanied by steadily *increasing* crime, that theory seems increasingly dubious. In criminologist Franklin Zimring's recent book *The Great American Crime Decline*, he found that during the 1990s crime in Canada dropped by about 30 percent in most categories, while the prison population *decreased*—a stark contrast to the "lock 'em up" policies in the United States. In addition, a recent report by the Police Executive Research Forum called *A Gathering Storm—Violent Crime in America* acknowledged that economic factors may be playing a significant role in the recent crime increases, a turnabout from the 1990s, when the economic expansion of the Clinton years was not identified as having a significant role in the decade's declining crime rates. In a chapter called "Cities Within Cities," the *Gathering Storm* authors argue that sections of cities like Boston and Savannah with high poverty rates are responsible for much of the crime increases: "In Boston, where shootings are increasing, Dr. Anthony Braga of the Kennedy School of Government at Harvard University reported that 10 locations equaling one percent of the city was generating 33 percent of crimes involving a firearm. He described these locations as being 'disadvantaged with high unemployment rates and numerous single-headed households whose problems are entrenched.'"

While the idea that bad neighborhoods breed high crime rates is certainly nothing new, skyrocketing income inequality in America is a very recent phenomenon. In an August 2006 *New York Times* column, economist Paul Krugman dubbed the period stretching from 1980 to the present day "The New Gilded Age," which is characterized by "big [income] gains at the very top, stagnation below." Krugman continues, "Between 1980 and 2004, real wages in manufacturing fell 1 percent, while the real income of the richest 1 percent—people with incomes of more than $277,000 in 2004—rose 135 percent." Tellingly, as crime spiked in 2005, so too did income inequality. That year, the top 1 percent of Americans—those with incomes of more than $348,000—received their largest share of national income since 1928. The share of national income by the top 1 percent in 2005 was up significantly—an astonishing 19.8 percent—from even the previous year. So it's no surprise that in the New Gilded Age America's "cities within cities" have grown poorer and much, much more dangerous. With crime and income inequality rising, American cities may soon resemble Sao Paulo, Brazil, which investigative reporter William Langewiesche memorably described as a city of "little fortresses for the wealthy" ringed by pockets of poverty.

The resurgence in crime—2005 saw the largest single-year percent increase in violent crime in fourteen years according to the *Gathering Storm* authors—comes at a particularly dangerous time: law enforcement resources are dwindling in cities like Minneapolis, Boston, and Detroit; income inequality is rising still; the more than twenty years of harsh, inequitable federal sentencing policy have eroded trust in law enforcement among minorities; and not only has the availability of drugs remained fairly steady, but their price has declined significantly as well. It's a sprawling problem, but the solution may begin simply: refocus drug enforcement on drug dealers who engage in truly harmful behavior instead of those caught selling a specific amount of a drug. "All drug dealers supply drugs," wrote UCLA public policy professor Mark Kleiman in the January–February 2007 issue of the *American Interest*. "Only some use violence, or operate flagrantly, or employ juveniles as apprentice dealers. The current system of enforcement, which bases targeting and sentencing primarily on drug volume, should be replaced with a system focused on conduct. If we target and severely sentence the nastiest dealers rather than the biggest ones, we can greatly reduce the amount of gunfire, the damage drug dealing does to the neighborhoods around it, and the attractive nuisance the drug trade offers to teenagers."

Targeting dangerous dealers will replace a system that excessively punishes defendants caught with insignificant amounts of drugs, while also putting an end to the cottage industry of cooperators, many of whom simply provide information about fellow retail-level dealers in exchange for lighter sentences. Finally, cooperators themselves need to be given much greater scrutiny: limits should be placed on the number of times an individual can receive a 5K motion (thereby eliminating the phenomenon of savvy 5K game players, who return to the streets after cooperating to commit even more crime); assertions made by cooperators must be corroborated by prosecutors with evidence (which would end the practice of building indictments solely with cooperator testimony); and cooperators who give false statements to a grand jury or commit perjury on the witness stand should have their deals torn up or even face indictment.

Such reforms would restore faith in the criminal justice system and by extension would help encourage witnesses to come forward with information to prosecutors: in inner-city neighborhoods, much of the stigma of "snitching" is derived from a sense that cooperators are helping to perpetuate an unjust criminal justice system. As David Kennedy, the director of the Center for Crime Prevention and Crime Control at the John Jay College of Criminal Justice told the *Atlantic Monthly* in April 2007, "this [mistrust of law enforcement] is the reward we have reaped for 20 years of profligate drug enforcement in these communities." If we do not act soon to bolster state and local law enforcement resources and redirect drug enforcement toward truly bad actors on the streets, we can expect a frightening future in which handwringing over *Stop Snitching* will seem quaint.

ENDNOTES

PROLOGUE: SAYS WHO? COOPERATORS AND INFORMANTS REPLACE INVESTIGATIVE WORK

1   *"Says who?"*: Transcript of jury trial before the Honorable Edward R. Korman, United States Chief District Judge, *United States v. Lorenzo et al*, CR–00966.

3   *One federal agent*: Affidavit in Support of Seizure Warrant, *Lorenzo*.

3   *Rather than*: Memorandum in Support of the Pre-trial Motions of Defendants Irving Lorenzo, Christopher Lorenzo, MI Records Inc., and iG Records, Inc., *Lorenzo*.

3   *The Lorenzo case*: Jeff Leeds, "Hip-Hop Producer Surrenders in Money Laundering Case," *New York Times*, January 27, 2005. During the press conference NYPD Commissioner Raymond Kelly, joined by agents from the IRS and ATF (Bureau of Alcohol, Tobacco and Firearms), proclaimed, "If you're going to be involved in money laundering, drug dealing or murder, we're going to be coming after you."

4   *the most untrustworthy*: Transcript of jury trial, *Lorenzo*.

4   *I have general ideas*: Transcript of jury trial, *Lorenzo*.

5   *If telling a lie*: Transcript of jury trial, *Lorenzo*.

6   *A handwritten note*: Transcript of jury trial, *Lorenzo*.

7   *I was a wreck*: Interview with Gerald Lefcourt, December 2005.

7   *It was a very weak case*: John Marzulli, "'Gottis' Beat Rap: Irv and Chris Not Guilty in Money Laundering Case," *New York Daily News*, December 3, 2005.

INTRODUCTION: SECTION 5K1.1 AND THE
RISE OF THE COOPERATOR INSTITUTION

9   *On April 19, 2007*: "Stop Snitchin': Rapper Cam'ron: Snitching Hurts His Business, 'Code of Ethics,'" *60 Minutes*, April 19, 2007.

9   *Soon after the segment*: Glenn Beck, "Al Sharpton Speaks Out Against Rap Artist Cam'ron," CNN, April 23, 2007, http://transcripts.cnn .com/TRANSCRIPTS/0704/23/gb.01.html.

9   *The Cam'ron controversy also felt*: David S. Bernstein, "It's Gotta Be the Shirts: Menino's Attempt to Win the Confidence of Kids in the 'Hood Will Have the Opposite Effect," *Boston Phoenix*, December 9–15, 2005, http://bostonphoenix.com/boston/news_features/top/ features/documents/05133928.asp.

10   *In June 2006*: Kris Ex, "Busta: On Music, Murder and Defying the Law," *XXL*, June 2006; Cheo Coker, "Busta: The Untold Story," *Vibe*, June 2006.

10   *Everybody in law enforcement*: Rick Hampson, "Anti-Snitch Campaign Riles Police, Prosecutors; Is It a Grass-Roots Backlash Against Criminals Turned Informers or Intimidation?" *USA Today*, March 29, 2006.

10   *New York Times columnist*: Clyde Haberman, "Rappers, As a Rule, Do Not Sing," *New York Times*, February 24, 2006.

11   *Perhaps this was because*: Andrew Jacobs, "When Rappers Keep Their Mouths Shut Tight," *New York Times*, February 19, 2006.

11   *Because the anticrime bills established*: Anti-Drug Abuse Act of 1988, H.R. 5210: "An amendment to impose minimum mandatory criminal penalties for possession of the drug 'crack,' based on a sliding scale: A five year minimum sentence would be imposed for a first conviction of possession of at least five grams of the drug"; http://thomas .loc.gov/cgi-bin/bdquery/z?d100:HR05210:@@@L&summ2=m&.

11   *Cooperation is so crucial*: United States Sentencing Commission, §5K1.1. Substantial Assistance to Authorities (Policy Statement):

Upon motion of the government stating that the defendant has provided substantial assistance in the investigation or prosecution of another person who has committed an offense, the court may depart from the guidelines.

(a) The appropriate reduction shall be determined by the court for reasons stated that may include, but are not limited to, consideration of the following: (1) the court's evaluation of the significance and usefulness of the defendant's assistance, taking into consideration the government's evaluation of the assistance rendered; (2) the truthfulness, completeness, and reliability of any information or testimony provided by the defendant; (3) the nature and extent of the defendant's assistance; (4) any injury suffered, or any danger or risk of injury to the defendant or his family resulting from his assistance; (5) the timeliness of the defendant's assistance.

11   *The anticrime bills created a scenario*: Interview with Robert Simels, March 31, 2006.

12   *Defendants who are most in the know*: Stephen J. Schulhofer, "Rethinking Mandatory Minimums," *Wake Forest Law Review* 28 (1993): 199–222.

12   *The more culpable you are*: Interview with Simels, March 31, 2006.

12   *Indeed, the percentage of low-level*: The Sentencing Project, *The Federal Prison Population: A Statistical Analysis*, January 2006, http://www .sentencingproject.org/pdfs/federalprison.pdf.

12   *Nearly 127,000 people*: Marc Mauer, Ryan S. King, and Malcolm C. Young, *The Meaning of "Life": Long Prison Sentences in Context*, The Sentencing Project, May 2004.

12   *If I can keep my clients*: Interview with Andrew White, May 2006.

13   *By contrast, the anticrime bills*: United States Code, Title 18, §3553:

   Except as provided in paragraph (2), the court shall impose a sentence of the kind, and within the range, referred to in subsection (a)(4) unless the court finds that there exists an aggravating or mitigating circumstance of a kind, or to a degree, not adequately taken into consideration by the Sentencing Commission in formulating the guidelines that should result in a sentence different from that described. In determining whether a circumstance was adequately taken into consideration, the court shall consider only the sentencing guidelines, policy statements, and official commentary of the Sentencing Commission.

13   *In the pre-guidelines era*: Interview with Martin Stolar, December 2006.

13   *Mandatory minimum sentences are not justifiable*: Jonathan P. Caulkins, C. Peter Rydell, William L. Schwabe, and James Chiesa, *Mandatory Minimum Drug Sentences: Throwing Away the Key or Taxpayers' Money?* The Rand Corporation, 1997.

13   *Over the past thirty years*: Interview with Gerald Lefcourt, December 2005.

14   *Similarly, Andrew White characterizes*: Interview with White, May 2006.

14   *One of the most powerful tools*: Federal Rules of Evidence, Rule 404(b): Character Evidence Not Admissible To Prove Conduct; Exceptions; Other Crimes:

   (a) Character evidence generally

   Evidence of a person's character or a trait of character is not admissible for the purpose of proving action in conformity therewith on a particular occasion, except:

(1) Character of accused—Evidence of a pertinent trait of character offered by an accused, or by the prosecution to rebut the same, or if evidence of a trait of character of the alleged victim of the crime is offered by an accused and admitted under Rule 404 (a)(2), evidence of the same trait of character of the accused offered by the prosecution;

(2) Character of alleged victim—Evidence of a pertinent trait of character of the alleged victim of the crime offered by an accused, or by the prosecution to rebut the same, or evidence of a character trait of peacefulness of the alleged victim offered by the prosecution in a homicide case to rebut evidence that the alleged victim was the first aggressor;

(3) Character of witness—Evidence of the character of a witness, as provided in rules 607, 608, and 609.

(b) Other crimes, wrongs, or acts

Evidence of other crimes, wrongs, or acts is not admissible to prove the character of a person in order to show action in conformity therewith. It may, however, be admissible for other purposes, such as proof of motive, opportunity, intent, preparation, plan, knowledge, identity, or absence of mistake or accident, provided that upon request by the accused, the prosecution in a criminal case shall provide reasonable notice in advance of trial, or during trial if the court excuses pretrial notice on good cause shown, of the general nature of any such evidence it intends to introduce at trial.

14 *When I was a prosecutor*: Interview with White, May 2006.

15 *U.S. Supreme Court Justice Samuel Alito*: United States v. Murray, 103 F.3d 310, 316 (3d Cir. 1997). From Alito's opinion:

The admission of evidence that is allowed by Rule 404(b) is not disfavored, but trial judges need to exercise particular care in admitting such evidence. This is so for at least two reasons. First, the line between what is permitted and what is prohibited under Rule 404(b) is sometimes quite subtle. Second, Rule 404(b) evidence sometimes carries a substantial danger of unfair prejudice and thus raises serious questions under Federal Rules of Evidence 403. Therefore, it is advisable for a trial judge to insist that a party offering Rule 404(b) evidence place on the record a clear explanation of the chain of inferences leading from the evidence in question to a fact "that is of consequence to the determination of the action."

15 *Generally 404 notice*: Interview with Simels, March 31, 2006.

15 *One result of punitive*: Northwestern Law School Center on Wrongful Convictions: http://www.law.northwestern.edu/depts/clinic/wrongful/mission.htm

15 *As of year-end 2005*: James Vicini, "U.S. Has the Most Prisoners in the World," Reuters, December 9, 2006.

16   *Moreover, black and Hispanic men*: Eric Eckholm, "Plight Deepens for Black Men, Studies Warn," *New York Times*, March 20, 2006.

16   *A June 2006 Washington Post poll*: Steven A. Holmes and Richard Morin, "Black Men Torn Between Promise and Doubt," *Washington Post*, June 4, 2006.

16   *Indeed, U.S. District Judge Robert W. Sweet*: "Drug Wars," PBS *Front-line*, October 4, 2000; http://www.pbs.org/wgbh/pages/frontline/shows/drugs/symposium/panel2.html.

16   *Sweet's characterization*: Paige M. Harrison and Allen J. Beck, PhD, *Bureau of Justice Statistics Bulletin: Prison and Jail Inmates at Midyear 2005*: "An estimated 12% of black males, 3.7% of Hispanic males, and 1.7% of white males in their late twenties were in prison or jail"; http://www.ojp.usdoj.gov/bjs/pub/pdf/pjim05.pdf.

17   *My focus here*: Harrison and Beck, *Bureau of Justice Statistics Bulletin*.

17   *Findings from the*: Bureau of Justice Statistics, "Prison Statistics: Summary Findings," http://www.ojp.usdoj.gov/bjs/prisons.htm.

CHAPTER 1. FEEDING THE FEDERAL BEAST: GIULIANI DAY, CONGRESS'S ANTICRIME BILLS, AND CANDY BAR JUSTICE

19   *Don't start crying*: United Press International, "Domestic News," January 9, 1984.

20   *The plan for the stepped-up drug enforcement*: Marcia Chambers, "Going Cold Turkey in Alphabetville," *New York Times*, February 19, 1984.

20   *I was shocked by what*: Chambers, "Going Cold Turkey in Alphabetville."

20   *After Ortiz's attorney made*: Associated Press, "Heroin Dealer, 18, Gets 6 Year Term," January 10, 1984.

20   *Unsurprisingly, in a city wracked*: Nichols W. Jenny, *New York State Statistical Briefs*, Rockefeller Institute of Government, July 2002.

21   *It was a disaster*: Interview with Robert Silbering, May 17, 2006.

21   *An examination of Federal Day*: William Glaberson, "Giuliani's Powerful Image Under Campaign Scrutiny," *New York Times*, July 11, 1989.

21   *The judges would say*: Interview with Silbering, May 17, 2006.

22   *The small percentage of defendants*: Andrew D. Leipold, "Why Are Federal Judges So Acquittal Prone?" *Washington University Law Quarterly* 83, no. 1 (spring 2005); http://law.wustl.edu/WULR/83–1/

23   *Since the mid-1990s*: Bureau of Justice Statistics, *Bureau of Justice Statistics Bulletin: Prison and Jail Inmates at Midyear 2005*.

23   *In 1978 Senator Edward Kennedy*: United States Sentencing Commission, "Introduction to the Sentencing Reform Act," http://www.ussc.gov/15_year/chap1.pdf.

23   *Efforts to revise criminal law*: Interview with Eric Sterling, May 31, 2006.

23   *This change in tack*: Lloyd D. Johnston, PhD, Patrick M. O'Malley, PhD, Jerald G. Bachman, PhD, and John E. Schulenberg, PhD (University of Michigan Institute for Social Research), *Monitoring the Future: National Results on Adolescent Drug Use: Overview of Key Findings 2005*.

24   *There were shoot-outs*: Interview with Sterling, May 31, 2006.

24   *One of the most notorious incidents*: Toni Locy, "For Jailed Kingpins, a Cocaine Kinship," *Washington Post*, August 19, 1996.

25   *We need one person*: Leslie Maitland, "U.S. Plans New Drive on Narcotics," *New York Times*, October 9, 1982.

25   *There was enormous consternation*: Interview with Sterling, May 31, 2006.

25   *During the spring of 1983*: United States Sentencing Commission, "Introduction to the Sentencing Reform Act."

25   *The role of the USSC*: United States Sentencing Commission, "Introduction to the Sentencing Reform Act."

25   *Indeed, the sentencing guidelines*: Erik Luna, *Misguided Guidelines: A Critique of Federal Sentencing*, Cato Institute, November 1, 2002.

26   *The sentencing guidelines took*: Interview with Eric P. Berlin, fall 2006.

26   *Judges were permitted to refuse bail*: United States Sentencing Commission, "Introduction to the Sentencing Reform Act."

26   *You can go back many years*: Leslie Maitland Werner, "Congress Moving on Major Changes in Criminal Law," *New York Times*, October 3, 1983.

26   *Sentencing is no longer for*: Eric P. Berlin, "The Federal Sentencing Guidelines' Failure to Eliminate Sentencing Disparity: Governmental Manipulations Before Arrest," *Wisconsin Law Review* (1993): 187–230.

27   *The sentencing guidelines replaced*: United States Sentencing Commission, "Introduction to the Sentencing Reform Act."

27   *But thanks to external pressures*: Congress Scan, "Senate Crime Bills Have Something for Everyone," *ABA Journal* (May 1984).

27   *The whole process*: Interview with Sterling, May 31, 2006.

27   *Berlin says that*: Interview with Berlin, fall 2006.

27   *On June 19, 1986*: Gary Reinmus, "Cocaine 'Trigger' in Bias Death," *Chicago Tribune*, June 25, 1986.

28   *During the summer of 1986*: Interview with Sterling, May 31, 2006.

28   *A former hustler who*: Ethan Brown, *Queens Reigns Supreme: Fat Cat, 50 Cent and the Rise of the Hip-Hop Hustler* (New York: Anchor, 2005).

28   *He's like a wounded lion*: Peter Blauner, "Fat Cat and the Crack Wars: Brash Young Dealers Muscle the Drug Establishment," *New York*, November 7, 1987.

28   *A 1985 study*: Katherine Greider, "Crackpot Ideas," *Mother Jones*, July/August 1995.

29   *Medical studies would later*: Gary A. Emmett, MD, "What Happened to Crack Babies?" *The Federation of American Scientists' Drug Policy Analysis Bulletin*, February 1998.

29   *Hysteria about the drug war*: Interview with Sterling, May 31, 2006.

29   *When Congress returned*: The Anti-Drug Abuse Act of 1986, HR 5484: "A bill to strengthen Federal efforts to encourage foreign cooperation in eradicating illicit drug crops and in halting international drug traffic, to improve enforcement of Federal drug laws and enhance interdiction of illicit drug shipments, to provide strong Federal leadership in establishing effective drug abuse prevention and education programs, to expand Federal support for drug abuse treatment and rehabilitation efforts, and for other purposes."

30   *Congress was totally illiterate*: Interview with Sterling, May 31, 2006.

30   *The bail denial*: Interview with Robert Simels, March 31, 2006.

30   *Indeed, immediately following*: John Scalia, *Federal Drug Offenders 1999, with Trends 1984–1999*, Bureau of Justice Statistics Special Report:

   U.S. district courts may impose a sentence above or below the sentencing range established by the Federal sentencing guidelines if the circumstances of a particular case were not adequately addressed by the guidelines. Judicial departures from the guidelines are nonetheless required to conform to applicable statutory minimums and maximums. *Upon the motion of the U.S. attorney, a district court may impose a sentence below the applicable guideline sentencing range and below the applicable statutory minimum if the defendant provided 'substantial assistance' to the Government in the investigation or prosecution of another* (U.S.S.G. §5K1.1 and 18 U.S.C. 3553(e)).

31   *We fought the Department*: Interview with Sterling, May 31, 2006.

31   *In the wake of Byrne's murder*: Interview with Sterling, May 31, 2006.

31   *If drug traffickers have become*: Monte R. Young and Anemona Hartocollis, "A Street Lined with Sorrow: 10,000 Cops Salute Rookie Slain Guarding Drug Witness," *Newsday*, March 1, 1988.

31   *George H. W. Bush hit the campaign trail*: "Candidate Ads: 1988 George Bush, Revolving Door," http://www.insidepolitics.org/ps111/candidateads.html. Inside Politics gives this description of the ad:

   (Dissonant sounds are heard: a drum . . . music . . . metal stairs.) "As governor, Michael Dukakis vetoed mandatory sentences for drug dealers." (A guard with a rifle climbs the circular stairs of a prison watchtower. The words "The Dukakis Furlough Program" are superimposed on the bottom of the prison visual.) "He vetoed the death penalty.'" (A guard with a gun walks along a barbed wire fence.) "His revolving door prison policy gave weekend furloughs to first-degree murderers not eligible for parole." (A revolving door formed by bars rotates as men in prison clothing walk in and back out the door in a long line. The words "268 Escaped" are superimposed.) "While out, many committed other crimes like kidnapping and rape." (The camera comes in for a closer shot of the prisoners in slow motion revolving through the door.) "And many are still at large." (The words "And Many Are Still At Large" are superimposed.) "Now Michael Dukakis says he wants to do for America what he's done for Massachusetts." (The picture changes to a guard on a roof with a watchtower in the background.) "America can't afford that risk!" (A small color picture of Bush appears, and the words "Paid for by Bush/Quayle '88" appear in small print.)

32   *If you look at the way*: Dick Kirschten, "How the 'Furlough Issue' Grew and Dominated the Campaign," *National Journal*, October 29, 1988.

32   *Along with creating*: The Anti-Drug Abuse Act of 1988 H.R. 5210: "A bill to prevent the manufacturing, distribution, and use of illegal drugs, and for other purposes."

32   *With us today*: President Ronald Reagan, "Remarks on Signing the Anti-Drug Abuse Act of 1988," November 18, 1988, Ronald Reagan Presidential Library, http://www.reagan.utexas.edu/archives/speeches/1988/111888c.htm.

33   *So, after spiking*: Jenny, *New York State Statistical Briefs*.

33   *From 1991 to 1998*: Marc Mauer and Jenni Gainsborough, *Diminishing Returns: Crime and Incarceration in the 1990s*, The Sentencing Project, September 2000. FBI Uniform Crime Reports can be found online at http://www.fbi.gov/ucr/ucr.htm.

33   *But while increasing incarceration rates*: Steven D. Levitt, "Understanding Why Crime Fell in the 1990s: Four Factors that Explain the Decline and Six that Do Not," *Journal of Economic Perspectives* 18, no. 1 (winter 2004).

34   *Younger brothers of the gang*: Interview with Mark A. R. Kleiman, June 12, 2006.

34   *So at the beginning of 1994*: The Violent Crime Control and Law Enforcement Act of 1994, H.R. 3355: "To amend the Omnibus Crime Control and Safe Streets Act of 1968 to allow grants to increase police presence, to expand and improve cooperative efforts between law enforcement agencies and members of the community to address crime and disorder problems, and otherwise to enhance public safety."

34   *Caught in the political crosswinds*: The Violent Crime Control and Law Enforcement Act of 1994.

35   *The proposed law*: Peter Beinart, "The Good Fight: Peter Beinart Responds," http://www.dailykos.com/story/2006/6/2/105025/7716.

35   *The legislation offered incentives*: Bureau of Justice Statistics, *Truth in Sentencing in State Prisons*, http://www.ojp.usdoj.gov/bjs/abstract/tssp.htm.

35   *These laws would quickly become*: Mary Zahn, "Inmates Less Motivated, Wardens Find; With No Way to Earn Time Off, Desperation Is More Common, They Say," *Wisconsin Journal Sentinel*, November 21, 2004.

35   *Wisconsin wardens also complained*: Zahn, "Inmates Less Motivated."

35   *How did such*: Anthony Lewis, "Abroad at Home: Crime and Politics," *New York Times*, September 16, 1994.

35   *But while the bill*: Steve Chapman, "Invisible COPS," *Slate*, November 12, 2001.

36   *But did the more than threefold*: Scalia, *Federal Drug Offenders 1999*: "Between 1984 and 1999, the number of defendants charged with a drug offense in the Federal courts increased from 11,854 to 29,306."

36   *Conversely, in the UK*: "In a Spin: Britain Wants to Tackle Money Laundering; Good Luck," *Economist*, May 27, 2006.

36   *The few studies that do exist*: DAWN (Drug Abuse Warning Network), http://dawninfo.samhsa.gov: "The Drug Abuse Warning Network (DAWN) is a public health surveillance system that monitors drug-related visits to hospital emergency department (EDs) and drug-related deaths investigated by medical examiners and coroners (ME/Cs)."

37   *But they do not provide a complete*: Peter Reuter and David Boyum, "An Analytic Assessment of US Drug Policy," AEI Press, February 2005.

37   *Nonetheless, it's clear from both*: Lloyd D. Johnston, PhD, Patrick M. O'Malley, PhD, Jerald G. Bachman, PhD, and John E. Schulenberg, PhD, University of Michigan Institute for Social Research, *Monitoring the Future: National Results on Adolescent Drug Use, Overview of Key Findings 2005*.

38   *On the twentieth anniversary of*: Michael E. Ruane and Paul Duggan, "Promise Thrown Away: Two Decades After Cocaine Killed U-Md. Basketball Star Len Bias, a Candlelight Vigil Spotlights the Toll of Drug Abuse," *Washington Post*, June 9, 2006.

38   *If cocaine usage*: Johnston et al., *Monitoring the Future*.

38   *In a May 1997*: Peter Reuter, "Punishing Without Reflection," *Federation of American Scientists' Drug Policy Analysis Bulletin*, May 1997, http://fas.org/drugs/issue2.htm#1.

39   *The situation with illegal drugs*: Interview with Sterling, May 31, 2006.

39   *Direct expenditures on crime*: Bureau of Justice Statistics, "Key Crime and Justice Facts at a Glance," http://www.ojp.usdoj.gov/bjs/glance.htm.

39   *The use of criminal informants*: Alexandra Natapoff, "Snitching: The Institutional and Communal Consequences," *University of Cincinnati Law Review* 73 (2004).

39   *They'll even volunteer to cooperate*: Interview with Cheryl Stein, spring 2006.

39   *As the cooperation process*: Natapoff, "Snitching."

40   *Targets are selected by informants*: Interview with Sterling, May 31, 2006.

40   *Cooperating witnesses claim*: Testimony of A. J. Kramer, Federal Defender for the District of Columbia, before the United States Sentencing Commission Public Hearing on Cocaine and Sentencing Policy, November 14, 2006.

40   *With low-level dealers*: U.S. Department of Justice, *Federal Cocaine Offenses: An Analysis of Crack and Powder Penalties*, March 19, 2002.

41   *Similarly, in 2001*: U.S. Department of Justice, *Federal Cocaine Offenses*.

41   *The targeting of low-level players*: Scalia, *Federal Drug Offenders 1999*.

41   *As of year-end 2005*: Harrison and Beck, *Prisoners in 2005*.

CHAPTER 2. BAD TO WORSE: SNITCHING SCANDALS, CODDLED COOPERATORS

44   *Perhaps the most notorious*: Taylor Branch, *At Canaan's Edge: America in the King Years 1965–1968* (New York: Simon and Schuster, 2006).

44   *Agent Kemp*: Gary May, *The Informant: The FBI, the Ku Klux Klan, and the Murder of Viola Liuzzo* (New Haven: Yale University Press, 2005).

45   *The next morning, Hoover*: Branch, *At Canaan's Edge*.

45   *Nearly a decade after the Liuzzo*: Church Committee, *Book III: Supplementary Detailed Staff Reports on Intelligence Activities and the Rights of Americans*, 1976.

45   *Rowe was also present*: Church Committee, *Vol. 6: Federal Bureau of Investigation*, 1976.

46   *Bergman and the Liuzzo family*: Bergman v. United States, 565 F. Supp. 1353, 1415 (W.D. Mich. 1983).

46   *The committee's report noted that*: Church Committee, *Book III*.

46   *In response to the Church Committee's*: "FBI Oversight: Hearings Before the Subcommittee on Civil and Constitutional Rights of the House Committee on the Judiciary, 94th Congress (1976)."

47   *The Levi Guidelines had*: Department of Justice Inspector General Glenn Fine, "The Federal Bureau of Investigation's Compliance with the Attorney General's Investigative Guidelines," September 2005.

47   *Attorney General Benjamin Civiletti*: "Final Report of the Senate Select Committee to Study Undercover Activities (Civiletti Informant Guidelines §F.2), 1982."

47   *From 1982 to the spring of 1983:* "Attorney General's Guidelines for Domestic Security Investigations: Hearings Before the Subcommittee on Security and Terrorism of the Senate Committee on the Judiciary, 98th Congress, 1983."

48   *After considering the Senate subcommittee's:* Department of Justice press release, March 7, 1983.

48   *Smith lowered the evidentiary:* "FBI Domestic Security Guidelines: Oversight Hearings Before the Subcommittee on Civil and Constitutional Rights of the House Committee on the Judiciary, 98th Congress."

48   *This would prove:* Robert L. Jackson and Ronald J. Ostrow, "Old 'Ghosts' to Protest Presser, FBI Men Swore," *Los Angeles Times*, February 13, 1987.

48   *Starting in the late 1970s:* "The Friends of Jackie Presser," *Time*, September 2, 1985; William Serrin, "Jackie Presser's Secret Lives Detailed in Government Files," *New York Times*, March 27, 1989.

49   *The sticky legal and ethical:* Shelley Murphy, "Ex-Agent Testifies to Probe of Bulger: Says Senate Chief Targeted in '83 Case," *Boston Globe*, June 20, 2006.

49   *A federal judge in the case:* Department of Justice Inspector General Glenn Fine, "The Federal Bureau of Investigation's Compliance with the Attorney General's Investigative Guidelines," September 2005.

50   *While Bulger remains at large:* "Henchman Tells of Whitey's Black Deeds," *60 Minutes*, March 12, 2006.

50   *in early 2001:* Department of Justice Guidelines Regarding the Use of Confidential Informants, January 8, 2001, http://www.usdoj.gov/ag/readingroom/ciguidelines.htm

50   *a sprawling 314-page report:* Dan Eggen, "FBI Agents Often Break Informant Rules; Study Finds Confidentiality Breaches," *Washington Post*, September 13, 2005; Department of Justice Inspector General Glenn Fine, "The Federal Bureau of Investigation's Compliance with the Attorney General's Investigative Guidelines," September 2005.

51   *But in a federal criminal justice system dominated:* Bureau of Justice Statistics, *Drug Arrests by Age 1970–2005*, http://www.ojp.usdoj.gov/bjs/glance/drug.htm.

51   *Informants are an investigative tool:* Interview with Gerald Shargel, August 2006.

52   *Defendants know that 5K motions:* Interview with Shargel, August 2006.

52   *Incredibly, defendants who do not:* Federal Rules of Criminal Procedure, VII Post Conviction Procedures, Rule 35 (http://www.law.cornell.edu/rules/frcrmp/Rule35.htm):

Rule 35. Correcting or Reducing a Sentence

(a) Correcting Clear Error.

Within 7 days after sentencing, the court may correct a sentence that resulted from arithmetical, technical, or other clear error.

(b) Reducing a Sentence for Substantial Assistance.

(1) In General.

Upon the government's motion made within one year of sentencing, the court may reduce a sentence if:

(A) the defendant, after sentencing, provided substantial assistance in investigating or prosecuting another person; and

(B) reducing the sentence accords with the Sentencing Commission's guidelines and policy statements.

(2) Later Motion.

Upon the government's motion made more than one year after sentencing, the court may reduce a sentence if the defendant's substantial assistance involved:

(A) information not known to the defendant until one year or more after sentencing;

(B) information provided by the defendant to the government within one year of sentencing, but which did not become useful to the government until more than one year after sentencing; or

(C) information the usefulness of which could not reasonably have been anticipated by the defendant until more than one year after sentencing and which was promptly provided to the government after its usefulness was reasonably apparent to the defendant.

(3) Evaluating Substantial Assistance.

In evaluating whether the defendant has provided substantial assistance, the court may consider the defendant's presentence assistance.

(4) Below Statutory Minimum.

When acting under Rule 35(b), the court may reduce the sentence to a level below the minimum sentence established by statute.

53   A lot of people, particularly: "Henchman Tells of Whitey's Black Deeds."

CHAPTER 3. KING TUT'S THIRD STRIKE: THE MURDER OF TUPAC, THREE STRIKES LEGISLATION, AND THE FALL OF BROOKLYN'S MOST STORIED HUSTLER

55   Just after nine AM on October 4: Interview with Walter "King Tut" Johnson, spring 2006; United States v. Walter Johnson, CR–00932.

56   *Though Johnson had a criminal record*: Walter Johnson; Samuel Buell, "Letter in opposition to the pre-trial motions of Walter Johnson," January 10, 1997.

56   *What's up, Wally*: Interview with Johnson, spring 2006.

56   *Flamhaft later filed*: Interview with Stephen Flamhaft, spring 2006.

57   *His fear turned to paralysis*: Special Agent Robert Schmitt, "Arrest Report of Walter Johnson, #742008–97–005": "He denied any involvement in the robbery and shooting of rapper Tupac Shakur."

57   *Told of Johnson's recollection*: Interview with Samuel Buell, September 7, 2006.

58   *Though Johnson has the most*: Interview with Johnson, spring 2006.

59   *On October 7, 1982*: From the transcript of *Walter Johnson*:
       On August 8, 1983, Johnson was convicted of Robbery in the Second Degree (a Class C Felony) in Queens County Supreme Court for an October 7, 1982 armed robbery in which Johnson and accomplices boarded a New York City transit bus in Queens and robbed the passengers at gunpoint as the bus traveled into Brooklyn. . . . On September 12, 1983 Johnson was convicted of Robbery in the First Degree (a Class B Felony) in Kings County Supreme Court for a June 23, 1982 armed robbery in which Johnson and accomplices robbed worshippers at gunpoint among hundreds gathered at the Kingdom Hall of the Jehovah's Witnesses in East New York.

59   *But Johnson's luck with the law*: Seth Faison, "3 Officers Hurt in Shootouts with Suspects in 2 Robberies," *New York Times*, January 16, 1993.

61   *Though Johnson had a long*: The Notorious B.I.G., "Gimme the Loot," *Ready to Die* (compact disc), Bad Boy, 1994.

61   *In 1995, when Shakur was incarcerated*: Kevin Powell, "Ready to Live," *Vibe*, April 1995.

62   *Dr. Leon Pachter said*: Interview with Dr. Leon Pachter conducted by former *Vibe* editor Serena Kim for Ethan Brown, "The Score: In the Beef-Obsessed World of Gangsta Rap, Managers like Jimmy 'Henchmen' Rosemond Are the Real Bad Boys Who Move in Silence," *Vibe*, December 2005.

63   *The theory that Johnson attacked*: Tupac Shakur, Tupac as "Makaveli," "Against All Odds," *Don Killuminati, The 7 Day Theory*, compact disc, Death Row, 1996.

64   *When Johnson arrived at U.S. District Court*: Walter Johnson.

64   *One informant claimed*: Laura Williams, "Feds Hope to Bury 'King Tut,'" *New York Daily News*, October 27, 1996.

64   *Yet another informant claimed*: Laura Williams, "Suspect in '94 Shoot of Tupac," *New York Daily News*, October 25, 1996.

64   *Even more damaging*: Derrick Parker with Matt Diehl, *Notorious C.O.P.: The Inside Story of the Tupac, Biggie, and Jam Master Jay Investigations from the NYPD's First "Hip-Hop Cop"* (New York: St. Martin's Press, 2006).

64   *We hope this*: Williams, "Feds Hope to Bury 'King Tut.'"

65   *Shakur and a gaggle of informants*: Special Agent Robert Schmitt, "Arrest Report of Walter Johnson, #742008–97–005": "Among the items recovered in the search were several pairs of gloves, several ski masks, a Halloween mask, two cellular telephones and other miscellaneous papers and items."

65   *Early in the morning of March 15, 1995*: Transcript of *Walter Johnson*.

68   *A night that began*: United States v. Jay-Tee Spurgeon, CR–00335.

71   *Spurgeon didn't dare let*: United States v. Spencer Bowens, CR–00110.

72   *For fifteen years*: *Walter Johnson*; Buell, "Letter in opposition to the pre-trial motions of Walter Johnson."

72   *A Daily News headline*: Williams, "Feds Hope to Bury 'King Tut.'"

72   *I am not a snitch*: From *Walter Johnson*.

73   *The U.S. Attorney's Office*: Interview with Kevin Keating, spring 2006.

73   *Former Assistant U.S. Attorney Samuel Buell*: Interview with Samuel Buell, September 7, 2006.

73   *In a court filing soon after*: From *Walter Johnson*:
      Affirmation: Both factually and procedurally this is an unusual case. The theory of the Government's case at trial was that Johnson, with the assistance of unindicted co-conspirators, engaged in a series of attempted robberies against the same victim . . . in an unsuccessful effort to steal narcotics from the victim. At trial, the only eyewitness providing testimony implicating Johnson in these attempted robberies was Crystal Winslow. In a confusing, and somewhat, inconsistent verdict which undoubtedly reflected the jury's concern over the credibility of Ms. Winslow, the jury found as follows . . .

74   *on April 25, 1996*: Jay-Tee Spurgeon.

75   *In the spring of 2002*: Sworn affidavit of Burgess Chad Flowers, May 21, 2002.

75   *Another Leavenworth inmate*: Sworn affidavit of James A. Mitchell, May 17, 2000.

75   *Interestingly, Isaac has long been*: Interview with Dexter Isaac, spring 2005.

75   *Even more tellingly*: Interview with source close to Bowens, July 2007; interview with William Sewell, private detective hired by Bowens, July 2007.

76   *It's also worth noting that in 1998*: United States v. Dexter Isaac, CR–00497.

76   *During the spring of 2005:* Interview with Johnson, spring 2006.

76   *Johnson also worried that:* PR Newswire, "The Family of Christopher G. L. Wallace (Notorious B.I.G.) Responds to 'Irresponsible' *Los Angeles Times* Article," September 6, 2002.

77   *Though Johnson was not aware of it:* United States v. *The Premises Known and Described as 108–41 159th Street, Apartment 1F, Queens, New York,* Affidavit in support of search warrant by William Courtney, a detective with the New York City Police Department cross-designated as a special agent of the Intelligence Squad of the Federal Bureau of Investigation.

77   *Furthermore, just as Johnson finished:* Johnnie L. Roberts, "Hip-Hop Probe: The US Attorney Has Launched a Quiet Probe into the Hip-Hop Music Business," *Newsweek,* March 4, 2005.

77   *It is not unusual for the feds:* United States v. Kenneth McGriff, CR–00514.

78   *A source close to the case:* Ethan Brown, "Who Wants 50 Dead?" *Rolling Stone,* April 3, 2003.

78   *Johnson's attorney Keating:* Interview with Keating, spring 2006.

78   *Sam Buell, the former assistant U.S. Attorney:* Interview with Buell, September 7, 2006.

78   *50 Cent has also name-checked Johnson:* 50 Cent, "Many Men," *Get Rich or Die Tryin',* compact disc, Interscope, 2003.

CHAPTER 4. LINE 'EM UP AND INDICT 'EM: THE COOPERATOR CASTING CALL THAT BROUGHT DOWN EUKA WADLINGTON

82   *I wasn't really taking care:* Transcript of United States v. Euka Wadlington, CR–00242.

82   *In September 1996:* United States. v. George Harper, CR–00112; United States v. Deleon Gadison, CR–00112.

82   *A few months later, in April 1997:* United States v. Terry Hildebrandt, CR–1013.

83   *In Chicago, everyone from street hustlers:* Interview with Euka Wadlington, November 14, 2006.

87   *In early 1997, Clinton cops:* Transcript of Euka Wadlington.

89   *He hit me with the guilt trip:* Interview with Wadlington, November 14, 2006.

90   *As Wadlington feared:* Euka Wadlington.

91   *It was too stressful:* Romaine Dukes, "Sworn Affidavit of Romaine Dukes," December 26, 2002.

92   *When cops warned Hood:* Transcript of Euka Wadlington; Terrance Hood, "Sworn Affidavit of Terrance Hood," February 7, 2003.

93   *On April 7, 1999*: Leonard Goodman, "Brief and Argument for Defendant-Appellant Euka Wadlington," United States Court of Appeals for the Eighth Circuit.

93   *Such hardball tactics would provide*: Leonard Goodman, *United States v. Euka Wadlington*, Petition for a Writ of Certiorari.

94   *If I were you*: Transcript of *Euka Wadlington*; Goodman, "Brief and Argument for Defendant-Appellant Euka Wadlington."

95   *You know a little bit*: Transcript of *Euka Wadlington*.

98   *When a federal prosecutor says*: Interview with Leonard Goodman, fall 2006.

CHAPTER 5. MARK'S BAD TRIP: THE SHAKY SCIENCE THAT LED TO INCREASED PENALTIES FOR ECSTASY DEALING AND THE DEALER WHO TURNED COOPERATOR BECAUSE OF THEM

Author's note: When I interviewed the cooperator whose story is recounted here, he had yet to receive a 5K motion from the prosecutor in his case, so his cooperation was a secret. In order to ensure his safety on the streets (and to prevent retribution from prosecutors for revealing the inner workings of the cooperation process), many details—from his name to the city in which he resides—have been changed. The essential facts about his case, however, have not been altered in any way.

100   *Prison sentences were relatively light*: Marsha Rosenbaum, PhD, "Ecstasy: America's New Reefer Madness," *Journal of Psychoactive Drugs* (April–June 2002), http://www.drugpolicy.org/library/ecstasy_reefer.cfm.

102   *Seizures of Ecstasy*: "Statement of Commissioner Raymond Kelly, Customs: Before the U.S. Senate Caucus on International Narcotics Control—Hearing on Ecstasy Trafficking and Use," July 25, 2000. From Commissioner Kelly's statement: "For the past several years, the United States Customs Service has witnessed an unprecedented rise in the smuggling of Ecstasy. The numbers speak for themselves: in 1999, Customs seized 3 and a half million tablets of the drug, *a seven-fold increase over the 400,000 tablets seized in 1997*. We've already shattered that record in the first half of 2000, with seizures so far totaling about eight million tablets" (emphasis mine; http://www.cbp.gov/xp/cgov/newsroom/commissioner/speeches_statements/archives/2000/jul252000.xml).

102   *Perhaps the most profound shift*: Una McCann and George Ricaurte, "Positron Emission Tomographic Evidence of Toxic Effect of MDMA

('Ecstasy') on Brain Serotonin Neurons in Human Beings," *Lancet* 352, October 31, 1998, http://www.erowid.org/chemicals/mdma/references/journal/1998_mccann_lancet_1/.

102 *Armed with Ricaurte and McCann's*: Rick Doblin, "Exaggerating MDMA's Risks to Justify a Prohibitionist Policy," Multidisciplinary Association for Psychedelic Studies, January 16, 2004, http://www.maps.org/mdma/rd011604.html.

103 *During the spring of 2000*: Chuck Grassley, "Grassley Seeks Prompt Response to Drug Used by Teens," Congressional Press Releases, May 23, 2000.

103 *In his public comments*: Chuck Grassley, "Grassley Seeks Prompt Response to Drug Used by Teens," Congressional Press Releases, May 23, 2000.

103 *The Ecstasy Anti-Proliferation Act became law*: Jonathan P. Caulkins, "Should the U.S. Direct More Law Enforcement Efforts at XTC?" Rand Corporation Drug Policy Research Center, June 2000. Caulkins's paper was presented to the Subcommittee on Crime of the House Committee on the Judiciary, June 15, 2000.

103 *Still, after the bill's passage*: United States Sentencing Commission, "2001 Public Hearing," March 19, 2001, http://www.ussc.gov/hearings/Pubhrng2001.htm.

103 *It kills the serotonin*: Judge Diana E. Murphy, "Statement of Diana E. Murphy Before the Senate Caucus on International Narcotics Control," March 21, 2001, http://www.ussc.gov/testimony/ecstasytestimony2.pdf.

104 *Mueller was even more emphatic*: United States Sentencing Commission, "2001 Public Hearing."

104 *The scientists and drug policy experts*: United States Sentencing Commission, "2001 Public Hearing."

104 *We left feeling like*: Interview with Rick Doblin, fall 2006.

104 *Defendants convicted of selling*: Judge Diana E. Murphy, "America at Risk: The Ecstasy Threat," Senate Caucus on International Narcotics Control, March 21, 2001, http://drugcaucus.senate.gov/ecstasymurphy.html.

104 *This is a wholly political*: Karen Gullo, "Guidelines Stiffened for Selling Ecstasy," Associated Press, March 21, 2001.

108 *Although cooperation agreements*: Alexandra Natapoff, "Snitching: The Institutional and Communal Consequences," *University of Cincinnati Law Review* 73 (2004).

108 *Indeed, criminal defense attorney*: Interview with Robert Simels, July 2007.

109 *The DEA agent likely asked*: United States Department of Justice, *Information Bulletin: Crystal Methamphetamine*, August 2002, http://www.usdoj.gov/ndic/pubs1/1837/index.htm.

112   *In the spring of 2002, just one year*: David Concar wrote in his article "Ecstasy on the Brain," "Some say it will kill you or poison your brain, others that it's a safe enough high if you take precautions. Despite official campaigns highlighting Ecstasy's dangers, the drug has never been more popular with clubbers. Are they recklessly risking brain damage or worse, sensibly ignoring anti-drug propaganda?" (*New Scientist*, April 20, 2002).

113   *I spoke with a man*: Interview conducted spring 2003.

113   *An interview with Ricaurte-McCann subjects*: Donald G. McNeil Jr., "Research on Ecstasy Is Clouded by Errors," *New York Times*, December 2, 2003.

114   *Ricaurte's reputation was dealt another*: Donald G. McNeil Jr., "Report of Ecstasy Drug's Risks Is Retracted," *New York Times*, September 6, 2003; "Retraction of Ricaurte et al. Science 297," *Science* 301, September 12, 2003, http://www.sciencemag.org/cgi/content/full/sci;301/5639/1479b.

114   *During the 2001 USSC hearings*: United States Sentencing Commission, "2001 Public Hearing."

114   *More importantly, no effort has been made*: "E Is for Evidence," *New Scientist*, April 20, 2002.

115   *Indeed, the very first judge*: United States Court of Appeals for the Eighth Circuit, *United States v. Gary James Lenfesty*.

117   *Even if retail hustlers like Mark*: Interview with Jon Caulkins, fall 2006.

CHAPTER 6. BROTHERHOOD OF THE BOOKSTORE:
THE $100,000 INFORMANT, THE THIRTY-FOURTH STREET BOMB PLOT, AND THE PREEMPTIVE INDICTMENT BROUGHT BY THE FEDS

120   *Early in the afternoon of October 9*: Transcript of *United States v. Shahwar Matin Siraj*, CR–00104.

121   *He was extremely helpful*: Transcript of *Shahwar Matin Siraj*.

123   *When he heard the call*: Craig Horowitz, "Anatomy of a Foiled Plot: Two Would-Be Bombers of the Herald Square Subway Station Find that Three Is a Crowd," *New York*, December 6, 2004.

123   *Siraj's life had been marked*: Transcript of *Shahwar Matin Siraj*.

124   *The politically savvy Eldawoody*: Interview with Martin Stolar, fall 2006.

128   *They asked Siraj*: Interview with Martin Stolar, fall of 2006.

129   *In a 2004 special terrorism-themed issue*: Horowitz, "Anatomy of a Foiled Plot."

129 *Just before Siraj went to trial*: Michelle Malkin, "Brooklyn Bridge Is Falling Down," http://michellemalkin.com/archives/005076.htm.

129 *Meanwhile, a lesser known right-wing blogger*: Bay Ridge Conservative, "Bay Ridge Islamic Center Terrorists Carry a Tune," April 28, 2006.

130 *In this climate, juries*: Interview with Juliette Kayyem, November 1, 2006.

130 *After the trial*: Jennifer 8. Lee, "Entrapment Evidence Lacking, Jurors Say," *New York Times*, May 25, 2006.

131 *Anyone who still disputes*: Heather MacDonald, "New York Cops: Still the Finest," *City Journal*, summer 2006.

131 *Incredibly, Eldawoody acknowledged*: Photocopy of Eldawoody letter to Senator Hillary Clinton appears in documents section.

132 *During the fall of 2006, Eldawoody also lamented*: Armen Keteyian, "The Cost of Cooperation: A Confidential Informant Who Helped Break Up a Terror Plot Opens Up," CBS News, September 14, 2006.

132 *In June 2006*: NBC News and NBC News Services, "FBI Arrests 7 in Alleged Terror Plot; Investigators Claim Men Conspired to Attack Sears Tower, Federal Building," NBC News, June 23, 2006; *United States v. Narseal Batiste*, CR–20373.

132 *Seas of David leader Narseal Batiste*: "CNN Security Watch: How Safe Are We?" CNN *American Morning*, June 23, 2006, http://transcripts.cnn.com/TRANSCRIPTS/0606/23/ltm.01.html.

133 *That designation should go to*: *United States v. Derrick Shareef*, CR–00919.

134 *But divining intent*: Amy Waldman wrote in her article "Prophetic Justice," "The United States is now prosecuting suspected terrorists on the basis of their intentions, not just their actions. But in the case of Islamic extremists, how can American jurors fairly weigh words and beliefs when Muslims themselves can't agree on what they mean?" (*Atlantic Monthly*, October 2006).

CHAPTER 7. JONATHAN LUNA'S LAST DAYS: THE RAP LABEL, THE ROGUE COOPERATOR, AND THE MURDERED PROSECUTOR

135 *Early on the morning of December 1, 2003*: *United States v. Walter Oriley Poindexter*, CR–00213.

135 *It should have been a typical*: Office of National Drug Control Policy, Drug Policy Information Clearinghouse, *Baltimore, Maryland Profile of Drug Indicators*, February 2005.

135 *In his four years*: Allan Lengel, "Online Sting Yields Gritty Testimony from FBI Agent Who Posed As Teen," *Washington Post*, December 4, 2002.

136   *History, says Andrew White*: Interview with Andrew C. White, January 2004.

136   *White may have been*: Transcript of *Walter Oriley Poindexter*.

139   *Eager to put the excruciating*: Transcript of *Walter Oriley Poindexter*.

139   *The only thing that*: Interview with White, January 2004.

139   *But Luna never stopped*: FBI timeline of Luna's last night: "12:57 AM Luna's debit card is used at an ATM located at the JFK Plaza in Newark, Delaware."

140   *After more than an hour*: FBI timeline of Luna's last night: "4:04 AM Luna's vehicle exits the Pennsylvania Turnpike at Exit 286 (old Exit 21), the Reading/Lancaster Interchange."

140   *An employee of Sensenig & Weaver*: Interview with Sensenig & Weaver employee, December 2004.

140   *stabbing Luna thirty-six times*: Lancaster County Coroner's Office, "Coroner's Investigation Form": "Body of deceased found face down in creek. . . . Primary cause of death: fresh water drowning/multiple stab wounds." Gail Gibson, "Search Uncovers Luna's Penknife: Federal Prosecutor, 38, Was Likely Stabbed with It," *Baltimore Sun*, February 13, 2004.

141   *Raised in a housing project*: Associated Press, "Slain Prosecutor Remembered," December 4, 2003.

141   *When the* New York Times *profiled*: "Say Something Good about South Bronx," Letters to the Editor, *New York Times*, November 26, 1991:

> To the Editor: As someone who grew up in the Mott Haven section of the Bronx and whose parents still live there, I could not help being offended at the title of your series on that South Bronx neighborhood, 'Life at the Bottom' (Nov. 5–8). Contrary to the images in the news media and in popular literature like Tom Wolfe's *Bonfire of the Vanities*, there is much hope and promise in Mott Haven. You and your readers should know that there are decent hard-working people like my parents who are struggling every day to make a life for themselves and their families in Mott Haven. My dad struggled in the restaurant business, while my mom stayed at home to raise my brother and me. Despite all the obstacles they had to contend with, I managed to make my way to Fordham University and the University of North Carolina School of Law. I don't deny that my neighborhood is being used as a dumping ground for New York City's unwanted homeless and drug addicted. The other boroughs should take on their fair share of the burden of providing shelter for such people. Perhaps it is time to look for what is good about places like the South Bronx.
>
> Jonathan Paul Luna
> Carrboro, N.C., Nov. 12, 1991.

141   *Jonathan stood out*: Interview with Reggie Shuford, January 2004.

142   *Senior partner James Sandman*: Interview with James Sandman, January 2004.

142   *I can't say personally that there's been*: Robert Schmidt, "Minority Lawyers and the D.C. Firm; Race, Culture and Sexism Make Integration at Law Offices Difficult," *Legal Times*, September 26, 1994.

142   *Baltimore was every bit*: Virginia B. Evans, "Members of Cator Gang Sentenced in Federal Drug Conspiracy," Maryland U.S. Attorney's Office press release, May 10, 2002.

143   *Jonathan was very adept*: Interview with White, January 2004.

143   *But if Luna's prosecutions*: Interview with former assistant U.S. attorney, January 2004.

143   *Assistant U.S. Attorney James Warwick*: Transcript of *Walter Oriley Poindexter*.

145   *We will find out who*: Gail Gibson, "Prosecutor of Drug Case Found Killed: Assistant U.S. Attorney for Md. Discovered Shot, Beaten and Stabbed in Pa.; 'We Will Find Out Who Did This'; Authorities Retrace Luna's Steps, Ask for Public's Help," *Baltimore Sun*, December 5, 2003.

145   *But in the wake of*: Department of Justice, "Statement of Attorney General John Ashcroft," December 4, 2003, http://www.usdoj.gov/opa/pr/2003/December/03_ag_665.htm:

      Today, we learned of the tragic death of District of Maryland Assistant United States Attorney Jonathan Luna. On behalf of the entire United States Department of Justice, I express our deepest condolences to Jonathan's family, colleagues and friends. We share his family's grief and will provide any support and assistance to help them through this difficult time. All appropriate resources will be dedicated to investigating this matter.

145   *This is a monumental*: Interview with Robert Reuland, spring 2007.

145   *Incredibly, not a week*: Gail Gibson, "Personal Motive Suspected in Killing of U.S. Prosecutor; Investigators Pursue Theory of Relationship That Turned Violent; Case Could Be Handed Off to Pa.," *Baltimore Sun*, December 6, 2003.

145   *As such, it was expected*: Gail Gibson and Gus Sentementes, "Decision in Slaying Probe Set for Today; Luna Case Could Go to Pa.; Sources Say Prosecutor Had Genital-Area Injuries," *Baltimore Sun*, December 8, 2003.

146   *a source close to Luna*: Interview with former assistant U.S. attorney, January 2004.

146   *The source says that DiBiagio*: Interview with former assistant U.S. attorney, January 2004.

146   *This is pretty ironic*: Interview with Thomas DiBiagio, spring 2007.

146   *But in 2004 the Sun*: Stephanie Hanes, "Luna Reportedly Feared Losing Job, Hired Lawyer; DiBiagio Told Staff He Lied about Prosecutor's Status to Protect Man's Family," *Baltimore Sun*, August 18, 2004.

147   *In 2004, DiBiagio sent*: "A Vote of No Confidence," *Washington Post*, July 20, 2004.

147   *After the e-mails were leaked*: Doug Donovan, "DiBiagio Gets Formal Rebuke from His Boss; Unusual Public Reprimand for Prosecutor's Directives; 'Protecting Office's Credibility'; Public Corruption Cases Must Get Superior's OK," *Baltimore Sun*, July 17, 2004.

147   *Justice Department officials*: Erich Rich, "Justice Admits U.S. Attorney Was Forced Out," *Washington Post*, March 7, 2007.

147   *In June 2005*: Interview with Chuck Grassley, spring 2007; Associated Press, "Report: FBI Committed Misconduct in Luna Probe," January 8, 2006.

147   *Smith-Love later received*: FBI National Press Office, "Jennifer Smith Love Named Special Agent in Charge of the Washington Field Office Criminal Division," November 27, 2006.

147   *At a May 2006 Judiciary Committee hearing*: Interview with Grassley, spring 2007; Chuck Grassley, "Prepared Statement of Senator Chuck Grassley, Oversight Hearing on the Department of Justice," July 18, 2006.

148   *During a hearing later that year*: Interview with Beth Levine, spokeswoman for Senator Chuck Grassley, January 2007; Senator Chuck Grassley, "Questions Submitted 'for the record' to FBI Director Robert Mueller":

Allegations of Misconduct by FBI Supervisor

On January 3, 2005, Agent Jennifer Smith-Love was promoted from the field to a position at FBI Headquarters. According to your answers to previous questions for the record, you approved this promotion while an investigation was still being conducted of her involvement in possible misconduct related to her handling of the investigation of the death of federal prosecutor Jonathan Luna.

(a) At the time you approved the promotion of Smith-Love, did you know she would be cleared by FBI/OPR of any misconduct? If so, how did you know that? If not, then why approve the promotion while the investigation is still pending?

(b) The head of FBI/OPR told staff in a briefing earlier this year the mission of the office would not be impaired by providing the Committee access to its final report on this matter. Please provide a copy of the report or a detailed explanation of the basis on which it is being withheld.

148 *Mike Kortan, an FBI spokesperson*: Interview with Mike Kortan, March 2007. The full FBI response is as follows:

After a thorough and independent investigation of allegations from the Baltimore Division—conducted by the FBI headquarters–based Inspection Division—the Office of Inspector General (OIG) later addressed a limited aspect of that larger investigation. The OIG looked specifically at whether the Inspection Division findings should have been referred to the Office of Professional Responsibility (OPR) to determine if discipline was warranted. As part of its investigation, the OIG reviewed the original investigative file, and referred to portions of it in its report, which early last year was provided to the FBI with the specific recommendations that the file be forwarded to OPR for adjudication. Those recommendations were followed. As a result, the actions of several employees were examined, and while no misconduct was found, performance issues were identified and for the on-board employees, remedial action was taken.

The OIG report was not—and has not been—released to the public. The report contains legally protected information, and OIG policy is designed to guard the privacy of employees and other individuals who cooperate with every expectation of privacy in these types of investigations.

Last year, the FBI implemented the vast majority of recommendations made by the Bell-Colwell Commission, an independent study—begun in 2003—of the FBI's disciplinary procedures and processes by a team headed by former Attorney General Griffin Bell and former FBI executive Dr. Lee Colwell. The commission took into account a full range of employee concerns and called for a number of practical recommendations designed to ensure fairness and efficiency in the disciplinary process, including the separation of investigative and adjudicative functions of the OPR.

Earlier, in a separate review, the Office of Inspector General investigated allegations of a double standard of discipline based on rank within the Bureau. The resulting reforms were designed to eliminate any actual or perceived discrepancy in the imposition of discipline in the FBI employee ranks. Those reforms were in place at the time of the Baltimore investigation.

148 *In May 2006*: Matthew Dolan, "Senate Targets Local FBI Agents; Judiciary Panel Opens Probe into Possible Perjury Related to Luna Case," *Baltimore Sun*, May 13, 2006.

148 *The main problem here*: Interview with Grassley, spring 2007.

149 *While it is true that*: Gibson, "Prosecutor of Drug Case Found Killed."

149 *It's commonplace for cooperators:* Interview with Renato Stabile, spring 2007.

149 *In Baltimore's Park Heights neighborhood: Skinny Suge Presents: Stop Fucking Snitching, Vol. 1,* DVD, One Love Films/Skinny Suge Records, 2004.

149 *When I spoke with Stash House's Walter:* Interview with Walter Oriley Poindexter, fall 2006.

149 *Grace's attorney, Joseph Balter:* Interview with Joseph Balter, spring 2007.

150 *DiBiagio admitted to me:* Interview with Thomas DiBiagio, spring 2007.

150 *Due to its problems:* Interview with Mark Cohen, fall 2006; Mark Cohen, "Letter to Inspector General Glenn A. Fine," December 2, 2005.

150 *It looks like the murder:* Interview with William Sewell, spring 2007.

150 *Similarly, Ed Martino:* Interview with Ed Martino, spring 2007.

151 *In February 2007:* Helen Colwell Adams, "Luna Inquest Pushed; Private Investigator Petitions Court to Force County Coroner to Seek Testimony in Death of Assistant U.S. Attorney Here," *Lancaster News,* February 25, 2007.

151 *Everybody was saying afterward:* Interview with White, January 2004.

CHAPTER 8. KILLER COOPERATORS: THE HARVEY FAMILY AND ST. GUILLEN MURDERS

Author's note: Much of the information in the chapter is drawn from evidence and witness testimony presented during the August 2006 trial of Ricky Javon Gray at the John Marshall Courts Building in Richmond, Virginia. Photocopies of Darryl Littlejohn's cooperation agreement with the Nassau County District Attorney's Office as well as the notes from the FBI's interview with Littlejohn in the Luc Stephen–Charles Thomas armed robbery case can be found in the documents section.

157 *And just one year before:* Dave Clinger, "Innovators: World of Mirth; Find Out How a Painting and Printmaking Major Created Carytown's Favorite Toy Store for Kids and Adults Alike," Richmond *Work Magazine,* January 12, 2005.

157 *Two candlelight vigils:* Tom Campbell, "Candlelight Vigil Outside House Draws Big Crowd," *Richmond Times-Dispatch,* January 5, 2006.

161 *I had a hard time imagining:* Page Akin Mudd, "Gray Gets Death Penalty," *Richmond Times-Dispatch,* August 23, 2006.

161   *The answer, unfortunately, is simple*: United States v. Ricky Javon Gray,
      CR–00212.

161   *The recognition of Gray's*: On September 21, 2001, Judge TS Ellis III
      granted the motion by the United States for "Reduction of Sentence
      Based on Defendant's [Gray's] Substantial Assistance to the United
      States." Ellis then ordered that "Deft's sentence is REDUCED to 60
      mos. w/ all other terms and conds. to remain in full effect" (*United
      States v. Ricky Gray*, CR–00212).

162   *In the mid-1990s Gray and nephew*: Jim Nolan and David Ress, "Defen-
      dants Have Long Records; Suspects in the Slayings of Two Families
      Spark Probes Up and Down Mid-Atlantic," *Richmond Times-Dispatch*,
      January 12, 2006.

162   *Both Morris Parker Jr.*: Interview with Morris Parker Jr., fall 2006.

163   *And just as in the Gray case*: United States v. Luc Stephen, CR–01214.

163   *Instead, news coverage focused*: Russell Berman, "Halt in New Liquor
      Permits Is Set for Parts of Manhattan," *New York Sun*, September 7,
      2006.

164   *Though Tacopina was understandably*: "Nassau County District Attor-
      ney's Office, Burglary and Narcotics Bureau Conditions of Coopera-
      tion, Rights and Responsibilities of Cooperating Individual," signed
      by Darryl Littlejohn (under the alias "Jonathan Blaze"), April 15,
      1997.

164   *I also told Tacopina that after*: United States v. Jonathan Blaze, CR–00105.

164   *But according to a source close to the case*: Interview conducted fall
      2006.

164   *Littlejohn's lack of connections*: Stephen, direct examination of Jonathan
      Blaze.

165   *In one interview Littlejohn included himself*: Interview with Jonathan
      Blaze, DOB: 11–11–64, address: 116–80 Foch Boulevard.

165   *Upon hearing the news*: Interview with Joseph Tacopina, August 2006.

166   *The St. Guillen family is refusing*: Raja Mishra, "St. Guillen Family
      Plans to Sue N.Y. for $100m," *Boston Globe*, May 27, 2006.

167   *Gravano's behavior after entering*: Chris Summers, "FBI and the Mafia:
      A Tale of Betrayal," *BBC News*, May 30, 2001.

168   *Though Hill has been arrested*: Interview with Robert Simels, March
      31, 2006.

168   *Littlejohn's former Queens associates*: Rob Stafford, "Meeting Imette's
      Family," *Dateline NBC*, March 11, 2006.

168   *When Littlejohn was indicted*: Nicholas Confessor and Kareem Fahim,
      "Club Bouncer Is Arraigned in Murder of Graduate Student," *New
      York Times*, March 24, 2006.

CHAPTER 9. *STOP SNITCHING*: THE BARBER, THE CORRUPT COPS, AND THE PROSECUTOR ON THE FRONTLINES OF THE BATTLE OVER WITNESS INTIMIDATION IN BALTIMORE

170   *Calling the State of Maryland*: Hearing for the *State of Maryland v. Rodney Thomas*, Clarence Mitchell Courthouse, October 11, 2006.

170   *Just two years earlier, Thomas*: Skinny Suge Presents: Stop Fucking Snitching, Vol. 1, DVD, One Love Films/Skinny Suge Records, 2004.

171   *The meandering, 108-minute*: John B. O'Donnell, Kimberly A.C. Wilson, and Jim Haner, "Justice Undone: How Itchy Man Beat the Rap: Charged with 2 Deaths and 12 Attempted Murders, Solothal Thomas Has Dodged Hard Time," *Baltimore Sun*, September 30, 2002.

171   *At one point the joking*: Gregory Kane, "'Stop Snitching' DVD Puts Homegrown NBA Star in Verbal Crossfire," *Baltimore Sun*, December 6, 2004.

171   *Think how bold criminals*: Julie Bykowicz, "Another Weapon in War on Witnesses; 'Snitch' DVD: City Prosecutors Say Threats and Attacks Permeate Nearly All the Violence Cases They Handle," *Baltimore Sun*, December 12, 2004.

173   *When I met Bethea in Baltimore*: Interview with Rodney Bethea, October 12, 2006.

177   *Three years previously*: Dan Rodricks, "Tragedy on E. Preston St. Can't Shake Faith in Future," *Baltimore Sun*, October 18, 2002.

178   *Maryland Congressman Elijah Cummings*: Kane, "'Stop Snitching' DVD Puts Homegrown NBA Star in Verbal Crossfire."

178   *Baltimore city police, meanwhile, vowed*: Ryan Davis, "Homemade DVDs about Informing Give Police Clues; Information from Film Has Led to Arrest; Anthony Has No Culpability," *Baltimore Sun*, December 4, 2004.

178   *The first thing people wanted to know*: Interview with Patricia Jessamy, October 12, 2006.

180   *We estimate that at least 25 percent*: Patricia Jessamy, "Culture of Intimidation (Testimony in Support of HB 248)," testimony before the Judiciary Committee, Maryland House of Delegates, February 17, 2005.

181   *On May 11, 2005, Baltimore city police*: United States v. William King and Antonio Murray, CR–00203.

183   *In August 2005, nearly one year*: Gregory Kane, "Who Knew? Some Good May Come of the 'Stop Snitching' DVD After All," *Baltimore Sun*, August 10, 2005.

184   *King is working!*: Transcript of *William King and Antonio Murray*.

192   *There is something fundamentally wrong*: Matthew Dolan, "Judge Criticizes Ex-Officer's 315 Year Sentence; Ex-City Officer Sentenced to Mandatory 315 Years for Fun Crimes, Robbing Drug Dealers," *Baltimore Sun*, June 17, 2006.

192   *In an interview with the* Sun: Dolan, "Judge Criticizes Ex-Officer's 315 Year Sentence."

192   *Baltimore City Police Commissioner Leonard*: Dolan, "Judge Criticizes Ex-Officer's 315 Year Sentence."

192   *In contrast, nonprofit organizations committed*: The November Coalition, "Dissenting Opinions: Judge Criticizes Ex-Officer's 315 Year Sentence," http://november.org/dissentingopinions/Motz.htm.

193   *But Bethea holds out hope*: Matthew Dolan, "2 More Plead Guilty in Drug Probe; U.S. Prosecutors Near Sweep in Investigation of Decade-Old Park Heights Operation," *Baltimore Sun*, October 20, 2006.

CHAPTER 10. A SESSION WITH SESSIONS: SENTENCING REFORM AND SNITCHING SOLUTIONS

195   *The truth is*: Interview with Senator Jeff Sessions, November 2006.

196   *When he was the U.S. attorney*: Sarah Wildman, "Closed Sessions: The Senator Who's Worse Than [Trent] Lott," *New Republic*, December 30, 2002.

197   *In July 2006, Sessions and a group*: United States Senator Jeff Sessions, "Sens. Sessions, Pryor, Cornyn and Salazar Introduce Drug Sentencing Reform Act," July 25, 2006, http://sessions.senate.gov/pressapp/record.cfm?id=259385; S. 3725, "A bill to reduce the disparity in punishment between crack and powder cocaine offenses, to more broadly focus the punishment for drug offenders on the seriousness of the offense and the culpability of the offender, and for other purposes."

198   *Soon after President Clinton's Violent Crime*: United States Sentencing Commission, "Special Report to the Congress: Cocaine and Federal Sentencing Policy," February 1995.

198   *Congress's disapproval of the USSC's proposal*: S. 1254, "A bill to disapprove of amendments to the Federal Sentencing Guidelines relating to lowering of crack sentences and sentences for money laundering and transactions in property derived from unlawful activity" (http://thomas.loc.gov/cgi-bin/query/D?c104:2:./temp/~c104pI8a1r::).

199   *Upon signing the legislation that fall*: "Presidential Signing Statement on Signing S. 1254," October 30, 1995.

199 *The USSC recommended that the amount*: United States Sentencing Commission, "Special Report to the Congress: Cocaine and Federal Sentencing Policy," April 1997, http://www.ussc.gov/r_congress/ NEWCRACK.PDF.

199 *Just one year later, Senator Sessions*: United States Senator Jeff Sessions, "Sen. Sessions Introduces Drug Sentencing Reform Act," December 20, 2001, http://sessions.senate.gov/pressapp/record.cfm?id=180169.

200 *The USSC complied by issuing*: United States Sentencing Commission, "Report to the Congress: Cocaine and Federal Sentencing Policy," May 2002, http://www.ussc.gov/r_congress/02crack/2002crackrpt.htm.

201 *Inspired by the USSC's new report*: HR 1435, "To amend the Controlled Substances Act and the Controlled Substances Import and Export Act to eliminate certain mandatory minimum penalties relating to crack cocaine offenses."

201 *Two years later, Rangel revived*: H.R. 2456, "To amend the Controlled Substances Act and the Controlled Substances Import and Export Act to eliminate certain mandatory minimum penalties relating to crack cocaine offenses."

201 *In United States v. Booker*: *United States v. Booker* (04–104) 543 U.S. 220 (2005); No. 04–104, 375 F.3d 508, affirmed and remanded; and No. 04–105, vacated and remanded. http://www.law.cornell.edu/ supct/html/04–104.ZO.html.

202 *In August 2006, Larry Schwartztol*: Larry Schwartztol, "Rocks and Powder: Will Congress Listen to the Courts and Fix Drug Sentencing?" *Slate*, August 23, 2006.

202 *Indeed, in his dissenting*: Lyle Dennison, "Salvaging the Guidelines? The 2/20/07 Arguments," SCOTUS Blog, http://www.scotusblog.com/ movabletype/archives/2007/02/salvaging_the_g.html.

202 *Scalia's prediction has turned out*: James H. Feldman Jr., "Booker Appellate Update: Reasonableness Review," *The Law Offices of Alan Ellis* [bulletin], Issue 21, fall 2006.

203 *The case of Juan Castillo*: *United States v. Juan Castillo*, CR–00134; "Drug Sentence Departure Struck; Court Erred in Trading Own Ratio for Guideline's 100:1 Ratio," *New York Law Journal*, August 24, 2006.

206 *Yet that same week, the USSC*: R. Alexander Acosta, United States Attorney for the Southern District of Florida, "Testimony of the United States Department of Justice: Federal Cocaine Sentencing Policy," before the United States Sentencing Commission, November 14, 2006.

207 *Because crack is no longer*: Eric Sterling, "Take Another Crack at That Cocaine Law," *Los Angeles Times*, November 13, 2006.

207 *When U.S. District Judge Reggie B. Walton:* Reggie B. Walton, "Testimony of Judge Reggie B. Walton Presented to the United States Sentencing Commission on November 14, 2006 on Sentencing Disparity of Crack and Powder Cocaine Offenses."

208 *The burden of this ever-expanding:* Bureau of Justice Statistics, "Direct Expenditure by Criminal Justice Function, 1982–2004: Direct expenditure for each of the major criminal justice functions (police, corrections, judicial) has been increasing." http://www.ojp.usdoj.gov/bjs/glance/exptyp.htm.

209 *Some criminal justice experts:* Alexandra Natapoff, "Snitching: The Institutional and Communal Consequences," *University of Cincinnati Law Review* 73 (2004).

209 *Incredibly, Mosley's involvement:* A photocopy of Mosley's cooperation agreement appears in the documents section.

211 *Everything Secret Degenerates:* The House Committee on Government Reform, "Everything Secret Degenerates: The FBI's Use of Murderers as Informants." http://www.gpoaccess.gov/serialset/creports/everything-secret.html.

211 *In 5K agreements:* Natapoff, "Snitching."

212 *When President Clinton and the Democratic-majority:* Al Franken, "Block that Rush!" *Nation,* June 19, 2000.

213 *Just after the midterm election in 2006:* Thomas Edsall, "The Struggle Within," *New York Times,* November 25, 2006.

EPILOGUE: CASE CLOSED? ARE *STOP SNITCHING* AND WITNESS INTIMIDATION LEADING TO LOW CLEARANCE RATES AND A RETURN TO THE "BAD OLD DAYS" OF THE 1980S?

215 *We have deputies:* Interview with Patricia Jessamy, October 12, 2006.

216 *The FBI reported that in the first half:* FBI National Press Office, "Preliminary Crime Statistics for January–June 2006," December 18, 2006.

216 *Though criminologists cannot say:* John Tierney, "The Crime Mystery," TierneyLab, *New York Times,* February 16, 2007, http://tierneylab.blogs.nytimes.com/2007/02/16/the-crime-mystery/

216 *New Orleans has now eclipsed:* Brendan McCarthy, "Study: Murder Rate Is Even Higher," *Times-Picayune,* March 12, 2007.

216 *Now matter how you parse it:* McCarthy, "Study."

217 *A study released by the* Baltimore Examiner: Luke Broadwater, "Murder City: Two Die Every Three Days," *Baltimore Examiner,* March 2, 2007.

217   *Similarly, in March 2007 New Orleans*: Laura Maggi, "Riley, Jordan Unveil New Agency Policies; Changes Should Foster Cooperation on Fighting Crime," *Times-Picayune*, March 16, 2007.

217   *Indeed, criminologist Scharf*: Interview with Peter Scharf, spring 2007.

218   *Law enforcement points to*: FBI, "Uniform Crime Reports," http://www .fbi.gov/ucr/ucr.htm#cius.

218   *In New Orleans, fear of reprisals*: Jarvis DeBerry, "Can I Get a Witness?" *Times-Picayune*, March 18, 2007.

218   *In New Orleans, former mayoral*: Interview with Leo Watermeier, spring 2007.

219   *Unfortunately, a freed*: Ken Foster, "A Promising Case Gives Way to Chaos," *Times-Picayune*, July 8, 2007; Gwen Filosa, "N.O. District Attorney Rejects Scapegoat Role; City Council Hearing Has Eddie Jordan Once Again Defending His Office," *Times-Picayune*, July 19, 2007.

220   *In Detroit, a city that like New Orleans*: Pam Belluck, "Detroit Police Cast a Wide Net Over 'Witnesses,'" *New York Times*, April 11, 2001.

220   *In an extraordinary March 18*: DeBerry, "Can I Get a Witness?"

221   *New Orleans District Attorney Jordan even*: Laura Maggi, "Riley, Jordan Unveil New Agency Policies," *Times-Picayune*, March 16, 2007.

221   *In criminologist Franklin Zimring's*: Franklin E. Zimring, *The Great American Crime Decline* (Studies in Crime and Public Policy; Oxford: Oxford University Press, 2007).

221   *In addition, a recent report by the Police Executive Research*: Police Executive Research Forum, *A Gathering Storm—Violent Crime in America*, October 2006.

222   *In a chapter called "Cities Within Cities"*: Police Executive Research Forum, *A Gathering Storm*.

222   *In an August 2006 New York Times column*: Paul Krugman, "Wages, Wealth and Politics," *New York Times*, August 18, 2006.

222   *Tellingly, as crime spiked in 2005*: David Cay Johnston, "Income Gap Is Widening, Data Shows," *New York Times*, March 29, 2007.

222   *With crime and income inequality rising*: William Langewiesche, "City of Fear," *Vanity Fair*, April 2007.

223   *All drug dealers supply*: Mark A. R. Kleiman, "Dopey, Boozy, Smoky— And Stupid," *American Interest*, January–February 2007.

224   *As David Kennedy, the director*: Jeremy Kahn, "The Story of a Snitch," *Atlantic Monthly*, April 2007.

DOCUMENTS

DMB:WAB:caz

UNITED STATES DISTRICT COURT
FOR THE MIDDLE DISTRICT OF PENNSYLVANIA

UNITED STATES OF AMERICA	)	CRIMINAL NO. 1:CR-92-199-01
	)	(JUDGE KOSIK)
v.	)	
	)	
EMANUEL MOSLEY	)	

CERTIFICATE OF SERVICE

The undersigned hereby certifies that he is an employee in the Office of the United States Attorney for the Middle District of Pennsylvania and is a person of such age and discretion to be competent to serve papers.

That this *Bth* day of October 1995, he served a copy of the attached

MOTION FOR GUIDELINE DEPARTURE
PURSUANT TO U.S.S.G. § 5K1.1 AND 18 U.S.C. § 3553(e)

by placing said copy in a postpaid envelope addressed to the person hereinafter named, at the place and address stated below, which is the last known address, and by depositing said envelope and contents in the United States Mail at Harrisburg, Pennsylvania.

ADDRESSEE(S):
Paul S. Brenner, Esquire
401 Broadway, Suite 306
New York, NY 10013

WILLIAM A. BEHE
Assistant U.S. Attorney

5K Motion for hitman Emanuel Mosley who later cooperated in the trial of Kenneth "Supreme" McGriff.

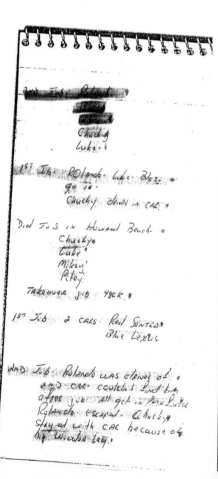

Notes of FBI interview with Darryl Littlejohn.

United States District Court
District of Maryland

UNITED STATES OF AMERICA   WARRANT FOR ARREST

v.

ANTONIA MURRAY   Case No. JFM-05-CR-0203

TO: The United States Marshal and any
      Authorized United States Officer

YOU ARE HEREBY COMMANDED to arrest   ANTONIO MURRAY

                                              Name

and bring him/her forthwith to the nearest magistrate judge to answer a(n)

[X] Indictment [ ] Information [ ] Complaint [ ] Order of Court [ ] Violation Notice [ ] Probation Violation Petition

charging him or her with (brief description of offense):   CONSPIRACY TO INTERFERE WITH
COMMERCE BY ROBBERY AND EXTORTION; CONSPIRACY TO POSSESS WITH INTENT TO
DISTRIBUTE NARCOTICS; CONSPIRACY TO POSSESS FIREARMS IN FURTHERANCE OF A CRIME OF
VIOLENCE AND A DRUG TRAFFICKING CRIME

in violation of Title 18; 21   United States Code, Section(s) 1951;846; 924(o)

Felicia C. Cannon   Clerk, U.S. District Court
Name of Issuing Officer   Title of Issuing Officer

(By) Deputy Clerk   May 11, 2005   Baltimore, MD
                                   Date and Location

Bail fixed at $ by U.S. MAGISTRATE JUDGE PAUL W. GRIMM
                                        Name of Judicial Officer

RETURN		
This warrant was received and executed with the arrest of the above-named defendant at BALTIMORE MARYLAND		
Date Received 5/12/05	Name and Title of Arresting Officer D U S M LEN NIEDORA	Signature of Arresting Officer
Date of Arrest 5/12/05		

U.S. DISTRICT COURT (Rev. 12/1999) - Bench Warrant

Arrest warrant for
Baltimore cop
Antonio Murray.

**IN THE UNITED STATES DISTRICT COURT
FOR THE DISTRICT OF MARYLAND**

UNITED STATES OF AMERICA,   *

v.   FILED ENTERED
                               LODGED RECEIVED   CRIMINAL NO. S-02-0220

WARREN GRACE,   JUN 07 2002   (SEALED)
Defendants.

ORDER

Upon motion by the government and there being no objection on the part of defendant,

IT IS HEREBY ORDERED that defendant's conditions of release be modified as follows:

1. Defendant is to be placed under 24 hour house arrest at 2506 Edgecombe Circle North, Baltimore, Maryland 21215;

2. Defendant is to be placed under electronic monitoring by the Pre-Trial Services Office;

3. Defendant shall be allowed to leave his residence to meet with agents from the FBI and/ or his attorney.

SO ORDERED.

                              06/07/02
                    United States District Judge

Conditions of release
for Warren Grace,
cooperator in the
Stash House case.

Darryl Littlejohn informant agreement with Nassau County D.A.

Informant Eldawoody's letter to Hillary Clinton in the Siraj case.

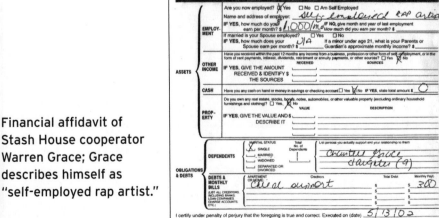

Arrest warrant for Baltimore cop William King.

Financial affidavit of Stash House cooperator Warren Grace; Grace describes himself as "self-employed rap artist."

Walter Johnson, AKA "TUT"

INVESTIGATION No. (Include Suspect No.)
742008-97-0005

6. TYPE OF REPORT (Check applicable boxes)		7. BUREAU PROGRAM		8. PROJECT(S)
PRELIMINARY	COLLATERAL (Request)	X TITLE I	FIREARMS	TARGETED OFFENDER
		TITLE II		TERRORIST/EXTREMIST
X STATUS	COLLATERAL (Reply)	TITLE VII		OCD
		TITLE II	EXPLOSIVES	ITAR
FINAL	INTELLIGENCE	TITLE XI		SEAR
		TOBACCO		OMO
SUPPLEMENTAL	REFERRAL (Internal)	ALCOHOL		X OTHER (Specify) VIOLENT CRIME

9. DETAILS:

On October 24, 1996, Special Agents Schmitt and McGrane along with members of the NYPD placed Walter Johnson under arrest at the New York State Supreme Court Building at 360 Adams Street in Brooklyn, at approximately 10:00AM. Johnson asked if he was being arrested for murder. Special Agent Schmitt read Johnson his rights at approximately 10:50AM, in the presence of S/A McGrane. Subsequently, Johnson was debriefed, and made the following statements:

He knows Sean Coombs, AKA "Puff Daddy", and that Coombs lent him one

10. SUBMITTED BY (Name) Robert Schmitt	11. TITLE AND OFFICE Special Agent, New York Five	12. DATE 11/12/96
13. REVIEWED BY (Name) Guy Spiotto	14. TITLE AND OFFICE Group Supervisor, New York V	15. DATE / /
16. APPROVED BY (Name)	17. TITLE AND OFFICE	18. DATE / /

Exhibit B

Walter "King Tut" Johnson arrest report.

Walter Johnson, AKA "TUT"

INVESTIGATION No. (Include Suspect No.)
742008-97-0005

6. TYPE OF REPORT (Check applicable boxes)		7. BUREAU PROGRAM		8. PROJECT(S)
PRELIMINARY	COLLATERAL (Request)	X TITLE I	FIREARMS	TARGETED OFFENDER
		TITLE II		TERRORIST/EXTREMIST
X STATUS	COLLATERAL (Reply)	TITLE VII		OCD
		TITLE II	EXPLOSIVES	ITAR
FINAL	INTELLIGENCE	TITLE XI		SEAR
		TOBACCO		OMO
SUPPLEMENTAL	REFERRAL (Internal)	ALCOHOL		X OTHER (Specify) VIOLENT CRIME

9. DETAILS:

On October 24, 1996, Special Agents Schmitt and McGrane along with members of the NYPD placed Walter Johnson under arrest at the New York State Supreme Court Building at 360 Adams Street in Brooklyn, at approximately 10:00AM. Johnson asked if he was being arrested for murder. Special Agent Schmitt read Johnson his rights at approximately 10:50AM, in the presence of S/A McGrane. Subsequently, Johnson was debriefed, and made the following statements:

He knows Sean Coombs, AKA "Puff Daddy", and that Coombs lent him one

10. SUBMITTED BY (Name) Robert Schmitt	11. TITLE AND OFFICE Special Agent, New York Five	12. DATE 11/12/96
13. REVIEWED BY (Name) Guy Spiotto	14. TITLE AND OFFICE Group Supervisor, New York V	15. DATE / /
16. APPROVED BY (Name)	17. TITLE AND OFFICE	18. DATE / /

Exhibit B

INDEX

PublicAffairs is a publishing house founded in 1997. It is a tribute to the standards, values, and flair of three persons who have served as mentors to countless reporters, writers, editors, and book people of all kinds, including me.

I.F. STONE, proprietor of *I. F. Stone's Weekly*, combined a commitment to the First Amendment with entrepreneurial zeal and reporting skill and became one of the great independent journalists in American history. At the age of eighty, Izzy published *The Trial of Socrates*, which was a national bestseller. He wrote the book after he taught himself ancient Greek.

BENJAMIN C. BRADLEE was for nearly thirty years the charismatic editorial leader of *The Washington Post*. It was Ben who gave the *Post* the range and courage to pursue such historic issues as Watergate. He supported his reporters with a tenacity that made them fearless and it is no accident that so many became authors of influential, best-selling books.

ROBERT L. BERNSTEIN, the chief executive of Random House for more than a quarter century, guided one of the nation's premier publishing houses. Bob was personally responsible for many books of political dissent and argument that challenged tyranny around the globe. He is also the founder and longtime chair of Human Rights Watch, one of the most respected human rights organizations in the world.

.   .   .

For fifty years, the banner of Public Affairs Press was carried by its owner Morris B. Schnapper, who published Gandhi, Nasser, Toynbee, Truman, and about 1,500 other authors. In 1983, Schnapper was described by *The Washington Post* as "a redoubtable gadfly." His legacy will endure in the books to come.

Peter Osnos, *Founder and Editor-at-Large*